BEING "IN CHRIST"
WE HAVE VICTORY!

"If anyone be '**in Christ**,'
he is a new creation, old things
(your old life) are passed away, behold all things
(your new life) are become new."
II Corinthians 5:17

DR. GLEN E. CLIFTON

WestBow
PRESS
A DIVISION OF THOMAS NELSON

Copyright © 2012 by Dr. Glen E. Clifton.

All rights reserved. No part of this book may be used or reproduced by any means, graphic, electronic, or mechanical, including photocopying, recording, taping or by any information storage retrieval system without the written permission of the publisher except in the case of brief quotations embodied in critical articles and reviews.

WestBow Press books may be ordered through booksellers or by contacting:

WestBow Press
A Division of Thomas Nelson
1663 Liberty Drive
Bloomington, IN 47403
www.westbowpress.com
1-(866) 928-1240

Because of the dynamic nature of the Internet, any web addresses or links contained in this book may have changed since publication and may no longer be valid. The views expressed in this work are solely those of the author and do not necessarily reflect the views of the publisher, and the publisher hereby disclaims any responsibility for them.

Any people depicted in stock imagery provided by Thinkstock are models, and such images are being used for illustrative purposes only.

Certain stock imagery © Thinkstock.

ISBN: 978-1-4497-6027-4 (sc)
ISBN: 978-1-4497-6028-1 (hc)
ISBN: 978-1-4497-6026-7 (e)

Library of Congress Control Number: 2012913189

Some Scripture taken from the King James Version of the Bible.

Some Scripture taken from the New King James Version. Copyright 1979, 1980, 1982 by Thomas Nelson, inc. Used by permission. All rights reserved.

Some Scripture taken from the Holy Bible, New International Version®. Copyright © 1973, 1978, 1984 Biblica. Used by permission of Zondervan. All rights reserved.

Printed in the United States of America

WestBow Press rev. date: 08/30/2012

Dr. Darrell W. Robinson, former head of Evangelism of the Home Mission Board of the Southern Baptist Convention, and former Vice President of the S.B.C. He currently leads Evangelism and Missions Conferences nationally and internationally, **Dr. Robinson states**, "The book, **Being "In Christ," We Have Victory,** is based solidly on Biblical principles and is practically relevant to everyday life. Dr. Glen Clifton gives the sound basis for our encouragement and daily victory as we continue to experience all God has for us **"IN CHRIST!"** I am delighted to recommend it for every Believer to read to enhance their growth in Christ. Also, I highly recommend it to every non-believer for their experience in coming to a personal relationship with Jesus Christ Himself and not simply becoming religious."

Dr. David O. Dykes, is pastor of the 15,000 member Green Acres Baptist Church in Tyler, Texas. This church, under his leadership averages about 1,000 new members each year, with over 250 baptisms for the past 21 years, and are #1 in mission giving in the SBC. **Dr. Dykes states**, "In this book, Pastor Glen Clifton has latched on to one of the most important phrases in the entire Bible. To recognize who we are '**in Christ**' is the genuine key to living a life beyond ourselves. He skillfully mixes Biblical exposition with interesting illustrations that make this truth come to life. You will be richly blessed by reading this book."

Texas Pastor, Dr. Rocky Weatherford states, "I am glad to recommend this book. It is essential that the Church wake up to the danger of "easy believe-ism" that threatens the purity of the Body of Christ. Dr. Clifton has addressed this critical need with an exceptionally readable, easy to understand book. I enthusiastically recommend this work to anyone committed to strengthening the Church. Thanks for sharing it with me...this stuff will preach. As a matter of fact, I have used some of it."

Rev. Robert N. Bennett, First Baptist Church of Stewart Florida, states, "Just completed reading **"In Christ"** by Dr. Glen Clifton. This in depth study of our blessed position **"In Christ"** is a wonderful resource for Pastors, Sunday School teachers and believers alike. The great themes of transformation, justification, sanctification and glorification are punctuated with pointed analogies throughout every chapter. Thank you brother Clifton for reminding us that "In Christ" we have the "Victory!"

DEDICATION

This book is dedicated to my wife Dee (Delia M. Joiner—Clifton). From 1953 we have been friends. She became my love, my loving wife, the mother of our children (Pamela, Stephen, Mark and Joel), my companion in ministry. Through all my ups and downs, she continued to encourage and assist me as my partner.

For almost a year, during the writing of this book, she has been extremely ill. Much of this writing took place as she slept. Being in three Hospitals (one twice), two Nursing Facilities, and home nursing care, and many doctor visits, she battles on.

Each day as I pray, and as I claim Philippians 4:13,19, God has been faithful in hearing and answering my prayers. As you read, **Being "In Christ," We have Victory!**, please join me in a prayer for her health regained.

ACKNOWLEDGMENTS

I would like to acknowledge the following individuals for helping me with this manuscript from spelling, corrections, elimination of duplicate messages, as well as adding some clarification of certain sentences.

First, I'd like to thank **Don Cass** for writing the **Forward** for this book. He has been a pastor, and a full-time Evangelist across the Southern Baptist Convention. He just recently retired as Evangelism Director for the Southern Baptists of Texas Convention.

Second, I would show my heartfelt appreciation to **Richard and Beth Childs,** graduates of Southern Seminary, and Assoc. Pastor of First Baptist Church of Ft. Pierce, FL. Their reading, correcting and suggestions were totally essential to the completion of the manuscript.

Third, A huge thanks to **Rev. Robert N. Bennett,** Pastor to Senior Adults at First Baptist Church in Stuart, FL, where he has served for over 18 years. He has served Southern Baptist churches from Tennessee to Florida for over 40 years. He and wife Nancy are Gospel Recording artists.

Fourth, I want to thank **two men** who attend our local Savannah Club Worship Group where I share weekly Bible Studies. **Salvatore "'Sal' Franco,** former professor of languages in Rhode Island and at IRCC, here in Port St. Lucie. With a Catholic background, I had the privilege of leading him to a relationship with Christ and baptizing him in the Atlantic Ocean, with six other seniors. **George Waddy,** who after 34 years of teaching English in Upstate New York, and in the N.Y. State Prison System, gave me great advice and corrections to grammar, spelling and sentence structure.

DISCLAIMER

In my efforts to write this book, I have gleaned from over 55 years of sermon preparation, in which I quoted many individuals in my sermons without always writing down their names or the source. I have preached thousands of sermons and read scores of commentaries, and other thousands of pages of books, teachings and the sermons of others. The ideas and illustrations were taken from my experiences, along with many other sources. Where I could, I gave personal recognition. If you desire, I encourage you to use any of the thoughts and stories. As a teen-age preacher attending Baylor University, I received from Dr. W. Herschel Ford a box of free books, (his sermons) at the F.B.C. of El Paso, TX. We all said, "When better sermons are preached . . . we'll preach 'em." And we did!

FOREWORD

There are some things every follower of Jesus should know. My friend Glen Clifton has written a book that is filled with truths all of us should know. The content is built around the verse in II Corinthians 5:17, "If anyone be **in Christ,** he is a new creation, old things are passed away, behold all things have become new."

Every person who follows Jesus has a new life, so radically new that Jesus likened it to being "born again". However, the author of this book has focused on two words within II Corinthians 5:17 which helps us understand the impact of the rest of the verse. The words are, **"in Christ."** With God's guidance and years of studying the Word of God, Glen Clifton has skillfully exposed the depth of meaning which always follows being **"in Christ."**

Warren W. Wiersbe wrote in his book, **Being a Child of God**," "There is a vast difference between age and maturity. Age is a quantity of years, while maturity is a quality of experience." **Novelist F. Scott Fitzgerald wrote** about people who "go from one childhood to another," and he says, that kind of person is with us today. They don't know the difference between being childlike and being childish. They go through life trapping people into becoming surrogate parents whose main task is to pamper and protect them. Consequently, they never grow up; they just grow old." **John Debrine once stated,** "Christians will either grow in grace or groan in disgrace." This a book, once you read it, you will want to read it again because its content will stimulate spiritual growth. The author writes from the overflow of his own spiritual pilgrimage.

Pastoring local churches for many years, helping people biblically address the challenges of life, and seeking out answers to his own life's needs has set this author on the path of spiritual maturity you sense in the pages of this wonderful book. It will drive you to scripture, cause you to worship God through grateful praise and thanksgiving, and will inspire you to want to tell others how they too can be **"in Christ."**

You will learn how God chose you, graciously forgave you, loves you, imputes righteousness to you, supplies every need you have in life, will one day raise you from the dead and give you the ultimate victory! This book will be like a valued gift which God will use to bless you beyond words. Read it and rejoice!

Don Cass
Pastor, Evangelist and recently retired
Director of Evangelism for
The Southern Baptists of Texas Convention

CONTENTS

ACKNOWLEDGMENTS vii
DISCLAIMER ix
FOREWORD xi
INTRODUCTION: Being "In Christ!" xv
PREFACE: Being "In Christ," We Have Victory!............................xvii

Chapter 1:   'Blessed' and 'Chosen' by God Before Creation!........................ 1
Chapter 2:   Given "Grace" Before the World Was Created......................... 22
Chapter 3:   'Redeemed' and 'Forgiven' for All Your Sins 39
Chapter 4:   'Redeemed' by God With an 'Inseparable', 'Inescapable' Love. 58
Chapter 5:   'Justified' Before God, and the 'Righteousness' of God in Christ is 'Imputed' to You. 76
Chapter 6:   'Assurance' That You Are a 'New Creation' and a 'Child of God!' 97
Chapter 7:   'Seated in the Heavenly Places,' Even While You Live On Earth. 116
Chapter 8:   "In Christ" You Are Being 'Sanctified' and Made 'Holy'........ 137
Chapter 9:   "In Christ" Everything You Really 'Need' Will Be Supplied. 150
Chapter 10: "In Christ" the 'Peace of God' Will 'Guard' Your Heart and Mind. 171
Chapter 11: "In Christ" You Have 'Eternal Life' 189
Chapter 12: You Will be 'Raised From the Dead' at the Coming of the Lord. 211
Chapter 13: "In Christ," We Have Ultimate 'VICTORY!' 230

IN CONCLUSION: "Are You "In Christ"? 253

INTRODUCTION
Being "In Christ!"

Spiritual growth is critical, but until those of us in the church, who **claim to be Christians, realize who we are "In Christ,"** it will be impossible for us to go forward in the faith of our Lord.

This brief study emphasizes this fact: that to be "In Christ," means you are now so identified with Jesus, that God always views you in connection with Christ. Your spiritual identity is never viewed apart from Christ. **Most Christians just don't understand** that God has **imputed righteousness** to us, as well as the forgiveness of sins.

Sometimes this is hard to fathom, because of our limited understanding. **For the Christian, God is our Father!** Because of our union, being **"in Christ," we are adopted by God into His family.** He is our Father, and we are His children. **Paul writes,** "He predestined us to **adoption as sons** through Jesus Christ to Himself." **Because of this adoption**, we have an intimate relationship with Him. We are to refer to God as **"Abba,"** the Greek equivalent of the term **"Daddy,"** (Romans 8:15; Galatians 4:6).

Unfortunately, Spiritual Growth isn't the major topic in most churches today. **Today's contemporary church** is filled with leadership who are placing emphasis, **not** on spiritual growth, but on dramatic experiences, outward excitement, instant solutions to spiritual problems, the health and wealth/prosperity gospel, or how to get wealthy financially through God. They overemphasize physical healing and other spiritual fads, **rather than emphasizing true discipleship** and **growth in grace** in the Lord Jesus Christ—**the basics** that grow a dynamic New Testament church. (II Peter 3:18).

Because of this familial relationship, we know that **we are secure 'In Christ.'** As Christians, we may see ourselves in sin and in need of forgiveness, because we are out of fellowship with our Lord. **We must realize** that because we are **covered** by the **blood** of His Son, Jesus, **God sees us as** perfect and complete in Christ. **Paul exhorted the Ephesians** to "walk in a manner worthy of the calling with which you have been called." (Ephesians 4:1) Because we now have been placed in His family, "when we sin, we have an **advocate** with the Father, Jesus Christ the righteous. And He, Himself is the propitiation for our sins . . ." (I John 2:1,2) **Our advocate** (attorney) propitiates us (automatically restores us) favorable before our Father.

I urge you to read and reread carefully all the scriptures given below.

Dr. Glen Clifton

PREFACE
Being "In Christ," We Have Victory!

"If anyone be **'in Christ,'** he is a new creation, old things (your old life) are passed away, behold all things (especially your life) are become new." II Corinthians 5:17

This phrase **"in Christ,"** is probably one of the most simple, revealing and exciting doctrinal statements in the Word of God. **Christian, what kind of words** do you use to **define** your own salvation experience? Are they words like: redemption, atonement, reconciliation, propitiation, justification? Most people just don't relate to those big $100. words. **Salvation, simply put, means to be "in Christ."**

Did you know that being **'in Christ'** is one of Paul's favorite teachings to impress on us our position with God, since we have been redeemed. **Being 'in Christ' means** belonging to Jesus, having a personal relationship with Him, being in 'unity' with Him. **This word, 'in' tells the world who we are!** "In' gives information about our state of being, about our self. This word, **'in'** demonstrates many things. Anyone can be **in** love, in great health, **in** bad health, **in** the marines, **in** ministry, **in** banking, **into** golf, **into** music. **Question:** Does being **'in Christ,'** describe who you are? **Are you one of God's children,** as Paul describes in Galatians 4:19?

It's amazing when you first realize the wonderful **benefits** of being **"in Christ."** We realize that we are "remade" as individuals. Although we occupy the same body and are still the same person, **several changes** have taken place, and will continue. **Paul tells us that when** "we are baptized into Christ," we are then raised up to "walk in newness of life." (Romans 6:4). **This baptism** referred to here **is a spiritual baptism** by the Holy Spirit of God, and is totally different from **water baptism upon being saved.**

The phrase **"in Christ,"** occurs one hundred and thirty **(130) times** in the New Testament. It is used **twenty seven (27)** times in Ephesians alone. Let me remind you, **Jesus said,** "You in me and I in you." (John 15:4). **How wonderful!** You, as a believer, **are "in Christ,"** and Christ is in you (the believer). **Being "in Christ Jesus"** is an **astonishing reality.** It is a **breathtaking experience** to be **"in Christ,"** in agreement in Christ. **united to Christ. bound** to Christ. **If you** are **"in Christ,"** do you know what it means to you.?

I hope you realize that: those **"in Christ"** have all that Jesus has. You may ask, "What do you mean, brother Glen?" **Here's what the Word of God says in John 1:12,** "As many as received Him (Jesus), He gave to them the right to become the children of God, to those who believe on His name. **And in Romans 8:16, 17,** "The (Holy) Spirit Himself bears witness with our spirit that we are children of God, and if children, then **heirs**—heirs of God and joint heirs with Christ . . ."

I know this is hard for some to accept, understand, and/or believe. **We must remember** that these are the **Words of the Infinite God,** and it's sometimes hard for our finite minds to comprehend. **LISTEN: When we are "in Christ," Christ's riches** are our riches, **His righteousness** is our righteousness, and **His power** is our power to have. **Please, open your mind as we study the Word together, and discover what it means to be "In Christ."**

Spiritual growth comes through **understanding** and **practicing** the truths of the Word of God. Multitudes of **spiritual blessings are yours** when you unlock and understand the major truths of the Scripture.

Being "in Christ" is **everything** for the Christian! **It is so important** that after we accept Jesus as our Lord and Savior, **we must realize** that we are to be transformed into His image. **The Holy Spirit Who resides** inside us now, is the **only One Who** can make us like Christ Jesus. "Beloved, now we are children of God; and it has not yet been revealed what we shall be, but we know that when He is revealed, we shall be like Him, for we shall see Him as He is." (I John 3:2)

In this study it is my desire that **we, who are "in Christ,"** will learn how God manifests Himself **in** and **through** us.

CHAPTER ONE

"In Christ" You Were 'Blessed' and 'Chosen' by God Before Creation!

God's Word states in Ephesians 1:3-4, "Blessed be to the God and Father of our Lord Jesus Christ, who has blessed us with all (every) spiritual blessings in the heavenly places **in Christ. God chose us "in Him"** before the foundation of the world, that we should be holy and without blemish before Him in love."

The Apostle Paul begins his greeting to the Ephesians with the word **"blessed." Webster defines** "Blessed" as, "of or enjoying happiness. specifically enjoying the bliss of Heaven." **It carries the idea of that which** "brings pleasure, contentment, or good fortune." Simply stated, it is that state of being that we all want to enjoy. **Now, let's be honest,** we all like blessings don't we? There **isn't a person reading** this that does not enjoy a blessing! And, certainly, **we are a blessed people!**

Paul begins his greeting to the saints (Christians) at Ephesus by praising God for having blessed us with so many blessings . . . in fact, **'all'** blessings (v. 3). **That little three letter word** tells us that **in the Lord**, we find every single thing we need to live the Christian life. God has **held nothing back** from His children. When He saved us, **He gave us** everything we needed to serve Him. **We have everything** we need right now to be content, to be successful, to be obedient, to be useful to the Kingdom and to be happy in Jesus! **We received everything** Jesus had to offer us! **We received it** at that very moment when we were saved.

He begins in verse 4 with the thought of the **foreknowledge** of the Almighty. This verse **deals with the matter of election.** For some reason, **God, in His wisdom, chose me** before the world was formed. **He knew me** before He formed me in my mother's womb, (Jeremiah 1:5), and He had already determined that I would be in His family. **I cannot explain election** and all the ramifications of it, **but I am still going to rejoice in it!** One of the greatest spiritual blessings we enjoy as saved people is the fact that **we were chosen "in Christ"** by the grace of God. **The Apostle Paul,** under the inspiration of the Holy Spirit, **explains this** in **Romans 8:28-31. God loved me** even though **He knew all about me! Praise God!**

God hasn't blessed us with every **'conceivable'** blessing. Paul doesn't say that God has blessed us with **every 'physical'** blessing. He says that God has blessed us with **every 'spiritual' blessing.** The blessings that He will talk about come specifically through the work of the Holy Spirit. **Later, Paul will write about** why we need to be "filled with the Spirit" (Eph. 5:18). **As we are filled** with the Spirit, **we will experience** more and more the blessings that God has for us as Christians.

One young mom wrote, "One day **I asked my two-year-old** daughter, Catherine, where her slippers were. **"Downstairs** in the kitchen," she told me. **"What are they doing** there?" I asked. **"Nothing,"** she replied. **"They can't walk** because they **don't have feet** in them right now." **The Holy Spirit gives** us 'unction,' or 'feet,' like Catherine said, to go and do the things of God.

The question now arises, what are these spiritual blessings? Pardon, adoption, redemption, the earnest (guarantee) of the Spirit, sanctification, peace, glorification, etc., referred to in many scriptures, blessings which individual Christians enjoy. (Galatians 4:5; 5:22, 23; Colossians 3:15; II Corinthians 1:22; 5:22).

We saints while still in this body on earth, are enjoying some of the blessings which we will enjoy in heaven. We call this our **spiritual 'position.'** We do not currently and physically live in heaven. But we have a position here and in heaven. **Paul will tell us later** that we are "seated in the heavenlies" (Ephesians. 2:6).

What does this mean?

Perhaps you **read about** the lady named **Hetty Green. For many years** Hetty Green was called **America's greatest miser.** When she **died in 1916,** she left an **estate valued at $100 million,** an especially vast fortune for that day. But she was **so miserly** that she ate **cold oatmeal** in order to save the expense of heating the water. When her **son had a severe leg injury,** she took so long trying to find a **free clinic** to treat him that his **leg had to be amputated** because of advanced infection.

It has been said that she hastened her own death by bringing on a fit of apoplexy while arguing the merits of skim milk because it was cheaper than whole milk.

For her to possess such great assets but to live so miserably, to live the **life of a pauper** when her **wealth** was so **tremendous,** was very foolish. Paul teaches us in his letter to the Ephesians, that many of the **benefits, and the blessings,** which are ours today, **are unappreciated** by so many of us. This results in **some Christians** living in what **Thoreau** would call, "lives of quiet desperation." Let me add: the **reason many don't know** of the wealth, the blessings, and the benefits of God ... **that are now ours** ... is because we **don't read** the handbook ... the Word of Almighty God, the Bible. **Unfortunately,** the church today is filled with many Biblical illiterates.

Many who struggle with the Christian life, who **seldom** experience joy, who wrestle with finding peace, **do so because** they do not know **how rich God** has **made them.** That is Paul's concern in Ephesians. We see most of **the purpose of his teaching** in this letter, in his **prayer in 1:18**: "I pray also that the eyes of your heart may be enlightened in order that you may know the hope to which he has called you, the riches of his glorious inheritance in the saints, and his incomparably great power for us who believe." **You may want to read that verse again!**

The overall thrust of the book of Ephesians is to **expose us to the riches** that we have from trusting in Christ, and to learn to see how it affects our lives. **God doesn't want us living a miserable existence like Hetty Green,** who **had some incredible resources at her disposal,** but didn't take advantage of what she had available to her.

James stated, "Every good thing bestowed and every perfect gift is from above, coming down from the Father of lights, with whom there is no variation, or shifting shadow. In the exercise of His will He brought us forth by the word of truth, so that we might be, as it were, the first fruits among His creatures" (James 1:17-18).

In churches across our land and around the world, **Christians sing:**

> "Praise God from whom all blessings flow.
> Praise Him all creatures here below.
> Praise Him above, ye heavenly host.
> Praise Father, Son, and Holy Ghost."

—Thomas Ken

We also sing

> "Come Thou fount of every blessing,
> Tune my heart to sing Thy praise
> Streams of mercy, never ceasing,
> Call for songs of highest praise."

—Robert Robinson

The theology of these songs of praise certainly agrees with Paul's teaching, and that of the rest of the apostles. In Ephesians 1:3, Paul not only praises God for His bountiful blessings, but he calls for us to join with him. In the broadest sense, every blessing comes from God, including our material blessings (Matthew 5:45; Acts 14:17; 17:24-28). But in our text, Paul draws attention only to the **"spiritual" blessings,** every one of which originates with God and **many of which await us** in the **"heavenly places."**

Our blessings are "in the heavenlies" because our Lord, the source of all blessings, **dwells there** and this is **where we will experience them** to the full (see Ephesians 2:6; Hebrews 11:13-16; 1 Peter 1:4). **Paul describes** these things as "blessings in heavenly places." This **literally means** that these blessings are things that **originated in heaven.** They are **not** earthly blessings, but they are heavenly blessings! In the most **literal sense,** they are "Heavenly Things!"

God has blessed us! It is something **He has done.** It is **all because of grace,** His unmerited, undeserved favor. He has done everything; **you can do nothing except receive it.** There is only one way to find yourself in this verse, and that is by the words of the **old hymn,** by Augustus Toplady, "Nothing in my hands I bring; simply to thy cross I cling." **There is nothing** you can do except to **receive it,** but receiving this blessing **means you can do all things** through Christ who strengthens you. **Why would God do** such a thing? There is nothing we can say in response to this except for what **Paul said:** "Blessed be the God and Father of our Lord Jesus Christ, who has blessed us with every spiritual blessing in the heavenly places in Christ." **Because He has blessed us in His election,** we receive all the blessings, while He receives all the glory!

In the late 1960's, while pastor of the First Baptist Church in Pleasanton—Livermore, California, my sons got a **2-wheel scooter. We lived** in the **outskirts** of Pleasanton where they could ride in open fields. Mark and Joel were riding around on that thing like race drivers in the field. **Joel, the youngest,** came up to me and he said, "Dad, why did God make Honda QA50's?" **I had no idea how to answer the question,** and so I just made something up: "Well, Joel, I guess it's because He **wanted little guys like you to have fun."** "No, Dad! **for His own glory!"** Touché. He had actually been **listening to a sermon** I had preached a week earlier. **He was exactly right! Everything** in this world is for God's own glory. But my friends, if you really believe that, **that's life re-orienting. Everything is for His glory!** Everything!

On T.V. they were interviewing a woman who was 23 years old when she was working as a **stewardess on an Air Florida jet** that took off from Washington, D.C. **You may remember the story** of that Air Florida jet that never made it any further than the 14th Street Bridge. **She was one of the survivors. All she remembers** of **that crash** is the fear in the faces of the people, and in **coming up for air** in the **freezing river** and being rescued. **She had never prayed** in her life until that day. She had **never gone to church.** She is now **teaching a Sunday School class** in a church in Miami, Florida. She has **three beautiful children**, she's **married** to a Christian man, and she, **in her interview, said,** "God used that to **change my life for my eternal good and for His own glory.**" That's exactly right. She understands exactly what Paul is getting at.

In our Scripture, in **Verse 4,** there is an **extraordinary statement.** **"God chose us 'in Christ,'"** which indicates that **it is a matter of His grace** and **not** our personal worth. It is **not** by our "works of righteousness which we have done, **but according to His mercy He saved us** . . . through Jesus Christ our Savior." (Titus 3:5,6). We do not have to earn this exalted position **"in Christ." It is already ours** through our salvation in the Lord Jesus Christ. **We are secure forever "in Christ."**

A shipwrecked man writes a **message,** places it in a **secure, capped bottle,** and **throws it** into the sea, in the **hope** that it may **reach some shore.** But will not the **water damage and destroy it? No;** for, while it is cast into the sea, it is **first sealed** in a bottle—and **so it arrives.** Yes, in Philippi, with all its destructive influences, but **"in Christ,"** so **they are secure,** and so, **in spite** of all **antagonistic** forces, **they arrive** at "the haven where they would be." With all the temptations, evil and distractions of the world, how can a holy life be lived in such unholy surroundings?

Just like the little water-spider going down to the bottom of that **pond.** It doesn't really belong there, **even as we believers** are: "in the world" . . . but not of it, (John 17:11,16). **The little creature** has the queer, and amazing, ability of weaving a **bubble of air** around itself, and hidden in that it **is able to pursue** its way even amid such **adverse conditions,** in the water, but in the bubble!

Wayne Barber shares, "If you ever see anything good in me, you know, it didn't come from me. **It came from He Who** is in me and Whose I am (and Who I am in). **It came from** the Lord Jesus Christ Himself." **It's the same with you,** when you see something in me that is good, remember it is not me, **it must be Christ in me. The ability to be faithful** as well as the ability concerning our responsibilities to Christ, is an **ability that comes from** our being **in Him** and **Him being in us.**

Remember: Everything you have is **in a Person,** and His name is **Jesus.** And if you'll **come to Him** and **bow down** to Him, **you will begin experience** inwardly what you've been looking for all along. **The key is a repentant and submissive heart.** When you are ready to bow, at that very moment, you attain access to the things that are yours **in Christ Jesus** because they're all available in Christ. **The problem with most of us is,** we look for these things, (spiritual blessings), **everywhere except** where they are found. And, if we don't have our needs met spiritually **in Christ,** they'll never be met anywhere else.

Remember: In these verses, Paul expounds on the **idea of a believer's new identity,** using the phrase **in Christ** or its synonyms (over 160 times in some form, in Him, in the Beloved, in Christ, in Christ Jesus, in the Lord). The words, **"In Christ,"** summarizes the **profound truth** that believers are now and forever in **spiritual union** with the Lord Jesus Christ. This **mysterious spiritual truth** is one of the **most significant teachings** in the New Testament.

Charles Ryrie states, Probably the **most important doctrinal fact** underpinning the spiritual life is the believer's **union with Christ.** It is **foundational to the truth** of co-crucifixion of the Christian with Christ (Romans 6:6; Galatians 2:20), which in turn is the basis for freedom from the power of sin.

Remember that freedom in Christ is not the **right** to do as one pleases but the **power** to please God by doing what is **right**! Unfortunately, this concept is little understood, unbalanced in its presentation, and unused in its application. **What does this concept mean?** My own definition is simply this: To be **in Christ** is the redeemed man's new environment in the sphere of **resurrection life.**

These thoughts are beyond my understanding. **Listen:** Reading these verses, **We were 'planned'** by the Father from the beginning **for His glory. We were 'purchased'** at an expensive price **by His Son** at Calvary. **We were 'preserved'** by the Spirit in order that we may be with Him forever. **Each person** of the **Triune God** was involved in these truths of **God's family secrets. Why?** "to the praise of His glory." (vs.12, 14)

Having been a Scuba diver since the mid 1960's, when I was first certified in California, I've always dreamed of searching for lost treasure. Watching the **History Channel** recently I watched **a treasure-hunting** company find a sunken galleon with hundreds of millions of dollars worth of coins. **The Christian life** is really a **treasure hunt** as you **progressively discover** the vast wealth **that already is yours** because you are now **"in Christ."** From the moment He saves you, **God bestows on you, as Paul puts it,** "every spiritual blessing in the heavenly places in Christ."

And this lifetime is just the beginning, because throughout eternity we will go on discovering the riches of God's grace, which He lavished upon us (Ephesians 1:7-8).

William Randolph Hearst, wealthy newspaper and magazine publisher, once read about an extremely **valuable piece of art,** which he decided he must **add** to his extensive collection. He instructed his agent to scour the galleries of the world to **find this masterpiece.** He was determined to own it at any price. **After many months** of painstaking search, the **agent reported** that the piece **already belonged** to Mr. Hearst and had been **stored in one of his warehouses** for many years. How many **Christians are unaware** of the many treasures that the Father has given us.

The first half of the book of Ephesians tells us about the **treasures** that we **already have as Christians.** In the **last half** of the book Paul will tell us how we are to live as Christians. I think it's very important as we learn about what we're supposed to be doing as Christians that **we first know what we already have.**

For those of you who like a challenge in your Bible Study, **don't get all upset about the words, 'election,' 'choosing,' 'predestination,'** etc. Remember: You and I didn't do the choosing. **He chose us!**

I believe it was **Charles Spurgeon** who once said, "God chose me before I came into the world, because if He'd waited until I got here, He never would have chosen me." **In other words,** you and I are **not chosen** because of our goodness, our works of righteousness, our benevolence, our expertise, or anything else, **God chose us because of His love for us! He can do this because HE IS GOD,** and He can do anything He desires . . . . and He desires to choose us!

We like to quote Romans 8:28, which states, "And we know that all things work together for good to those who love God, **to those who are the called** according to **His purpose.**" We all know and like to quote the first part, but we usually leave the last part out . . . . about being **called for His purpose.**

Much of today's pulpit presentation is: "ask Jesus into your heart," "make a decision for Christ," "accept Jesus as your personal Savior," etc. **Please know this: this alone is not a full Biblical terminology or**

teaching. In an effort to make the gospel palatable and easy, the gospel has been watered down, and the truth of salvation diluted. **The message that Jesus proclaimed** calls us to **discipleship.** It is a call to **submissive obedience. Having written that,** let me quickly state, I became a Christian as a boy, by asking Jesus into my life. **I'm not sure** at the time if I understood about the "Lordship of Christ." **But, I guarantee you,** that as soon as I **heard and understood** that "Jesus is Lord," **He was the Lord of my life.**

John 1:12 sets two conditions of receiving Jesus and **believing** Jesus: "But to all who RECEIVED him, who BELIEVE in his name, he gave authority to become children of God." **Receiving Jesus means** that **when Jesus offers Himself** to you, you welcome him into your life for what he is. If he comes to you as **Savior,** you welcome his salvation. If he comes to you as **Leader,** you welcome his leadership. **If he comes to you as Provider, you welcome his provision. If** he comes to you as **Counselor,** you welcome his counsel. If he comes to you as **Protector,** you welcome his protection. If he comes to you as **Authority,** you welcome his authority. If he comes to you as **King,** you welcome his rule. **Receiving Jesus means** taking Jesus into your life for **who He is.** It does not mean a kind of peaceful co-existence with a Christ who makes no claims, as though he can stay in the house as long as he doesn't play his music so loud.

Much of our preaching/teaching today has become fuzzy. **There is no call** for repentance, commitment, surrender, and separation from the world, or living a life that produces fruit. **Someone once said,** "cheap grace produces a cheap ineffective salvation, which produces a meaningless faith." **This is not a saving faith!** Saving faith is **more than just understanding some facts** and deciding for Jesus.

Much of the so-called evangelism today is a push for decisions, statistics, pitches, aisle-walking, hand shaking, gimmicks, prefabricated presentations, emotional manipulation and even intimidation. **The aftermath of this** is evident as we see our churches being filled with those who profess faith, with no commitment, resulting that the truth of Christ has had no impact on their behavior. **Unfortunately, many** who have "walked the aisle, been baptized, joined the church, etc." **have been deluded into believing they are saved, when they are not!**

This verse, Ephesians 1:4 tells us that "God chose us!" This is according to His plan. **God the Father** planned the church. **God the Son** paid for the church. **God the Holy Spirit** protects the church. **We must understand** that we are not the originators, the promoters, the sustainers, or the consummators of our salvation and the church. **God planned our salvation in eternity before** there ever was a you or me in this world.

A little boy was once asked, "Have you found Jesus?" The little **boy answered,** "Sir, I didn't know He was lost. But, I know this . . . I was lost, and He found me." **Friend, you don't find Jesus. He finds you.** Whether you and I understand it or not, **God's choosing** goes back to the sovereignty of the wisdom and goodness of God alone. **God's divine choosing,** according to verse 1, was for a divine purpose: "that we should be holy and without blemish before Him in love."

He chose us "that we should be holy." **He chose** us in order to **sanctify us** (set us apart). **His sanctification makes us holy. Paul asks the question,** "Shall we continue in sin that grace may abound? God forbid. How shall we who are dead to sin, live any longer therein?" (Romans 6:1,2), **Listen: Grace** is **not** a **license** to sin. If you are continually living in sin, with no regard for the Lord, you are not saved.

We are not chosen because we are **holy and blameless,** nor does the grammar allow us to read this. **God's choice** only extends to our holiness without specifying whom He has chosen. **The Puritan Thomas Watson said it best:** "Let us then ascribe the whole work of grace to the pleasure of God's will. God did not choose us because we were worthy, but by choosing us he makes us worthy."

He chose to make us holy and blameless, and then **sent His Son to save us** so that this choice could be fulfilled. **Holiness is** the end, the **central purpose** of salvation, not a fringe benefit of it, that seems almost optional. **Are you holy and blameless** before Him in love? **Are you more** so than you were a year ago? **Are you more** so than the day you were saved? **Do you want to be? It is your destiny! Hallelujah!**

Let me illustrate: Let us imagine that God tells a little boy, "You are **chosen** to play **baseball** in the major leagues." **Will he loaf, skip** practice, **not** hustle, because **God has told him** he will be successful anyway? **That is what many people seem** to think this doctrine leads to. But they have never been that little boy. Imagine him well. **Will this be his response?** Not if he loves the game! For **if he is really elected,** that election **works itself out** by implanting that **love in him.** And if he loves the game, **his election** to the major leagues will be a **great incentive** and encouragement to **play his best** and give a **full effort,** for he knows that **even if he stumbles** in the short run his efforts are destined to be rewarded.

It may come as **a surprise** that the **first benefit of our riches in Christ** is the one which **sends Christians** into such **apoplexy** (a sudden paralysis with total to partial loss of consciousness . . . both an angry fit). If you ever want to **throw a grenade** into a **Christian gathering,** just **ask people** if God foreordains everything that shall come to pass? **Ask them** if they believe in predestination. **Ask them** about election. And we need to remember: **It is what the Bible says,** and **not what we** say or think.

J.I. Packer has stated, "**The secret** to **soul-fattening Bible study** is to ask first the question '**What does this passage teach me about my God?**'" So often **we go to the Bible and ask,** 'How does this help me to be a better husband or father?' 'How does this help me be a better man?' Those aren't bad questions; **those are good questions!** Far too many **people go** to the Bible **to prove** what they already believe or think, not for correction and instruction.

Christians desperately **need** to be **reminded** of the fact that **God is the One** who is **most important in this life;** because we forget that, and want our opinion to be heard. What does God say through His Word? That is the question. **That's why** the **first principle of theology is** "There is a God"; and the **second principle is** "You are not Him." It is **vital** as we continue on in our **Christian life to remember both** those principles of theology: **There is a God, and I am not Him.** In the midst of **our troubles,** in the midst of the **difficulties and trials** and **disappointments** of life, our world tends to shrink and our eyes tend to turn in on ourselves. We think that is **most important in our life is getting out of whatever fix** we are in. We think the most **important thing that God can do is to accommodate** us in that. And **it's not.**

God elected (chose) us that we should **be "without blame."** A **believer "In Christ"** is seen by God as having no blame. **This means** that your life has been changed. If there is no evidence of a change . . . you are not of the elect. **Since Christ died for you,** you cannot say, "I'm not one of the elect." **You are** of the elect if you hear His voice. Jesus said, "whosoever will may come." **It was a wonderful thing** to hear His still, small voice when **He called me** to be a member of His family. Maybe I am not able to totally understand all this now, I just believe it, because He said it.

Ephesians 1:3, 4, "According as He hath chosen us in Him **before the foundation of the world** that we should be holy and without blame before Him, in love having predestined us unto the adoption of sons by Jesus Christ to Himself according to the good pleasure of His will to the praise of the glory of His grace." (Ephesians 1:5).

You may be thinking, "But I don't understand how God chooses." **Join the crowd** of mortal man. None of us understand it completely. Though I do not understand it, **I accept it and rejoice** in the knowledge that I was chosen in Him. **You may be asking,** "How can I know if God chose me or not?" **By accepting Jesus Christ** as your Lord and Savior, the moment you do, **you will discover** that you were chosen by Him. As with the disciples you will **hear His words,** "You have not chosen Me, but I have chosen you, and ordained that you should be My disciples, and that you should bring forth fruit." (John 15:16).

Some have a hard time accepting these verses. To make this crystal clear He said in I Corinthians 1:30 (literally): "From Him (God) you are in Christ Jesus." Or as the NASB says, "By His doing you are in Christ Jesus." **In other words,** it is just as though **Paul knew that someone would come along** some day and say that God does not choose those who are in Christ, but only chooses Christ and any who put themselves in Christ. **So he says, in verses 27-29,** that **God chose** the individuals who would make up the church in Christ. And he says in verse 30 that it is by God's doing that they are put in Christ.

We are not only chosen by God, but He **makes us "accepted,"** (v.6). He makes us **"graceful."** He makes us **"lovely."** God doesn't just **choose** you for His seventh grade **football team** and then place you on the **sidelines** and ask you to be the **waterboy.** You're **not just His "charity case"** when you are chosen. He makes you "graceful." He makes you "accepted," **as if He had chosen you** the **"Most Valuable Player"** for the team. (Ephesians 1:6).

The glorious, unshakable, objective foundation of your being a Christian is that God chose you to be one. **God put you "in Christ." We must say with Paul** (I Corinthians 1:26-31) "Consider your calling!" **Consider how** you came to be in Christ! Think about it. **It will take all boasting off of man** and put it all on God. **Verse 31** ends the section: "Let him who boasts boast in the Lord." (II Corinthians 10;17). This is the **boast of assurance.** This is the jubilation of considering our calling and our election, and **seeing that it's all of God, and feeling a tremendous peace and confidence and courage** and **strength** and **love** well up inside to keep us going in the face any opposition. Because, "who can bring any charge against God's elect?" (Rom. 8:33).

Let me reiterate: Your salvation did not begin with your choice to believe in Christ, a choice which was real and necessary. **Your salvation began before the creation of the universe** when **God planned** the history of redemption. **The Almighty ordained** the death and the resurrection of his Son, **and chose you** to be his own through Christ. This is **a great objective ground for assurance,** and we should consider it deeply.

Charles Spurgeon once wrote, "God called us **in Christ.** He **justified** us **in Christ.** He **sanctified** us **in Christ.** He will **perfect** us **in Christ.** He will **glorify** us **in Christ. We have everything in Christ,** and we have **nothing apart** from Christ." **The point** of these words, **"in Christ,"** is to take our thoughts away from anything in ourselves and to focus us on the merits and love of our Savior, Who gave Himself for us. **Although we must believe to be saved,** salvation is not to be traced to our faith or to anything else in us. Rather, **salvation is to be traced to God's eternal** purpose through Jesus Christ and all that He did for us. **We were not chosen** because of anything in us, **but rather we were chosen in Him.** Bless His name!

What a rich sentence this is that we are reading today! And the Apostle has **saved the best part of it for last.** The very **essence of every spiritual blessing** in the heavenly places is that it is **"in Christ"**. "In Christ," is perhaps the **deepest, richest, most profound phrase** in Scripture, and it is the key not only to this sentence but to the **whole book of Ephesians.** What does it mean?

William Barclay adds, that **when Paul spoke** of the Christian being **"in Christ,"** he meant that the Christian lives **"in Christ"** as a bird in the air, a fish in the water, the roots of a tree in the soil. **What makes the Christian different** is that he is always and everywhere conscious of the **encircling presence of Jesus Christ. It is nowhere else to be found.** "Blessed be the God and Father of our Lord Jesus Christ, who has blessed us with every spiritual blessing in the heavenly places **in Christ.**" (Ephesians 1:3).

"Jesus is the Way, the Truth, and the Life, and no one comes to the Father but by Him." (John 14:6) Here it **means at least that;** but it is **more** than that. For **Christ Himself** is the **very essence** of the blessing. It is all bound up in Him. **He is** its height and its depth, its final summation, its be all and end all, its Alpha and Omega, its beginning and its end. **"In Christ,"** we **have everything** that makes life good and worth living, yea, even for an eternity; **apart from Him we have nothing.**

In salvation, what is there that **constitutes God's blessing? There is justification,** the forgiveness of our sins: it is **"in Christ';** it is nowhere else to be found. **What of the meaning of life** and the purpose of existence? **It is "in Christ';** it is nowhere else to be found. **What of peace** with

God, peace with ourselves, and peace with our fellow men! They are **"in Christ;"** it is nowhere else to be found. **What of love, joy, confidence? They are "in Christ";** it is nowhere else to be found. **What of eternal and abundant life?** They are **"in Christ";** it is nowhere else to be found. **The whole shebang!** They are **"in Christ";** it is nowhere else to be found.

I know some have a problem with these scriptures and Paul's teachings. **Question: Do you think** that a Sovereign, Almighty God would leave such an important plan of salvation (redemption) to **the rebellious will of humans? When man fell into sin, God didn't say,** "Oh no, now I have to modify My plan!" If He had done so, then He would be a changeable being, not the immutable (never changing) Sovereign of the universe.

Think about this, if He is not **sovereignly in control of all events** Who knows whether He may have to change His plan again in the future? How could we even know whether **His promises and plan** would finally prevail, if He is not sovereign over all things, including the evil deeds of men?

And so it is that God chooses, not according to human will but **according to His own will.** The word **'chosen,'** in verse 4, means "to pick out for Himself," God chose for Himself those who would be a part of His family. **He chose us also,** "that we would be holy and blameless before Him." **Paul connects God's calling,** or **choosing us,** so that we will be holy. **In 2 Timothy 1:9,** he writes that God "has saved us and called us with a holy calling, not according to our works, but according to His own purpose and grace which was granted us in Christ Jesus from all eternity." **Hallelujah!**

"God chose us in Christ before the foundation of the world." **Before the creation of the universe** God thought of me. **Before I was, He saw me** and chose me for Himself. He did not choose me because He knew I would choose Him. He did not choose me because I was holy or good, but so that I might become holy and good.

Charles Spurgeon comments that, "One of the first doctrines of our holy faith is that of the **union** of all believing souls with Christ. We are **blessed with all spiritual blessings "in Christ."** Apart from Christ we are nothing, and can do nothing (John 15:5); **"in Christ"** we have "all spiritual blessings" **We are rich** as Christ is rich, when we are united to him by the living bond of faith.

The Apostle Paul says just as God the Father blessed us in Jesus Christ, **He also He chose us** from before the foundation of the world. Now let me say normally that **is a doctrine that we argue about.** It's a doctrine that we **debate about, but** you see, the **Apostle Paul sees it** as a **matter of praise and a matter of great comfort** in the Christian life. **Why?**

Paul breaking forth with this message to you and to the Christians who first heard this letter, that **just as God blessed you** with every spiritual blessing in the heavenly places "in Christ," **so also you need to know,** Christian, that from **before the** foundation of the world, **He set His love on you. Before you existed** in space and time, **He set His love on you,** so that **your love to Him** is simply the **response** of **His prior love to you.** He **did not choose you** because of something that you would do: **you chose Him** because of something that **He started** from before the foundation of the world, before time, as we know it, began. And **that young boy suddenly "got it!" God had first reached out** in saving love, "... **seeking me.** It was not I who found God, the Savior true; **no,** I was found of Thee." **Hallelujah!**

If you begin to try to understand that truth, your mind will boggle. That is a **fantastic statement,** isn't it? We struggle with it, and we question it. **We say,** "How could this be? How could God choose us, and yet still offer a choice that we must make?" And thus **we struggle between the doctrines** of the free will of man and the sovereign election of God. **Many have wrestled** with this great truth and have tried to explain it. Let's just learn to let God speak through the Bible.

It *is* true that we are chosen of God to be "in Christ." In John 6, **Jesus said,** "No one can come to me unless the Father who sent me draws him." (John 6:44). That's putting it plainly, isn't it? You cannot come to Christ unless you are drawn by the Father.

Growing up in Grade school and **Jr. High,** I think I held the **world's record in baseball** for the most number times striking out, never getting a hit. As I look back now I understand I was an **underdeveloped boy,** and smaller and younger than the others. Many times when it came to picking teams at recess or P.E., I was **often the last pick.** Boy, talk about self-esteem, mine was shot! It is a **rotten feeling** to **not** be "picked," **but this is not the case for the Christian.** The universe's **ultimate Team Captain** (Almighty God) has "picked" you to be His child! And, He is "on your side".

Please know: We are not afterthoughts in God's wisdom and His plan. **We are not accidental** members of His body. There are **no second class citizens** in the church of Jesus Christ; we are all equal, chosen of the Father, selected to be members of His family, added to the new creation, the new order that God is producing in this world. **What a fantastic privilege!**

We must also remember that it is **not** because of anything in us, as we'll see in a moment, but because of **everything in Him.** The **purpose of all this** is that we are to be holy and blameless. These great Biblical truths are so revolutionary, so radical, that **we hesitate** to believe them! **We hesitate** to apply them to ourselves despite the fact that they are true. **You may not always function properly as a Christian,** but you have the capacity to do so.

Most people refuse to think of themselves as **blameless** because they know that they have done many things for which they ought properly to be blamed. That is, **they have made choices,** deliberately, against light, and against knowledge of the results. **They have purposely done** that which they knew they ought not to have done. They **could have done otherwise** but didn't. And who is not in that boat? Therefore, they feel they are to be blamed. But they are confusing this word with another, because it is **not sinless.** Never having done anything wrong is sinlessness. But **you can be sinful** and still be blameless. Do you know how? By handling your sin in the right way.

Everything I am, and all I hope to be, is **rooted in God's freely choosing me.** And so **there is no ground for boasting** except in God. And in the face of fear and loss of assurance, and all my own defects, I repeat this word of trust: "Who shall bring any charge against the Lord's elect!" (Romans 8:33).

II Timothy 1:9, **says,** "God who hath saved us, called us with a holy calling not according to our works, but according to His own purpose and grace," **and listen to this,** "Which was given us in Christ Jesus before the world began." **This is amazing and incredible.** You and I, who are a part of the body of Jesus Christ, who know and love the Lord Jesus Christ, who are in His church, who have been saved, who have been born again, **are simply responding** to the divine decree of the eternal God made before the world began.

Listen: Nobody's a Johnny-come-lately in the body of Christ. **Everybody is master-planned in** because there is a vital area of responsibility that no one else can fulfill, and because there is **a unique purpose which God has designed** in His own love and wisdom to place upon you, some special and eternal blessing.

Why is it that we have such a **hard time accepting this?** Sometimes **we sing,** "Our God is an awesome God; He reigns from heaven above, with wisdom, power and love; Our God is an awesome God," a song of praise by Rich Mullins. **And then when we finish singing,** we make **comments** such as, "I just don't believe in all this election, choosing stuff," **or,** "I just don't accept the fact that God has planned all this," **or,** "I refuse to believe that God chose me before I knew who He was," **or,** "what about all the 'whosoever will's?" "I just don't accept. . . ." **Is Almighty God awesome, or is He not?**

Yes He is! Let me ask you a question, **"Do you pray?"** You say, "Yes." **To whom** do you pray?" "God!" **"Do you believe** that God is the source of all good things?" "Yes." **"Do you believe** that God answers prayer?" "Yes." **Well, when you answer yes to those questions, you acknowledge** that God is **Sovereign.** God is sovereign in all things in our lives. **Prayer is our acknowledgement** of our dependence on a sovereign God. **If God is sovereign** in all things in our lives, **He is also sovereign in our salvation.** Remember: **You did not** chose God, He chose you, **and He drew you to Christ. Christian, you did not** save yourself, He saved you. In His eternal wisdom, God has the right to do it as He chooses. **In** John 6:37, **Jesus said,** "All that the Father gives Me will come to Me, and the one who comes to Me I will certainly not cast out."

I have a friend who works in **East Texas.** He runs a **salvage yard. I call it a junk yard,** he calls it a salvage business. He's a **wonderful Christian.** He wears a **cap** that says **"Junk is Beautiful."** They have this **huge magnet on a crane,** and that thing will come over, drop down, get those cars and **pick those cars** up as if they were nothing but paper. It will swing them over, **demagnetize,** drop them down in this **big press** and pull away. Then they take this car, and smash it down. **The idea of that magnet** is what I want you to see. When you pull that **magnet over something, everything metal is irresistibly pulled right up to it.** That's **kind of the idea** that we have here when it **says that** "the Father must draw him to me." **God chose us,** and the way we know we are chosen is by the fact that we are drawn.

One night I was preaching on this. **A fellow came** running down the aisle at the end with **tears streaming** down his face. He said, "Oh, I've struggled with this. I **now know I'm chosen."** I said, **"How do you know** you're chosen?" He said, "Because I know I have **been strangely drawn unto Him."** How do you know you're chosen? **You're drawn.** That's the key. **Jesus taught** until the Father draws you, nobody can come unto me.

Friend, this is **pretty exciting stuff.** Being a Christian is pretty fabulous when you think about it in those terms. We are the **chosen.** We are the **elect.** We were His before the world began. We were the **inheritors** of His Kingdom before the world began. **We were the choice** to be in the Father's house forever before the world began. **In the study of theology,** we call it predestination, or election. **Before** the fall, before creation, before time, before anything. **God laid it all out.** It says here that He formed the body before the world began. **Hallelujah!**

Bible Teacher/Evangelist, **J. Wilbur Chapman** often spoke of the testimony of a certain man who attended one of his meetings: "**I got off at the Philadelphia, Pennsylvania depot as a tramp,** and for a year I **begged on the streets** for a living. One day **I touched a man** on the shoulder and said, "**Hey, mister,** can you **give me a dime?**" As soon **as I saw his face** I was shocked to see that **it was my own father.** I said, "**Father, Father, do you know me?**" Throwing his arms around me and with tears in his eyes, he said, "**Oh my son, at last I've found you!** I've found you. You want a dime? **Everything I have is yours!**" Think of it. I was a tramp. I stood begging my own father for ten cents, when **for 18 years** he had been **looking for me to give** me **all his fortune.**" **God has so much to give us ...**

In Matthew 25:34 **He said,** "It's the joy of the Father to give you the Kingdom which He prepared for you from before the foundation of the world." **Do you realize that** the Kingdom was ours then? **In I Peter 1:18-19, it says this;** "You were not redeemed with corruptible things like silver or gold, from your aimless conduct received by tradition from your fathers, But with the precious blood of Christ, as of a lamb without blemish and without spot who verily was foreordained before the foundation of the world."

The body of Christ was formed **before** the world began. **The Kingdom** was formed and we were given a place before the world began. Christ was crucified, as it were, before the world began. The whole master plan is simply being worked out and we're a part of it. **Things don't happen by chance.**

No wonder in Ephesians 2:10 he says, "For you are God's masterpiece." **You are God's masterpiece (His workmanship),** "Created in Christ Jesus unto good works which God has before ordained that you should walk in them." Understand: Your style of life was preordained before the world began. **Why did He do this?** "That we should be **holy** and, **without blemish,** before Him."

You say, "I can't make it. I'm a Christian, and I love Jesus Christ, **but I am such a sinner,** I am not without blame. I am not without blemish. I am not spotless. I am not holy." **Oh yes you are, when you say yes to Jesus!** You see, because **Paul is talking about your 'position' in Christ, not your practice. Positionally before God** you are holy. Why? Go back to **verse 4,** "He has chosen us in Him." We are in Christ, the end of verse 3. Because we are in Christ, His holiness is ours. **His righteousness** is imputed to us. **His spotlessness** is our spotlessness.

God states in these verses, that before God, you are holy and without blemish. Why? Because you're one with Christ. His blood covers your sin. **Your sin** is hidden from God. **His righteousness** is imputed to you as if you have a cape of righteousness covering you. **When God sees you,** He **sees only** the righteousness of Christ. That's your **position "in Christ."**.

Friend, listen to this. He's made a holy church, before God, **positionally.** We're all as holy as Jesus. Can you imagine that? You say, "God, is very kind." That's right! **That's what He's been saying** through this whole book here. He's is very gracious. Because we're in Him we're as secure as He is.

When you read the book of Hebrews you'll find that **salvation** there is even called **perfection.** It's called perfection! (Hebrews 6:1). **We are made holy** in Christ. Now I don't know about you but . . . this causes me to want to live it. Doesn't it you? At least to be grateful and show it in my life.

Look at the first part of Ephesians 1:5, "In love having predestinated us." You see, there's **only one reason** He did it. What was it? **Love!** "For God so . . . . what? . . . . loved the world." **It's always love.** And what is love? It is a **disposition in the heart** of God by which He determines to sacrifice Himself to meet the needs of others. **Love is not an emotion,** biblically. Love is an **act of selfless sacrifice.**

Jesus said, "Greater love hath no man than this; than that a man . . . what? . . . lay down his life for his friends." (John 15:13) **That's love, real love!** God determined that He would sacrifice Himself for us. And **in love He set His affection upon us** before the world began and said, "For those people I will die." **As love is the fulfilling** of the law, and **love is the fountain** from where their salvation flowed: **therefore, love must fill their hearts** towards God and each other, **and that love must be the motive** and end of all their words and works.

Let me finalize this section by saying, God knows who His elect are, not me. **God elected me and called me** to preach the Gospel to everyone

I can, and that **whoever will** may come. **He said,** "**whoever** shall call upon the name of the Lord shall be saved." (Romans 10:13). Those are my orders. **Someone said,** "until God gives me the roll-call of the elect, I am going to preach the 'whosoever will' Gospel."

Dwight Moody used to say, "The whosoever wills are the elect and the whosoever wont's are the non-elect." **The Lord extends an invitation** in the last chapter of the last book in the Bible, Revelation 22:17, "**The Spirit** and the bride say 'come!' and **let him** who hears say, 'come!' And **let him** who thirsts 'come.' **Whosoever** desires, let him take the water of life freely."

The story is told of a pastor, who, during the 19th Century, had **preached** on the **sovereignty of God.** After the service, a well-educated **woman** came up to him and **thanked him** for his sermon. **She said,** "O sir, it has done me good. All my life **I have been troubled** with the doctrine of election. I have studied it for more than twenty years in vain. But now **I know what has been the matter, I have never been entirely willing to let God be God.**" And friend, that's the problem with many of us, we are unwilling to let God be God!

In the upper room Jesus said to His own disciples, "You have not chosen Me, but I have chosen you." (John 15:16). **Just as God planned the universe,** He planned the **church.** You might ask, "What is His plan?" **Here it is:** "Just as He has **chosen us** in Him before the foundation of the world, that we should be holy and without blame before Him in love." (Ephesians 1:4).

Let's read it one more time: "Blessed be the God and Father of our Lord Jesus Christ, who hath blessed us with all spiritual blessings in heavenly places in Christ." Doesn't that **explain** it all? It **sums it all** up: that we can have nothing, nothing in this Christian life without Christ. **God has blessed us** by giving us and by putting us in Christ. **There's no stronger identification** than to say we are **"in Christ,"** because it means that Christ is our environment.

Like Patrick of old could say, "Christ before me, Christ behind me, Christ beside me, Christ above me, Christ beneath me, Christ in me, Christ outside me." You see **it is more** than the indwelling Christ. **It is more** than the Christ the size of an inch that fits in your heart, **but it means** that your whole being, your whole existence, **your whole environment is Christ.**

Probably one of the most romantic stories I ever heard was one which was **published** a number of years ago in **Reader's Digest. A happily married young woman was driving home** when she became involved in a **terrible collision.** Her body sustained **multiple injuries,** but the greatest damage was to **her head and face**. She survived the crash, but the **sight of her disfigured body was so horrifying,** her **husband never returned** to the hospital after his first visit. Instead, he **divorced her and remarried.**

The **injured woman came under the care** of a devoted and **talented plastic surgeon.** In spite of the fact that she had **no money,** seemed **hopelessly doomed** to live out her life **hideously disfigured,** the doctor would not give up. Using bone and flesh from other parts of her body, **he literally fashioned a new face,** creating, among other things, a nose and lips. **She was emotionally and spiritually shocked** by this tragedy. The **doctor saw her** frequently, **encouraging her** about the progress she had already made. He assured her that more improvement might come, over more time and many surgeries. **The doctor married this patient,** and persisted to refashion her face until she was able to resume a normal life, **her ugly, distorted face replaced by one** which was truly attractive.

The story of this doctor's love is one which ranks high in the annals of human love. It is a wonderfully romantic story. **Does anyone protest** because this doctor **chose to love** this unattractive woman? **Does anyone object** to the fact that the husband **first chooses** the woman he wishes to be his wife, and later the woman chooses whether or not she will marry him? **Why is the doctor's "(s)election"** of this woman to be his bride **different from God's choice** of those whom He will bless with salvation?

There is a major difference between this doctor and God, and between praise and protest which can be summed up in one word . . . **grace. The doctor was not put off** by this woman's outward appearance. **He chose her** because of something inside her, perhaps a deeper quality of character. **When God chose us,** it was **not because** of anything which He saw in us, that drew Him to us. **God does not find the basis** or motivation for election deep within us; **He finds it within Himself.** It is because of **His mercy,** compassion and grace that God has chosen us. **In the choice** of those whom He will save, **God brings about the good of His elect** and the demonstration of His own glory at the same time.

Being chosen of God is no reason for pride or boasting. It is only an occasion for humility and gratitude. Because divine election gives us no ground for boasting, **fallen men find it distasteful.** This text in Ephesians tells us that **divine election should be the basis for our praise.**

Everything I am and all I hope to be is rooted in **God's freely choosing me "in Christ."** My faith, my hope, my work is not the grounds of electing grace but only its effect. **There is no ground for boasting on my part**... except in God. And in the face of fear and loss of assurance and all my own defect, I speak this word of trust: "Who shall bring any charge against the Lord's elect!" (Romans 8:33).

> "All hail the power of Jesus Name, Let angels prostrate fall,
> Bring forth the royal diadem, and crown Him Lord of all.
> Ye chosen seed of Israel's race, Ye ransomed from the fall,
> Hail Him who saves you by His grace, and crown Him Lord of all."
>
> —Edward Perronet

CHAPTER TWO

"In Christ," You Were Given "Grace" Before the World Was Created

II Timothy 1:9-10 states, "Who (the Lord) has saved us, **and called us with a holy calling, not according to our works, but according to His purpose and grace,** which was given us '**in Christ Jesus**' before the ages (time) began, but now has been revealed by the appearing of our Savior Jesus Christ, who has abolished death and brought life and immortality to light through the gospel."

Unfortunately, for many believers, there is a tendency among us from time to time **to be ashamed** of who we are and what we have as Christians. There are times when **we will hope that no one finds out** that we are a believer. **Maybe** we are **ashamed to admit** that we love the Lord and are trusting Him to save our souls. **Or, maybe** we are **ashamed to speak up** in a discussion about doctrinal matters, because the truth from the Bible differs from what those around us believe. **Maybe** we are **ashamed to sell out completely** to the Lord, **as He desires. Maybe** there is **shame over some failure** in the past that haunts us and prevents us from being all the Lord wants us to be. **Whatever the reason,** God's people often find themselves ashamed of the Gospel, the Lord and of our relationship to Him.

In these verses, Paul is writing to a younger Pastor who is a little **discouraged** by the things going around him and in the life of his friends. **Paul seems to sense** the fact that **Timothy might be growing ashamed** of the Gospel because of the affliction, persecutions and trials that accompany it. **Paul wants Timothy to know** (and us), that there are **some things in life** of which we must **never be ashamed.**

This passage is designed to teach us that there are just **some blessings** of which God's children **should never be ashamed!**

Let me share a couple! We should never be ashamed to identify **yourself** with the cross of Jesus. It is the **cross that purchased** salvation! It is the cross that stands as the dividing line between saint and sinner, (1 Corinthians 1:18, 21)! **It is what happened on that cross** that day at Calvary that makes all the difference in life.

Likewise, we should never be ashamed **to identify ourselves** with the Gospel message. It may bring division, **it may bring** affliction, **it may bring** persecution, but **it is that very message** that penetrated your heart and brought you to the feet of a risen, saving Lord! The Gospel is "the power of God unto salvation," (Romans 1:16!) **Paul reminds Timothy to not be ashamed** of the people of God, including those like Paul who were imprisoned for the cause of Christ. **We should never be ashamed to identify ourselves** with that crowd that is serving the Lord! There is no finer group of people in the world than those who have left all to follow Him. They may be strange, they may be weird, they may be very different from us, but if they are saved, they are family! **We should never be ashamed** of that old-fashioned, worshiping, praising crowd. That's His crowd, it should be ours as well!

It's curious that while New Agers, (hippies updated and enlightened), will **outspokenly proclaim** pyramid power, or channelers, and crystals, **Christians struggle to mumble** that they believe Jesus is the Christ, the Risen Son of the Living God. **How about you? Here's a question for you.** Given the choice would you be **more embarrassed** to admit that your bodily functions are being monitored by microsensors in your clothing, or that you have put your trust in God? **I suspect that if Paul** were here this morning, he would say that **we are all too timid** and **ashamed** and **embarrassed** by the gospel. **(How can we be embarrassed by good news?).** He would say that we have a better spirit than that. We have a better love than that. **We know better. Live** what you know then, and **show** what you know. **Speak** what you know. **Amen!**

Paul reminds Timothy that we are "**saved**". This word is in a tense that **means it is a completed act.** We are saved and will **remain saved forever!** Praise God! We **have been delivered** from the depths of sin and are saved from the wrath of God. His salvation is precious because it is complete, perfect and eternal.

Timothy is also reminded that **our salvation** and **our calling** have nothing to do with who we are, or with anything we may have done. **We are saved by grace!** The "unmerited love and favor of God for sinners" was manifested toward us even **before the world was ever formed!** Before you and I were even conceived, before Adam was even formed, **grace had already been extended to you and me** through Christ Jesus. Even though **God knew all about us** and all about the things we would do, **still He extended His saving grace** toward us. **It was His grace** that loved us, sought us, called us, saved us, keep us and that will take us home.

Who we are and what we do have nothing to do with salvation. Ephesians 2:8-9 states, "For by grace you have been saved by grace, and that not of yourselves, it is the gift of God, not of works, lest anyone should boast."

What wonderful verses of Scripture these are! I hope you are as excited about studying them as I am to share some teaching with you. **Paul, knowing he is going to be put to death** very soon, speaks of Jesus abolishing death, which does seem strange. But keep in mind that the **sting of death is gone, Jesus removed it** and **to be absent from the body** is to be present with the Lord.

As Christians, we don't speak of death, **but of sleep,** and in reality, **it is a moving day** as our **spirit and soul moves out of this tent** (body) and into a **mansion** that the Lord is building for His own, an eternal body. **Thus, Christ removes** the sting of death! In knowing that, **why would we be fearful** to give people the Good News of Jesus Christ? **Our fate is sealed in Him.** As for others, outside of Christ, their fate is not! Thus, **they need to hear and receive Jesus** as Lord and Savior of their lives and no matter what may happen to us, **God has a plan** and He is in control, and even in death, **Satan loses! That is what this chapter is all about.**

Today's modern secular people either **trivialize** death or **live in total despair.** They refuse to speak or think about death. **They are gripped** by their fear of death, and **cover their fear** through plastic surgery or partying. Their parties are alcohol, drugs, or expensive toys, in order to make themselves unable to be realistic with the situations of real life. **And their fear is justified.** Every son of **Adam** is **spiritually dead,** that is, his soul is separate from God. **So they die physically,** that is separation of soul from body. And they will **also die eternal death,** or what we call second death, which is separation of soul and body from God forever. (Revelation 20). **Although their only hope is Christ,** they are always to busy, to preoccupied with the things of the world.

Listen to this explanation by the Holy Spirit, through Paul, to the Christians (the saints) in the church of Colossae, "**the mystery** which has been hidden from ages and from generations, but now has been revealed to His saints. **To them God willed** to make known what are the riches of the glory of **this mystery among the Gentiles, which is Christ in you,** the hope of glory." (Colossians 1:26-27).

About our salvation: We are not saved by works, but we are saved by God's purpose (His working) and grace. **These things God provided** for us before the world began. It was always in **God's plan** to save us. The plan just wasn't evident until Jesus came. **As Paul stated** to the Colossians, "it was a mystery, hidden through the ages." (1:26).

Our finite minds cannot comprehend the **wonderful fact that God's wonderful intention,** in Christ, was hidden in ages past, but now has been revealed in Christ through the Apostle Paul. **This mystery** in the Old Covenant was not revealed, but in Christ, **is now revealed** in the New Covenant. **Don't forget that this all started,** "before the ages began." **In other words, it began** in the mind of God, eternities ago. **We must remember** that **it is God Who reached down** and **saved** us. **He initiated the process** from before time eternal, **He wooed us** and **won us** by the **convicting ministry of His Spirit,** and He **will consummate** the process in His good time. **Truly there can be no boasting** on man's part, for all we ever did was turn farther away from the One Who created and redeemed us. **Inseparably linked** to our salvation, **is our calling.** "and called us with a holy calling." (II Timothy 1:9).

Our "holy calling" is not pleasure or **riches** or **achievement** or **recognition by mankind.** The Christian whose sole desire is for the things of this earth achieves nothing but frustration. **Unfortunately,** even for many Christians, **the greatest pursuit** of our day are the pursuit of **purpose, happiness and wealth** in life.

Isaac Singer, who is a Nobel Peace Prize winner for literature, once wrote in a **magazine article,** about his very **successful life. It described** in some detail how he lived a very full and rewarding life. But **at the end of the article,** Singer made a statement which I've never forgotten. "But you know the same questions bother me today which bothered me fifty years ago." And number one among these questions was, **"Why was I born?"** No doubt Mr. **Singer is not alone** in his **unfulfilled quest** for purpose and meaning in life.

I want to ask you, **"What is your purpose in life?"** Why are you here? What are the long-term goals that you want to bring to fruition? **And will you answer the most important question here? What is God's great goal for you?** Let me answer that for you. **God's great goal for your life and mine is to** "conform us to the image of His Son" (Romans 8:29).

The great purpose "set before" us is to be consumed with the calling of Christ-likeness and to relentlessly pursue this great goal, no matter what the cost. **Like the apostle Paul,** we should set as **our primary purpose** in life "to know Him, and the power of His resurrection, and the fellowship of His sufferings, being conformed to His death, if by any means I may attain to the resurrection from the dead." (Philippians 3:10,11) **In another letter Paul reminds the saints** that . . . **God has not called us** for the purpose of impurity (uncleanness), **but in sanctification** (holiness), (1Thessalonians 4:7).

"Who has **saved us** and **called us** with a holy calling, not according to our works, **but according to His own purpose and grace** . . . ." (II Timothy 1:9). **God's wonderful purpose** was hidden in ages past (a mystery), but now Paul, under the inspiration of the Holy Spirit, let us look into God's plan. **In the Old Covenant** it was a **secret,** but now in the New Testament it is **unveiled.** "which was given us in Christ Jesus before time began." **The mind of our Sovereign God had this plan** all along.

Dr. Karl Jung, the **famous psychologist** made the statement several years ago that **"Purposelessness is the neurosis of our day."** God has provided a totally satisfying answer to the question of purpose, but it is **important to note** that this answer is **"according to HIS OWN purpose." Until we are willing** to live life **for His purpose** then we will chafe at His answer for it **cuts across the grain** of **our natural desire** for personal happiness. God's purpose for our lives is **not** personal **happiness,** but personal **holiness** (Christ-likeness), (Romans 8:28,29).

This verse is God's effectual call of the **elect** to salvation. God has sanctified the believer (set the believer apart) from sin unto Himself, so that they are holy ones. **This calling results** in holiness: **imputed** (to credited another) justification, and **imparted** (to give) sanctification, and finally **completed** (finished) glorification. **This truth:** no works—just grace, **is the foundation** of the gospel. (Ephesians 2:8-9; Philippians 3:8-9). **The idea of verse 9 is,** that **our own works** have nothing to do in inducing God to call us.

Always remember: 'grace' is the only basis for **God's sustaining work** in believers **"in Christ Jesus."** The sacrifice of God's Son made God's salvation plan possible, because He became the substitute sacrifice for the sins of God's people. **Paul writes it this way,** "For He made Him (God the Father made God the Son), who knew no sin, to be sin for us, that we might become the righteousness of God in Him." (II Corinthians 5:21). **This is the heart of the gospel** . . . explaining how sinners can be reconciled to God through Christ Jesus.

"In this world," Paul said, literally, **"in this present age."** Where are you to show this change? In church? Well, that is a **nice place to start,** but the place **where it will really count** is at home, at work, at school. In other words, right in the center of life. That is where the change is to be manifest.

Question: Do your friends and co-workers see Jesus in you? **Do they even know** that you are a Christian?

A Christian man was once asked if he believed in the miracle of changing water to wine. He said, "Of course I do. I never watched Jesus change water into wine, but in our home **He changed alcohol into furniture for the wife and toys for the kids."**

Think about the connection between **God's grace,** and the **salvation** that is found **"in Christ."** Jesus is the distinguishing trait of God's grace on earth. **Titus 2:11 teaches us,** "The grace of God that brings salvation has appeared to all men." **We cannot be saved, however,** by grace of God outside of Jesus Christ. **In II Corinthians 8:9 Paul wrote,** "You know the grace of our Lord Jesus Christ, that though He was rich, yet for your sakes He became poor." **Listen: God's grace** is the **incarnation of God** in the sacrifice and death of His Son on the cross.

". . . according to His purpose and grace, which was given to us **"in Christ" Jesus** before time began, . . ." (v. 9). **There's that word "grace" again.** I wonder how well we understand it? **Grace** is **God's unmerited favor** and **supernatural enablement** and **empowerment** for salvation and **for daily** sanctification, empowering, strengthening aspect of grace. (I Corinthians 15:10; II Corinthians 12:9; and II Timothy 2:1). **Grace is everything for nothing** to those who **don't deserve** anything. **Justice is getting** what you deserve; **mercy is not getting** what you do deserve; **grace is getting** what you do not deserve.

Salvation and our calling have nothing to do with who we are, or with anything we may have done. **We are saved by grace!** The **"unmerited love and favor of God for sinners"** was manifested toward us even before the world was ever formed! **Before you and I** were conceived; even **before Adam** was formed, **grace had already** been extended to you and me through Christ Jesus. Even though **God knew all about us** and all about the things we would do, still He extended His saving grace toward us. **It was His grace** that loved us, sought us, called us, saved us, keeps us and **grace** will take us home. **Who we are** and **what we do** have nothing to do with it.

Ephesians 2:8-9 states, "For by grace are you saved by faith, and that not of yourselves, it is the gift of God, not of works, lest any one should boast." **Titus 3:5 states it similarly,** "not by works of righteousness which we have done, but according to His mercy He has saved us, through the washing of regeneration and renewing of the Holy Spirit." **In fact, our works and our so-called goodness** did nothing but condemn us. **Isaiah**

64:6 states, "All our righteousness is as filthy rags, and we all do fade (wither) like a leaf, and our iniquities (sins), like the wind carried us away." **Salvation is pure grace** from start to finish! **When we attempt** to add or do anything **to the grace** of God, **we have nullified salvation!**

Dwight L Moody said, "The **law** tells me how crooked I am. **Grace** comes along and straightens me out." **J. H. Jowett defined grace** as "holy love on the move." While **J.C. Ryle wrote,** "Grace in the heart of man is an exotic. It is a new principle from without, sent down from heaven and implanted in his soul." **and,** "The grace of God does not find men fit for salvation, but makes them so." stated **Augustine.**

Christian, listen: Grace is needed for every service, **mercy** for every failure and **peace** for every circumstance. **Accept** God's grace through faith, then **prove** his grace through works, **for God does not save us** by grace so that we might then live in disgrace (to His holy Name). **Know this:** The only limits to God's grace are the limits we put on it. **As heat** is opposed to cold, and **light** to darkness, **so grace** is opposed to sin. **"Fire and water** may as well agree in the same vessel **as grace and sin** in the same heart;" **so said Thomas Brooks. George Barlow wrote,** "Grace is what all need, what none can merit and what God alone can give." **Amen!**

Question: If grace is "in Christ," and **salvation** is "in Christ," then we need to **ask ourselves, "Am I 'in Christ?'"** If not, **what does God's Word teach** that we must do to get inside Christ? **There is no doubt** that a person must "call on the name of the Lord" as the Bible teaches (Romans 10:13). Is just 'calling' enough? Is just 'believing' enough? Is having 'faith' only enough?

Let me illustrate: A man is drowning, and he screams out for help, "save me!" If help is offered, the man who is drowning must do his part (reach up), just as the one who is offering the help must do his part (reach down). **Salvation is a combination** of God's grace plus man's faith. **Paul taught,** "For by grace are you save through faith, and that not of yourselves, it is the gift of God . . . not of works, lest anyone should boast. For we are His workmanship, created in Christ Jesus for good works, which God prepared beforehand that we should walk in them." (Ephesians 2:8-10)

There is absolutely no doubt that, in order to be saved, a person must have faith that Jesus is the Messiah, the Christ, the Son of God. But, just having faith or belief in certain facts about God, or just giving mental assent to the truths of God, is not enough. **God's Word teaches** that a man must repent (meaning: a person must change his way of thinking and acting). **When one repents, it means** that a person has a changed will, which leads to a changed way of thought.... **faith.**

In Acts 3:19 Peter preached, "Repent therefore and be converted, that your sins may be blotted out, so that times of refreshing may come from the presence of the Lord." **To be converted, a person cannot continue living** the same way he did before he confessed Christ as Lord and Savior.

The sinless Son of God "who knew no sin" **became** "sin for us." **God the Father treated Christ** as if He were a sinner, though He was not, and had Jesus die as a substitute to pay the penalty of sin for those who believe. **Jesus was treated as if He** was guilty of all the sins ever committed by all who would believe, though He committed no sin.

Our God is Sovereign and remains omniscient and incomprehensible and yet in many ways retains His simplicity. **He tells us** in His Word that He is not a God of confusion but of order. He is altogether good, altogether holy and altogether sovereign. **We must remember:** He chooses what He chooses according to His good pleasure. (Ephesians 1:4,5). It is in His pleasure that He moves. **God chooses** what is pleasing to Himself. **God is never pleased** to will or to do anything that is evil or contrary to His own will or goodness. **You can always rest assured** that God will never do anything that is evil, and will always have good things for His children. And, we'll never figure Him out! The Lord says, "My ways are higher than your ways, and My thoughts are higher than your thoughts." (Isaiah 55:8-9).

All this sounds, and is, so wonderful, but what we forget, or haven't learned is: Because God has saved us by His sovereign grace, **we should be willing to suffer** for the gospel. **Living in America, most** of our evangelical churches today preach (or pitch) the gospel as the **way to have an abundant life** (rich and always healthy in this world ... here and now. "Jesus did come **to offer** you **abundant life. Trust in Him** and He will give you peace, joy, and a truly happy life." **While all** of **those claims are true** if properly defined, what the **salesman** in the pulpit hasn't told the listener (potential customer), is that **your problems may grow much worse** after you have trusted in Christ.

For our finite minds, it's hard to understand that **God's wrath was poured out on Jesus** as if He was a sinner. **Jesus was truly** "wounded for our transgressions, He was bruised for our iniquities ... and by His stripes we are healed ... All we like sheep have gone astray ... and the Lord has laid on Him the iniquity (sin) of us all ... He was oppressed and afflicted, and they made His grave with the wicked."(Isaiah 53:5-9a).

When have you heard a sermon on these verses lately? In II Timothy 3:12, **Paul says,** "Indeed, all who desire to live godly in Christ Jesus will be persecuted." **When you read** verses 8 through 11, in the original Greek language, it is what English teachers call a "run-on" sentence. In II Timothy 1:8, **Paul exhorts Timothy not to** "be ashamed of the testimony of our Lord, or of me His prisoner, but join with me in suffering for the gospel according to the power of God."

When we preach Jesus as a better **way to personal "self-fulfillment,"** we are promoting an **Americanized message** that is **not identical** with the biblical gospel. What of a potential convert who is from a **Muslim background?** Will his life be **one of trouble-free happiness** if he trusts in Christ? **His family** will disown him and possibly kill him because he converted to Christianity. What if he is **from China?** He may **lose his job or** be sent to a labor camp on account of his Christian faith. It is time we **present a gospel that is worth suffering for!** In II Timothy 1:12, **Paul states,** "For this reason, I also suffer these things, but I am not ashamed."

Our text is sandwiched between an exhortation to **embrace suffering** for the gospel without shame and an example of one who had done so. The motive that Paul uses to **urge Timothy to embrace** suffering is the glorious gospel of God's sovereign grace. **He is saying that** we must get a grasp of the glorious truth that God **saved us** according to His own purpose and grace. **He granted to us** in Christ Jesus from all eternity, and **will give us** the strength to endure suffering for the sake of the gospel. **Remember,** these words are coming to us **from the Holy Spirit** through the **pen of a man** who is **facing imminent execution** because of the gospel. **So these truths are powerfully practical,** but we must understand and submit to them in order to benefit from them.

The **"good news"** was given to us **"in Christ" before the world was created.** This is God's eternal plan. It is the **only plan** whereby we might be saved. **If a person misses this plan** . . . he will miss salvation. There always has been, and there always will be opposition to this plan. For those who oppose it, and refuse it, they will be forever lost and separated from God for eternity.

God says, "You were saved before the foundation of the world." (v. 4). **God says,** "I wrote your name in the Lamb's Book of Life before the world was created." (Revelation 13:8). **God says,** "I saw you, and I knew you, and I called you, and I saved you before you were born." (Jeremiah 1:5). **We are saved,** and then, **we are called. God says we are saved** by the mercy, and the goodness, and the atonement, and the calling, and the elective purposes of heaven! **And in never** is a man saved with his own doing, in his own goodness, in his own merit, in his own holiness. **No!** "By the works of the law shall no flesh be justified." (Galatians 2:16).

Someone might say, "I'm my own man, I did it. I stand here on my own. I will walk into heaven head up. I didn't need any Savior. I didn't need any atonement. No blood gospel for me. I'm here by my own strength, by my own ability, by the worth and holiness and merit of my own life." **Remember,** "Not of works lest any man should boast," lest he say, "I did it." (Ref: Ephesians 2:8, 9).

Someone else might say, like the old ignorant country **fellow** on his first flight in an airplane **that said, "I never did put** my **full weight down** on that thing." **He just didn't think, because he was in it!** To live or to die, that's the way that a man is in Christ. I am either **depending upon Him,** I have either **given myself to Him,** or **I haven't.** It is one or the other. **I either commit a deposit** to the bank, or I hold it in my hands. **I either commit a package** to the FedEx, or I hold it in my hands. **I either commit my letter** to the Post Office or I hold it in my hands. **I cannot do both. So it is with the salvation** of God **in Christ,** not according to works. **I either give myself to Christ** and trust in Christ and look to Christ, or I'm trusting and looking to something or someone else. It's **not both!**

In the olden days, a man might be **placed in prison** for being in **debt,** and a friend or relative could go and **pay his debt** and then **announce** to the one in prison, **"You're free."** The man **was free** when his **debt was paid.** He **only knew it** when the **announcement** was made to him. **So it is with God's children** of mercy and faith. **We are saved in heaven,** in the mind and purpose and revealed call of God, **before the world was made.** And then **we hear the announcement** of it that day when the **Holy Spirit quickens us** and **in faith** we **trust in Jesus** for the gift of life from His gracious hands.

Listen: I know this is sometimes **hard to understand,** especially when reading or studying it for the first time. But, remember: We are listening and learning from **the infinite Almighty God,** not some finite person! **God says,** "My thoughts are not your thoughts, nor are your ways, My ways," says the Lord. "For as the heavens are higher than the earth, So are My ways higher than your ways, and My thoughts your thoughts." (Isaiah 55:8, 9). **And,** "... because the foolishness of God is wiser than men, and the weakness of God is stronger than men." (I Corinthians 1:25). **And,**

"Oh, the depth of the riches both of the wisdom and knowledge of God! How unsearchable are His judgments and His ways past finding out! For who has known the mind of the Lord?" (Romans 11:33, 34a).

John Wesley, founder of the Methodist church, would make this discovery in May of 1738, **that salvation is by grace,** and not by works. This fine, **upstanding man**, a graduate of Oxford University, with the world at his feet, decided **he would become a missionary** to do good to mankind. He set out on a ship, that would take himself to the shores of America, **and work as a missionary for God in America,** and do all kinds of good things. **And what did he discover?** He discovered **what the Apostle Paul** said of the Jews of his time: that they were going about to establish their own righteousness, not the righteousness of God, but their own righteousness.

Wesley discovered the all-important truth: that while he was engaged in missionary work in a foreign land, a foreign land to him, that is, **he actually wasn't a Christian! Let me repeat** . . . . He actually wasn't a Christian. He was trying to **earn his way** into the kingdom of heaven. Well, that's what Paul is reminding Timothy of here: that **all of our righteousness is as filthy rags.** Salvation is not something that he can work up; it's not something of human effort. It's something supernatural. It must come from outside of himself. **It must come from** the outpouring of the powerful, **sovereign God Himself!**

Friend, let me ask you again as you read this, a very, very simple question: what are you relying on for your salvation today? Are you relying on church membership? **Are you relying** upon the fact that you are a good, upstanding person? Have you been through **Mrs. Manners' course,** and you know all the rules of etiquette, and you're polite and you do good to your neighbor? **You never kick your dog. Paul is saying,** and these are his dying words! **That we are saved, not because of our works;** that of human efforts, effort expended by our own inner strength and abilities will achieve absolutely nothing in the sight of our holy and righteous God; **that if we are to be** saved, it **must come** from something entirely **from outside** of ourselves.

If you stumble here, and you **get it all wrong! Eternity hangs** on this issue. **Life and death hang** on this issue. Whether you spend an eternity in the presence of Christ or an eternity in hell **depends on your understanding** of this simple statement: that we are not saved because of our works, but by trusting in Jesus' finished work on the cross.

"**Jesus said unto His disciples,** 'I am the way, the truth and the life; no man comes unto the Father, but by me.'" (John 14:6). "Neither is there salvation in any other, for there is no other name under heaven given among men, whereby we must be saved." (Acts 4;12).

When a sinner is pardoned and restored to the favor of God, this again is declared to be **a work of grace.** If it is a work of grace, it is not founded upon anything in the sinner himself.

Several months ago I finished **re-reading** that amazing story, '**The Cross and the Switchblade,**' written by the late **David Wilkerson,** a story of what was going on in the **streets of New York City** among the **tough gang leaders** and **teen-age gangsters** there. **Wilkerson** was called '**the Hoodlum Priest**' of New York. **While I was pastor in California, I took our young people** to a "**teen challenge**" meeting in Anaheim. **We listened to Wilkerson** and **met Nicky Cruz,** who, **before his salvation,** had been a **leader** of one of the **worse gangs** in NYC.

Many of these were dope addicts, rapests, homosexuals, thieves, and murderers, **giving themselves over to the vilest** and the foulest of deeds, **yet because of the grace of God,** the gospel has penetrated even into those dark areas and is **transforming and delivering** them from drug addiction and the other hopeless, wearing, frightful things of their life. **God transformed them** into new creatures in Christ, intelligent men and women, living lawful lives. **God does this through grace, "in Christ."** Nicky Cruz has gone on to become an **ordained minister,** preaching the gospel due to the initial efforts of **David Wilkerson,** who was used of God to lead Nicky to Christ.

What is of grace is not of works! When we say that salvation is not of works, **we are saying** that **salvation is not** founded on anything in the believer himself. **Salvation,** in the Biblical sense, **is a wonderful display** of the unmerited love of Almighty God toward a fallen, sinful, depraved man.

In my helplessness and in my hopelessness, I am now, as a Christian, referred to in Jesus Christ. **It is Christ** who redeems us from the penalty of sin. **It is Christ** who delivers us from the chains of death. **It is Christ** who shall be our Advocate in the great judgment day that is yet to come. Our salvation is of God, our Savior the Lord Jesus, **and the righteousness which clothes the saints** is the righteousness of the Son of God. **As Revelation begins,** "Unto Him who loved us, and washed us in His own blood, and made us kings and priests unto God our Father; unto Him be glory and dominion and power forever and ever. Amen" (Revelation 1:5-6).

God's purpose and grace were revealed by the appearance of our Savior Jesus Christ: He fulfilled the eternal plan of God. **Jesus truly shows us** what God and His plan are all about. That's why we can never know Jesus too much. **God has revealed Himself** to us all in the person of Jesus Christ. Jesus reveals Him. Become a Ph.D. in the study of Jesus! **Why? He abolished death.** Death does not take anything from the Christian; it graduates them to glory!

The Christian has no place for "RIP" on his tombstone; "Rest In Peace" does **not** adequately describe our eternal fate. **Why not the letters "CAD"?** "Christ Abolished Death" would let everyone know that we are more alive than ever, enjoying the eternal glory of our Lord. **He brought life and immortality** to light through the gospel. The understanding of the after-life was murky at best in the Old Testament; but Jesus let us know more about heaven—and hell—than anyone else could. He created them!

Jesus brought the truth about our immortal state to life through His own resurrection, **He showed us** what our own immortal bodies would be like, and assured us that we would in fact have them. **These things make Jesus** a more **reliable spokesman** regarding the world beyond, more so than anyone who has a "near-death" experience.

God's plan of salvation began for us in eternity past, before time began. **It continued** with the appearing of our Savior Jesus Christ. **It became personal to us** when He saved us and called us. It **continues as we live** our holy calling, and **will one day** show itself in immortality—**eternal life! All men, everywhere, need to be saved!**

What great comfort there is in knowing that God purposed your salvation from all eternity. This comfort will give you assurance that He will finish what He began. As Paul put it Philippians 1:6, "For I am confident of this very thing, that He who began a good work in you will perfect it until the day of Christ Jesus." It will motivate you to grow in holiness. **There are many more practical benefits,** such as humility. 1 Corinthians 1:26-31, and confidence in witnessing. (Acts 4:27-31; 18:9-11; and II Timothy 2:10).

There's a little church in the mountains west of Boise, Idaho, that not long ago celebrated its centennial. The members **had an enactment** of the history of their church. **Townspeople dressed** in period costume portrayed the pastors who served their church over the years.

One of the former ministers was **played by an old logger** who had lived through much of the history of the church. The **logger had come to faith in Christ** as a result **of that pastor's ministry. He told of the efforts**

of the pastor to reach him when he was a hard-drinking, hard-living man with no interest in the gospel, **a man who once said he** "had never met a preacher he liked."

The minister was praying one day and complaining **that he'd never win the logger** to Christ, and that **even if he did** he wouldn't know what to do with him. **The Lord's answer came** to him in a way he could understand: **"Don't worry about a thing.—You 'catch' him, I'll 'clean' him."**

It's always a privilege to tell people about Christ. Salvation is "a holy calling, not according to our works, but according to His own purpose and grace" (II Timothy 1:9). Christian, **if we just keep fishing,** we'll **"catch" some**, and God will make the foulest clean, just as He has done for us.

For a man to suppose, to think, that he can save himself is a gross error and mistake. **Can a temple build itself?** We are God's temple, of God's own building. God is the architect and the planner. God is the builder, and God created the materials and gathered them out of which His temple is made. **Can creation create itself?** Creation never creates itself. Out of nothing, nothing comes. **Only by the divine eternal God** can there come out of nothing the universe in which we live and the establishment of our own souls and bodies. **In no wise,** in no time, in no place, out of nothing can something come.

Martin Neimoller was a Man with No Spirit of Fear—In **1934, Adolf Hitler** summoned German **church leaders** to his Berlin office to berate them for insufficiently supporting his programs. **Pastor Martin Niemoller** explained that he was concerned only for the welfare of the church and of the German people. **Hitler snapped,** "You confine yourself to the church. I'll take care of the German people." **Neimoller replied,** "You said that 'I will take care of the German people.' But we too, as Christians and churchmen, have a responsibility toward the German people. That responsibility was entrusted to us by God, and neither you nor anyone in this world has the power to take it from us."

Hitler listened in silence, but that evening his **Gestapo raided Neimoller's rectory,** and a few days later a **bomb exploded** in his church. During the months and years following, he was closely watched by the secret police, and in June **1937, he preached these words to his church,** "We have no more thought of using our own powers to escape the arm of the authorities than had the apostles of old. We must obey God rather than man." **He was soon arrested** and placed in solitary confinement.

Dr. Neimoller's trial began on February 7, 1938. That morning, a green-uniformed guard escorted the minister from his prison cell and through a series of underground passages toward the courtroom. **Niemoller was overcome** with terror and loneliness. **What would become of him?** Of his family? His church? What tortures awaited them all? The guard's face was impassive, and he was silent as stone. But as they exited a tunnel to ascend a final flight of stairs, **Niemoller heard a whisper.** At first he didn't know where it came from, for the voice was soft as a sigh. Then he **realized that the officer** was breathing into his ear the words of Proverbs 18:10, **"The name of the Lord is a strong tower; the righteous run to it and are safe."**

Neimoller's fear fell away, and the power of that verse sustained him through his trial and his **years in Nazi concentration camps.**

Ray Stedman has these comments: "We are expected **not only to be concerned** about **our struggles and problems,** but others' too, and we long to reach out to them to help them with their problems. **Nothing is more proof** to me that a person is filled with the Spirit than when he evidences concern for somebody else's problems. That is the spirit of love." **That is the spirit of being "in Christ."**

What a wonderful thing to teach a man to look up to God in all things. **We don't need** any **beads.** We don't need any **rosaries.** We don't need any **confessionals.** We don't need any **masses.** We don't need any **purgatories.** We don't need any **absolutions.** Actually, we don't need any priests, rabbi's or ministers. **Why? We have God,** we have **Christ!** We have **His Word,** His **promise,** His **salvation,** His **altar,** His **entrance,** His **anchor of faith!** That's enough. **What the Lord has said,** that will I believe. **What the Lord does will,** that will I do. **What the Lord has promised,** that will I build on. **What God has said,** that will I follow, **looking in triumph unto Jesus, the author and finisher of our faith. Amen!**

I read about a woman who had once **known much** of the **Bible by heart,** but as she **grew older her memory failed.** Her **favorite Bible verse** was **II Timothy 1:12:** "I know whom I have believed, and am persuaded that He is able to keep that which I have committed unto Him against that day." **In time, she forgot** the first **part** of the verse, but she **remembered the part** that said: "I am persuaded that He is **able to keep** that which I have committed unto Him against that day." **Then she forgot some more** of the verse, but she could be heard repeating the phrase: "He is able to keep that which I have committed unto Him." **Finally, she only** had **one**

word of the verse, and it was the word Him. **She would say: Him . . . Him . . . Him . . . . She had forgotten** all the Bible except for that **one word,** but in that one word **she had all of the Bible. Friend, that "Him" is Jesus!**

Death for the believer has been deprived of its power and terror by the removal of its sting, for death is now a believer's portal into the presence of our Lord. **The final and ultimate annihilation of death** is future when at the Great White Throne judgment "death and Hades are thrown into the lake of fire." (Revelation 20:14).

As I write this, it seems like I have had a stream of **phone calls about funerals** and **memorial services,** and I have another one day after tomorrow. **Death is** that unending **stalker** that is headed for each of us. **God says,** "It is appointed unto man once to die, and after this, the judgment." (Hebrews 9:27). **Perhaps, that is why mankind is frightened** of this thing called death.

Get this: God did not make us to die! But, we do. **Everyone dies.** Some in **old age,** but others in the blossom of **youth** and good health. Why is this? **Why do people die? The short answer is sin.** Not that the dead are more guilty than the living. But that's the point: everyone is guilty. **Paul said,** "All have sinned and come short of the glory of God." **With that sin came death,** death to our first parents, and to the whole human race.

Death is an **awful** thing, don't let anyone kid you. **It mocks** every plan, **breaks** every hope, and **poisons** the life we have long before it comes. **Someone has called Ecclesiastes the truest book** in the world. And rightly so. As long as death is there, life is not what it should be. It's "Vanity of vanities, all is vanity."

Have you ever felt that you had reached 'rock bottom'? It seemed that there was no way to turn, and no one to help? **Let me share a story on touching bottom. Crowds gathered each week** to hear the **soul-stirring sermons of Joseph Parker,** the famous pastor of London's City Temple in the late 19th century. **Then a crisis hit** him hard. **His wife died** after an agonizing illness. Parker later said he would not have allowed a dog to suffer as she did. **A heartbroken husband** whose prayers had gone unanswered, **he confessed publicly** that for a week he had even denied that God existed.

But Parker's loss of faith was only **temporary.** From that experience he gained a stronger personal trust in **Jesus' death-destroying resurrection** and began to testify: "I have touched the bottom, and it is sound."

Listen to this exclamation of triumph from the risen Christ as He proclaims His victory over the grave: "Do not be afraid; I am the First and the Last. I am He who lives, and was dead, and behold, I am alive forevermore." (Revelation 1:17, 18).

Death is our most venomous enemy, robbing us of joy and hope—**unless the triumph of Christ's resurrection** reverberates in our heart. As we believe in the mighty Victor over death, **doubt is banished** and light drives away the darkness. **Hold fast to that triumphant trust** as you struggle through life's worst crises.

J Vernon McGee, the great pastor/teacher states, "Although it is our business today to get out the Word of God, **there is no power in us,** there is no power in the church, but there is power in the Holy Spirit. **It is the Holy Spirit** Who moves through an individual or through the church or through a radio program. The question is whether we permit Him to do so." **Under the leadership and power** of the Holy Spirit, we can **never be ashamed of Jesus!**

Never be ashamed and **never be intimidated** about your faith. Though **we may be mocked** and **ridiculed** for what we believe, we can be sure that **God will vindicate** us in the end. **The Lord is "able to keep"** that which we have entrusted to him. **All** that we **may lose in this life** through following Christ **will be more than restored** in the eternity to come. **The truth will be known** to the entire universe. And **no one** who trusts his life to the promises of God **will be put to shame.**

Who we are "in Christ" is the **sum and substance** of everything we're taught in this day of grace. **God expects us** to understand who He has made us to be in His Son, and in fact, it is the **key issue** of successfully living the Christian life.

"Wonderful grace of Jesus, Greater than all my sin,
How shall my tongue describe it? Where shall it's praise begin?
Taking away my burden, Setting my spirit free,
For the wonderful grace of Jesus reaches me.
Wonderful grace of Jesus, Reaching the most defiled,
By its transforming power, Making me God's dear child.
Purchasing peace and heaven for all eternity,
For the wonderful grace of Jesus reaches me."

—Haldor Lillenas

CHAPTER THREE

"In Christ" You Are 'Redeemed' and 'Forgiven' for All Your Sins

The Bible says in Ephesians 1:7—8, **"In Him"** (Christ) we have redemption through his blood, the forgiveness of our trespasses (sins), according to the riches of His grace which He lavished (made to abound) toward us in all wisdom and prudence (discernment or insight)."

In this study, we come to verses 7-8 in the first chapter of **Paul's letter** to the Ephesians **where Paul states** the **specific action taken by Jesus Christ** to make our salvation possible. **He shed His blood** on Calvary's cross. **And so Paul writes,** "In him we have redemption through his blood, the forgiveness of sins, according to the riches of God's grace, which he lavished upon us . . ."

The idea of redemption finds its origin in **ancient warfare. Captives** were made **slaves** and put to work. Some of those captured were of importance and highly valued in their homeland. In such cases the captives could be set free if their home country could raise the funds to buy back their release. **During New Testament times there were 6 million slaves,** which was about **one-third** of the population, in the Roman Empire, and the **buying and selling of slaves** was a **major business.**

If a person wanted to free a loved one or friend who was a slave, he would have to buy that slave for himself and then grant him his freedom. **The Greek word Paul** uses here **for redemption** was used in the 1st century to designate **the purchasing** of a slave out of the market place by the payment of a price. **If a slave performed well,** he could buy his freedom or have another secure it for him if the right amount was paid to the owner.

During World War II, Auschwitz was the **first German concentration camp** to become a place of extermination. **The gas chambers** were in constant use. Because of the **great influx** of **new prisoners daily,** the Germans also began to use firing squads. One day the commandant selected **10 men from one barrack** to be **executed** by the **firing squad.** One of those selected was the **father of a large family.** When he was pulled from his place in line, **he fell to the ground,** and began to **beg for mercy.** The **Nazi official** was unresponsive until the man standing next to the one on the ground, a **Catholic priest** named **Maximillian Colbe,** stepped forward to offer his life in exchange for the man on his knees.

Surprisingly, the commandant agreed to such an exchange. But **instead** of being led away to the firing squad, the priest was **thrown into a tiny, damp cell** where he suffered the agonizing **death of starvation. When I read this,** I am deeply moved, as I'm sure you are, **by the sacrificial and unselfish love** that men like this Priest demonstrate toward other human beings.

But, O dear friend, there is an **infinitely greater display of love** which the Apostle Paul writes about in our text today. **It is the love of Jesus Christ** for you and for me that caused him to **go to the cross** and **shed his blood to redeem** us from the bondage of sin and all its consequences. **Also, He died not for one man** or even for a few men, or even for several. **Jesus came to die** for the sins of **the whole world.**

According to the Bible, we all come into this world **enslaved to sin.** By ourselves we cannot escape this slavery. But **through His death,** the **great exchange** can take place. **Jesus paid** the redemption **price to purchase us** for God and **set us free** from the bondage and consequences of sin. We then become new people, freed from sin, **because Jesus exchanged Himself** for us. **The riches of God's grace** are **seen** in **the price** that was **paid** for our **redemption.** The **word** translated **"redemption"** in verse 7 **literally means** "to be set free or released by the payment of a price." Your salvation has been **bought at a tremendous price,** at the price of nothing less precious than the blood of Christ, the Holy One of God.

Sin is a bondage of the will and of the **mind.** Sin make us all slaves! **Shakespeare** got it right in **King Richard III,** when **the hero** of the play **says,** "My conscience hath a thousand tongues, and every tongue brings in a separate tale. And every tale condemns me for a villain." We all need release. **The removal of our offensiveness** before God is what **Paul calls here: "forgiveness."** Redemption is **not complete** without a **pardon,** without the removal of sin. **Forgiveness** here means to let go, to send away or dismiss. **God remits our sins, refuses** to hold them against us. **Isaiah paints** a **wonderful picture** of this in Chapter 44, verse 22: "I have swept away your offenses like a cloud, your sins like the morning mist. Return to me, for I have redeemed you."

Human forgiveness is conditional. Someone will hurt us and we will struggle to reach a place of forgiveness. But, **when we do forgive,** we **rarely ever forget. No matter how hard we try,** what was done to us by the other person will always be there. **No matter how hard we try** to press those memories down, they always seem to float back to the surface again.

That is not how forgiveness works with God. When the **Lord forgives,** He also **forgets.** When God forgives, He takes sin and puts it away. **He takes our sins** and **treats them as if they were never committed** in the first place! That is the clear testimony of the Word of God, (Psalm 103:12; Isaiah 38:17; Isaiah 43:25; Jeremiah 50:20; Micah 7:19; 1 John 1:7).

This is what Paul wrote in Romans 5:20, "where sin increased, grace abounded all the more..." **Christian, please remember this:** we cannot sin beyond God's grace to forgive. **I wonder** if you are a believer. You know that **you have received the Lord** Jesus Christ, and you know that you've been cleansed and washed in His blood. **But in your Christian walk, somehow** you've made some **terrible mistakes.** You've made some **terrible choices** in your life, and you're having to **bear up** under those choices. **For some reason you're thinking** you're going to exhaust the power and the grace of God to forgive. **No!** You **cannot exhaust His grace to forgive.** He gave lavishly to us, in the Lord Jesus Christ, the forgiveness of sin. "**He lavished His grace upon us.**" You may never fully understand this truth, this side of Heaven, but **it is true!** Christian friend, **claim it... it's yours!**

Why is it that most just don't want to admit sin? The bad new is, it doesn't matter if you're black, white, Hispanic, or Asian; **sin has consigned you** to spend **eternity separated** from God in Hell. **Why?** Because of sin! "The wages of sin is death" (Gal 3:23), and **you are totally helpless** to fight those charges. **But there's Good News! Christ satisfied the demands of justice** when He suffered in your place at Calvary. **Ephesians 1:7 says,** "In him we have redemption through his blood, the forgiveness of sins, in accordance with the riches of God's grace."

Oh, did you notice that Paul didn't say God redeemed us "out of the riches of (His) grace." **He said** God redeemed us "in accordance with the riches of (His) grace." And there's a huge difference between salvation coming "out of His riches," and coming, "in accordance with His riches."

Let me give you an example of what I mean. Fortune 500 lists Bill Gates as **America's wealthiest man** who is worth multiplied billions. **Now** if Bill Gates **gave $100** to a charity that would be contributing **"out of"** his riches, and he'd never miss it. **But** if he **gave $100 million** to a charity that would be contributing **'in accordance with'** his riches! **And friend, that's just what Jesus did. The Cross** routs, pardons, and expunges every sin.

And our guilt isn't partially cancelled it's **fully canceled!** There's **power** in the **Blood** of Christ.

Let me ask you a question. I want you to pause, think, and **answer** this question in your mind **before you continue reading. The question is:** What do you think is your greatest need at this moment? **Are you sick?** You may think, "My greatest need is **to be healed** of this illness." If you're **unemployed,** are you thinking, **may think,** "My greatest need is to **get a good job** to provide for my needs." If you're single, you think, "My greatest need is for a spouse." If you're in a **difficult marriage,** you think, "My greatest need is for **harmony** in my marriage." If you have a **child** who has become **ensnared by drug abuse,** you may be thinking that your greatest need is for your child to be **free from this addiction.**

While **all of these are important needs, none of them** is your greatest need. **The greatest need** of every person, whether he recognizes it or not, is to have **God change his life and forgive his sins** before he dies and faces God's eternal punishment. Health, adequate money, and a happy family **are wonderful blessings,** but if you **die without God's forgiveness,** these blessings will be useless. **Your greatest need** is **to know** that God has forgiven your sins and that **you are reconciled** to the holy Judge of the universe.

This Scripture states that "redemption is through His blood." That was the price He paid for your forgiveness. **Peter states** it this way, "...with the precious blood of Christ, as of a lamb, without blemish and without spot." The blood of the precious Son of God is more precious than silver and gold. **The author of Hebrews tells us,** "according to the law almost all things are purified with blood, and without the shedding of blood there is no remission (forgiveness)—of sin." (Hebrews 9:22).

Who needs redemption? My reply is "those who have forfeited their inheritance." Is not our inheritance lost? **Yes.—As natural descendants of Adam,** we are **outcasts and aliens** from the family of God; our right and title to every spiritual gift, to every heavenly hope, **is forfeited.** We are the poorest and neediest of all the creation of God—**a withering curse** has blighted every faculty and power—**we live wretched** among the wretched for a few days, in the downward course which leads to "the blackness of darkness forever." **Thus we need redemption.**

Redemption supposes captivity and slavery, and is a **deliverance out** of it. God's elect by nature are in bondage to sin. Through the grace of Christ, **they are redeemed from all iniquity.** They are **ransomed** out of the hands of him that is stronger than they (Satan); and they are

freed from the law, its bondage, curse, and condemnation, and from every other enemy. **And Christ** is the author of this. **He was called to be the Redeemer** of his people from all eternity. **He was sent** in the **fullness of time,** to procure the redemption of them; to which He had a right, being their near kinsman; and for which He was every way fit, **being God as well as man.**

This redemption comes to them through the **blood of Christ,** which was freely shed on the cross to procure it; and **was a sufficient ransom,** or redemption price. It was not only the same blood with those who are redeemed, but the blood of an innocent person; and not of a mere man, but of one who is truly and properly God, as well as man. **As Paul stated,** "In whom (Jesus) we have redemption through His blood, the forgiveness of sins." (Colossians 1:7) We receive **the forgiveness of sins;** of all sins, original and actual, past, present, and of the sins to come, **through the blood of Christ,** which was shed for our redemption (our forgiveness).

The Almighty, Perfect, Righteous, Sovereign God **forgives on the basis** that a penalty has been paid for. This **was done when Jesus Christ shed** His rich, red royal blood on Calvary's cross. **The good news** is that the penalty has been executed. **The bad news** is that many have rejected Jesus' payment for their sin.

In certain circumstances people can even redeem something that is their own property. **A man** who urgently **needs money** may **decide to pawn his watch.** The pawn-broker will take the watch and give the man an amount of cash. But the watch **does not immediately** become the property of the pawn-broker. **For a certain period of time,** the watch, strictly speaking, remains the original man's property. **But when he wants to regain actual possession of his property,** he must **redeem it** within that time, that is, **buy it back**; and **the price** he will have to pay will, of course, **far exceed the amount** he originally received from the pawn-broker. **The purpose of redemption,** in the biblical sense, is always to bring people into God's freedom, and to enrich them with an eternal inheritance.

There's another story that I like about a **little boy,** who went through a **lot of trouble** to **make a boat.** And it was a rather **elaborate little boat,** a **nice** little boat, a **model** boat. **He took it to the river,** and it floated downstream. and he **lost the boat.** And he was **very much upset** by the fact that he had lost the boat. **One day,** he was **walking** down the street, and he **passed by a pawn shop.** As he looked in the window, **there was his boat.** But unfortunately, **they had a price on it.**

And so, he went home. Sometime later he managed to get the **money necessary.** He went in. **He put the money down,** and he **bought his boat.** And as he went out of the shop, **he was heard to say, "Now, boat, you're twice mine. I made you, and I bought you."** Well, **that's how we belong to Jesus.** We are **created** by God, and we have **been redeemed by Him,** "in whom we have redemption by his blood."

Redemption signifies that God can break those chains for us in this life if we will repent. **The act** of breaking the chain **is called forgiveness.** And **the cost of this release** is paid by Christ: "we have redemption" says the New Testament, "through his blood, the forgiveness of our sins" (Ephesians 1:7). Thus the chain is broken never to be re-placed. **The redemption Christ** has paid for is an eternal redemption (Hebrews 9:11-12). **We have freedom from the curse pronounced by God's law.** "Christ redeemed us from the curse of the law, having become sin (a curse) for us" (Galatians 3:13).

Redemption means release from slavery (v. 14; 4:30; Luke 21:28; Romans 3:24; 8:23; 1 Corinthians 1:30; Colossians 1:14; Hebrews 9:15; 11:35). **It involves buying back** and **setting free** by paying a **ransom price.** Jesus Christ has redeemed us from sin (Heb. 9:15), namely, set us free from slavery to it (Romans 6). **The blood,** representative of the life, of the perfect Sacrifice had to flow out of Him for this to happen (Romans 3:24-25; Hebrews 9:22). **The immediate result** of our liberation from sin's slavery is that God has forgiven our sins.

"Redemption through His blood." What a **glorious subject** this is! **Redemption presupposes** a very grave situation. **It presupposes** captivity, bondage, and slavery. **If we were not all a fallen,** captive, enslaved race, there would be no need for redemption. But God's elect, like all other people, are all children of wrath by nature. **Redemption means the complete deliverance** of sinners from captivity, bondage, and curse, into the glorious liberty of the sons of God—**By the purchase of His blood** and the **power of His grace. Redemption is the theme** of the Bible. It is promised, prophesied, portrayed, and proclaimed throughout the pages of inspiration. **Everything in the Old Testament pointed** to it. Everything in the **New Testament explains** and declares it.

It is important to notice that you only use the **word 'redeem' or 'redemption'** if you are **buying someone out** of prison and slavery, **or out of** the threat of death, into freedom, as stated earlier.

In the South—in the days of slavery—there was beautiful young black girl that was put on the slave block . . . **for sale.** A **man** who was known as a **brutal slave owner** began to bid on her. Every time he would bid, the girl would cringe and close her eyes in fear. **Another plantation owner,** seeing what was happening, began to bid on her. **He outbid** the cruel man and purchased her. **He paid the price** for her and began to walk away. **The girl followed him,** and he turned and said to her, "You misunderstand, and I didn't buy you because I needed a slave . . . . I bought you to set you free." **She stood there for a moment, stunned** at what she heard. She caught up to him again and fell on her knees and **shouted, "Why? I will serve you forever."**

That simple story illustrates the **basis** on which **the Lord Jesus, the Son of the Living God** wants to cleanse and save us, and wants us to serve Him. He loves you. **Jesus paid the price** for you by shedding His own blood for the forgiveness of your sin. **The good news: this is all yours** if you are willing to come to Him, repent of your sin, ask His forgiveness and accept Him as your Lord and Savior.

While still in the **slave-market of sin** as a captive of Satan, the **sinner is purchased by the Redeemer,** brought out of the market and set free. **This sinner is bought out** of all that he was, that he might be brought into what he never had been, **and is made a saint** which he would eternally be. **He ceased** to be a **slave** that he might **become a son.**

I have had cold, calloused, evil, hard-hearted, sinful men tell me, "Pastor, you just don't understand what I have done, the sins I have committed, the sorry, sinful life I have lived. **I know there is no hope for me."** I have been able to stand confidently before them and declare, **"My God is a God of hope . . . He is a God of the second chance!"** "But pastor, I have never cared anything about God, or church, or any of the religious things. I have a cold, hateful, and hard heart. **I don't understand how God** could take a **black heart**, and wash it with **red blood,** and make it **white as snow."**

Dear friend, "nor do I understand how a **brown cow,** can eat **green grass** and give **white milk or yellow butter** . . . **but she does!"** God's Word states, "Come now, and let us reason together," says the Lord. "Though your sins are like scarlet, they shall be a white as snow, and though they be red like crimson, they shall be as wool." (Isaiah 1:18). **We live in a crazy,**

mixed-up, confused, sinful world, and no one seems to know the way out of this concert of confusion.

Have you ever been around an orchestra? When I was in **grade school** I began playing the **violin.** When I got to Jr. Hi., I started with the **clarinet,** and even played and marched with the High School band. (gave 'em both up for football, **big mistake!**) I remember that when we came together and **warm up the instruments.** That's the **worst sound** you've ever heard in your life. **Then Mr. Worthington, the orchestra conductor** would walk up and **tap on the rostrum.** Everybody gets quiet, and all of those **strange sounds** somehow are orchestrated to the point that **they become harmonious** and understandable and appreciated.

The world we live in is allot like this. Things are going on in this world that are far beyond our understanding, **but God, the great conductor,** knows the piece. **He arranged it.** He is bringing those strange sounds together and orchestrating them so they make **sense to those of us that are believers.** How well **our salvation was thought through** by the Godhead before the foundation of this world. **He made a plan,** and He is carrying it out. **I want you to know He has the authority** and He has the power to carry out what He came up with before the foundation of the world. **There's a difference in authority and power.** For instance, **two men** may have a **gun.** Each has power. **One of them has a badge. He has the authority to use that power. Our Lord has both** the **authority** and the **power.**

When we trust Christ with our lives, then we are assured our sins are forgiven. Only through Jesus can we be brought into unity with God. It's only by the goodness of God that Jesus leads us to Him. When we choose Jesus, then Jesus alone will cleanse from all sin. **Jesus said,** "And I, if I am lifted up from the earth, will draw all peoples to Myself." (John 12:32). **The apostle John wrote,** "If we confess our sins, He is faithful and just to forgive us our sins and to cleanse us from all unrighteousness." (I John 1:9).

We must remember that our salvation is only the **beginning of our spiritual walk with God.** You may have seen the **T-shirts** or the **button** given out at the Youth Seminars which has the letters **PBPGINTWMY** on it. It is **designed,** of course, **to evoke the question,** "What does that mean?" **The answer,** obviously, is:

"PLEASE BE PATIENT, GOD IS NOT THROUGH WITH ME YET!"

Many people 'in the church,' have made salvation overly complicated. I have found that to many of those "in the church" have too many preconceived ideas, and opinions that **are not scriptural** about what salvation is.

I once read of a cowardly young soldier in the **army** of **Alexander the Great.** Whenever the **battle grew fierce**, the young soldier would yield or run and hide. **The general's pride was cut** because this timid **soldier** also bore the **name Alexander.** One day Alexander the Great sternly addressed him and said, **"Stop being a coward** or **change** that good **name."** The **call to all Christians** (you and me), is the same today. **May we faithfully** live up to all the name Christian implies.

Jesus "who gave Himself for us, that He might **redeem us** from all iniquity, and purify unto Himself a peculiar people, zealous of good works." (Titus 2:14). **Jesus Christ** "gave Himself for us." What does this mean? The **word translated "for"** means that He died in our behalf, in our place, as our substitute. He took our sins and paid the penalty for them. This is how God **demonstrated His grace** to the world. He gave His Son to die for the sins of men, **to redeem us to Himself.**

The truth taught in the **biblical doctrine of redemption** is that God did something for us that we could not do for ourselves. **We were enslaved** to sin and had **no power** or means to free ourselves. **God did not need our help** in paying the price. In fact, **it is an insult** to Christ if we think that we can add anything of our own to the great price that He paid. **If someone offered you a gift** that was worth thousands of dollars and you reached in your pocket to give him a penny to pay for it, you would insult him.

Jesus graciously paid it all. We can do nothing except to receive His gift and then live every day in light of what He so graciously and generously did for us. **The Apostle Peter exhorts us** to conduct ourselves in the fear of God and then adds in **1 Peter 1:18-19,** "knowing that you were not redeemed with perishable things like silver or gold from your futile way of life inherited from your forefathers, but with the precious blood, **the blood of Christ."**

The Scripture says, "In whom we have redemption through His blood, the forgive-ness of sins, according to the riches of his grace." **The price paid** that we might have life was an awesome price! **Christ died** so that we might have life. He took our sins. "He Who knew no sin, that we might become righteous and alive in Him." (II Corinthians 5:21). We are redeemed by the precious blood of Christ.

We can picture this experience as a **mother and her small child.** Little **Johnny is playing outside,** finds this nice **puddle of water,** he splashes and plays in the water, not even noticing that he is getting wet, and muddy. **There is mud** on his shoes, his pants his arms, his legs. There is even mud on his face. He **comes running to door** of the house, and **mother shouts, "NO YOU CAN'T COME IN HERE** with all that mud on you, you'd totally ruin the rugs and furniture. **There's no way** that mother is going to **allow little Johnny** to run around the house in that condition.

Now what can little Johnny **do** to make himself acceptable. He **can rub** at the mud but that just **smears** it all over himself even more. He can **jump back** into the puddle, but that will just make it worse. **No! He can't do anything** in and of himself to make himself fit to enter the house. **But mother, who loves** that little fellow very much, and knowing he wants to come in, **takes him and washes him** and **puts clean clothes** on him, and **gives him a big hug,** and now he can be in house! **Hallelujah! That's what Christ did for us** in a spiritual sense, **His blood washes** away the guilt of our sins, **He clothes us** with His robe of righteousness!

Someone has said, "If man's greatest need in life was **pleasure,** then God would have sent an entertainer. If man's greatest need had been **money,** then He would have sent a financial consultant. If man's greatest need would have been for **information,** He would have sent an educator. But **God in His infinite wisdom** knew that **man's greatest need was redemption**—and so He **sent a Savior.**

We need to remember that 'redemption' encompasses **more than 'forgiveness,'** but Paul mentions forgiveness because it is the first and foundational thing to know and experience when you are redeemed. **Forgiveness means** loosing or letting someone go from what binds him. **Trespasses are synonymous with "sins,"** the individual acts of sin, not sin in general. **Paul wants us to know** that our specific, shameful, embarrassing sins that **loom up in our memories to condemn us** are all **forgiven through the blood of Jesus Christ.**

All of us have transgressed the law of God. All of us will stand before the bar of justice. **All of us will stand before** the searching judgment of God, and that is why this word is so precious: that we have been given forgiveness of sins.

Professor Finlayson, of the Free Church College, **put this provocatively** (and read this carefully) when he said, "Hell is eternity in the presence of God." **He said, "I meant to say it that way."** Listen to it again: "Hell is eternity in the presence of God. Heaven is eternity in the presence of God **with a Mediator."**

I hope you see the point. To be in the presence of God eternally **without forgiveness** of sins, that **is hell.** But to be in eternity in the presence of God **with forgiveness** of sins, that is **heaven.** To have **a Mediator** (our divine lawyer, Jesus), who has borne our sins so that **our sins might be fully forgiven,** that we might have communion with God and with all those who trust in Him, that is heaven! **But to be before** the throne of God **without forgiveness, without the mercy** of the Mediator, that will be to receive the **sentence of hell.**

What is sin? It's a transgression; it is a trespass of God's commands. Whatever else we need in the Christian life, **we need forgiveness** before and more than anything else. **And here's the Apostle Paul reminding us** of God's forgiving grace, the forgiveness of our sins. Though we have broken God's law, God in Jesus Christ has forgiven us (Colossians 2:13). **God's undeserved bounty toward the sinner** was manifested by the **planned-in-eternity redemption** through the blood of the Lamb slain. (I Peter 1;18-20). Is it any wonder Paul says that **it will take all the ages to come** to show forth the exceeding riches of His grace?

Do you remember the judge's statement in the sentencing the **shoe bomber, Richard Reid** a few years ago? He had **attempted to blow up a jetliner** with an **explosive** he had hidden in his **shoe,** but, was unable to light it? In court he said that he had "done what he had done, or attempted to do what he had attempted to do, **in the name of the great Allah,** and that he was bringing judgment against the wicked infidels, and that, "**Oh! how he wished** that he had been able to kill himself and to kill these infidels," **And the judge said to him,** "Mr. Reid, on the Judgment Day, **God will judge** whether it was we who were evil or whether it was you who were evil."

All our righteous indignation wells up when we see someone through terrorism taking **innocent** lives, or attempting to take innocent lives, because we see obviously the very patent transgression of law and of morality. **Our Lord Jesus Christ said** to us many, many hundreds of years ago, "Take the log out of your own eye before you attempt to take the speck out of your brother's." **All of us have transgressed the law of God. All of us will stand** before the bar of justice. **All of us** will stand before the searching judgment of God, and that is why **this word is so precious:** that we have been **given forgiveness of sins.**

Just to be clear, what is: "The forgiveness of sins?" Out of all the many, many **blessings secured** for the sinner through redemption, **only this one** is mentioned. On the ground of **the shed blood** of His **Beloved**

Son, the **Father cancels all the sins** of the believing sinner and **gives him** a clean bill of pardon. **He assures His child** that, when once He has thus remitted the punishment for his sins, **He remembers them no more.** "For I will forgive their iniquity, and their sin, I will remember no more." (Jeremiah 31:34). "As far as the east is from the west, so far has He removed our transgressions from us." (Psalm 103:12).

Paul wrote to the Corinthian church, "Now all things are of God, Who has reconciled us to Himself through Jesus Christ, and has given us the ministry of reconciliation, that is, that God was in Christ reconciling the world to Himself, not imputing their trespasses to them, and has committed to us the word of reconciliation." (5;18-19).

We notice in these two verses **that our Sovereign God has accomplished** everything necessary for the newly converted person and newly transformed life. **Sinners, on their own,** cannot accomplish these things. **This verse teaches** that God has called every believer to proclaim the gospel of reconciliation to others. **God, by His own will** used His Son Jesus, the only acceptable and perfect sacrifice, as the means to reconcile sinners to Himself. **We must learn** that God wants Christians to accept the privilege of serving unbelievers by proclaiming a desire for them to be reconciled.

Peter states in his sermon at Pentecost, "And it shall come to pass that whoever calls on the name of the Lord shall be saved. Men of Israel, hear these words: Jesus of Nazareth, a Man attested by God to you by miracles, wonders, and signs which God did through Him in your midst, as you yourselves also know, Him (Jesus), being delivered by the determined purpose and foreknowledge of God, you have taken by lawless hands, and crucified, and put to death, whom God has raised up, having loosed the pains of death, because it was not possible the He should be held by it." (Acts 2:21-24).

This passage teaches, among other things, from eternity past (II Timothy 1:9; Revelation 13:8), **God predetermined** that Jesus would die an atoning death as part of His pre-ordained plan (4:27-28; 13:27-29). **The crucifixion** was predetermined by God for the redemption of His elect. **Jesus came to heal us** completely from the virus of sin.

Reconciliation is a change from enmity toward friendship, and is brought about by God alone. As stated, **"in Christ,"** we become a new creation. **This is only possible** through the compelling love of Jesus. The Father draws us to Him with an eternal love. His transforming, reconciling love comes into us through the Holy Spirit.

The **ultimate goal of the believer** is to be like Christ. (Romans 8:29; Philippians 3:12-14; I John 3:2). **By continually focusing on Jesus,** the Spirit continually transforms the believer more and more into His image. **The more you live** and **grow** in the knowledge of Christ, the more He is revealed in your life. (II Corinthians 3:17-18; Philippians 3:12-14). **This is a progressive sanctification** (setting you apart continuously for the work of God). This is a continued work of the Holy Spirit in you.

As a Christian we not only have forgiveness that takes care of the **negative** (our sins), but **positively** God gives us the equipment to understand Him and to walk through the world on a day to day basis. Isn't that fantastic? **By the wonderful grace of God,** He **forgives** our sin and **gives** us wisdom and insight in higher spiritual things. Then He deposits into our minds and pours through our hands and feet and mouths **principles for spiritual living** in the midst of a sinful world like ours. **When spiritual discernment** comes, we become wiser. God has taken us into His confidence.

Everyone must have forgiveness and salvation because of our sinfulness and character—"our sins, and . . . all unrighteousness". **How sadly sinful we are,** indeed! **We are not sinners because we sin: we sin** because we are sinners in character. **A dog** is not a dog because it barks: it barks because it's a dog. **A tree** is not a plum tree because it bears plums: it bears plums because it's a plum tree. **Actual sins** are the symptoms of the **deep seated malady** of a sinful character; and it is not merely the spots but the disease that the Great Physician would deal with, as we place ourselves in His hands.

We had all been kidnapped by sin, captured and cultivated by lawlessness and imperfection. All the world **is lost**, and needs to be redeemed, to be set free. God wants to deliver us from the evil one. **The Bible says that Christ** was our **ransom** . . . to set us free from sin. Once we come to Christ, we are delivered from the penalty of sin . . . which is death (physically and spiritually). By faith, **"in Christ" we are redeemed,** that is, to be set free from sin and death.

Many Christians tend to think that when God **wiped out the past,** and gave us a clean slate, and that **from now on** it is **up to us** to keep it clean. He gave us a new start once. **Now we are to struggle** to keep things straight. **But that paints God** as a **miser,** tight fisted with grace. **That is not true!** The Bible says, "With all wisdom and prudence God unveiled His Sovereign plan of redemption. God has not made His grace towards us to abound in a random manner, but His grace has abounded according to His divine wisdom and insight. **With all wisdom and prudence** God has unveiled **His Sovereign plan of redemption.**

Calvin Coolidge was the president of the United States in the **1920s,** and he was renowned for the **brevity** of his speech (he obviously wasn't a preacher!) **One Sunday** morning he **went to church** and, on returning home, **his wife,** who was unable to go because of **illness,** asked what the **subject the preacher** spoke about was, and he replied one word: 'Sin'. His frustrated wife said: 'Well, what did he say about sin?' Characteristically Coolidge said: **"He's agin' it"**—That, put very simply, **is the way God is,** and the way we should be regarding sin. **We ought to abhor it** with a holy hate.

Sometimes ministers, denominations and outspoken preachers seem to make salvation woefully complicated. **Our ideas and opinions** are brought into the discussion. We must remember and say, **"Jesus is my Lord and Savior!"** There is nothing that you can add to the equation of salvation, no matter what you do. When we make Jesus Lord, **He freely gives us all things** which are bestowed "through Christ" and His cross. (I Corinthians 1:30-31; Luke 2:10-11; Hebrews 4:1-8).

Here then is a statement of what Christ redeems his disciples from and what he redeems them for: "For the grace of God that brings salvation has appeared to all men. **It teaches us to say** 'No' to ungodliness and worldly passions, and to live self-controlled, upright and godly lives in this present age, while we wait for the blessed hope—the glorious appearing of our great God and Savior, Jesus Christ, who gave himself for us to redeem us from all wickedness and to purify for himself a people that are his very own, eager to do what is good." (Titus 2:11-14).

Paul wrote in a similar verse to Ephesians 1:7, 8, "In whom we have **redemption** through his blood, even the **forgiveness of sins,** according to the riches of His grace; which He has **lavished** on us...." (Colossians 1:14).

This redemption, this forgiveness is according to **the riches of His grace,** or to the riches of His grace, **which He 'lavished' upon us.** He's **not only drawing** our attention to costly grace; **He's not only calling** our attention to forgiving grace, **He's calling** our attention to **free grace.** That redemption has been given to us through **God's lavish grace. He not only** gave us redemption and "forgiveness of sins according to the riches of His grace," **but He 'lavished' these upon us!**

When God gives forgiveness, He **does not dig** down into a little pocket and **dig out a little** and say, "there's a little forgiveness, now make sure it lasts"... instead we see in these last words of our text that His grace and forgiveness is **"lavished upon us. What does** this word **"lavished"** mean? **When you lavish** something upon someone you **'heap it on' more and more. Lavished means** repeated portions, **again and again. When God redeems you** and forgives you he **doesn't give you** a **tiny bit** of forgiveness. **He pours it on!** He **gives you** a **new identity** as his **beloved child** in whom he is well-pleased. **Because God forgives you** and **totally accepts** you, regardless of what you have done, or what you have been, **you can accept yourself.** You are free!

Without Christ, **your soul was dead in sin,** then Christ took the punishment. **Christ took it!** Christ put it away! **Christ let you loose from** your sin and punishment! This is **something beyond** anything that **a psychologist** can do. This is beyond anything that **a hypnotist** can do. You can have **all the positive thinking** that you like. and **read all the books** about it, **and listen to all the tapes** about it, but **they can't give you,** through this therapy, **the forgiveness of sins.** For only **God, "in Christ,"** can do that.

But praise God, "in Christ," we have redemption through His blood, even the eternal forgiveness of our sins. **Sometimes we live** with **the consequences** of our sin. That is what's called **governmental** forgiveness. **There's restorative** forgiveness. **This often confuses young believers. They don't understand** that **if Christ has forgiven their past, present and future sins,** why is it that **if they slip up** today they **need to confess** their sins again? **It's simply this: because you are a child of God,** you are no longer in a relationship between **God who is a judge** and you who are a guilty sinner. **Do you understand?** That relationship's gone.

It is now God who is your Father and you **are His child. Your sins are gone: past, present and future;** but what you **need is restorative forgiveness.** That **means:** that sin, when **we commit it as Christians,** goes between our **fellowship and God—not our salvation,** but **our fellowship** between **us and God.** That is **why John says, in 1 John chapter 1 and verse 7:** "If we walk in the light, as he is in the light, we have fellowship one with another, and"—**verse 7**—"the blood of Jesus Christ his Son cleanses us from all sin."

"**If we confess** our sin"—what does that mean? Does that mean **God's not** going to forgive us as Christians? **Are we going to go to hell if** we don't confess **every little sin** that we do? **Do you know what confessing** your sin as a Christian is? **It's putting your hands up and saying:** "Lord, It's me again. I've done it again. Would You forgive me?

Take it away. **I don't want it to be between You and me.** I'm Your child, You're my Father; just take it away. **And I plead the blood,** I know there's power in the blood to **restore this fellowship** (not salvation), to me as Your child." **Remember David?** After all his abominable sins—laziness, adultery—lying—murder—etc. **He didn't pray,** "Restore my salvation, 'cause God I'm lost again." **No! He prayed,** "Restore to me the **joy** of Your salvation, and uphold me with Your generous Spirit." (Psalm 53:12). **"because I'm out of fellowship with You. I want my Father, because I've lost my joy and victory."**

If you are a believer, it is **crucial** for your **Christian life** that you understand and experience **on a daily basis** this liberating truth that **God forgives all of your sins** through the blood of Jesus Christ. **In II Peter 1:5-8,** Peter lists a number of virtues that you are to add to your faith so that you will be useful and fruitful in your walk with Christ. Then he adds II Pet. 1:9, "For he who lacks these qualities is blind or short-sighted, having forgotten his purification from his former sins." **The devil knows this,** which is **why he is the accuser** of the brethren. The saints **overcame** his accusations **because of the blood** of the Lamb. (Revelation 12:10-11).

This is how it **works practically. You are a believer** in Jesus Christ, but you have just sinned. **You disobeyed** a clear command in God's Word. Maybe it was anger or lust or foul language or stealing or whatever. **The Holy Spirit convicts** your heart through your knowledge of the Word that what you did was sin. **So, you repent** and **confess** your sin to God and appropriate His cleansing (1 John 1:9). So far so good!

But, then the enemy comes and **whispers,** "A fine Christian you are! **Do you really think** your sins are forgiven? **Ha! You're not even saved!** You're guilty and you know it. **Forget all of this nonsense** of being saved by grace!" How do you answer him? It would seem that he is right. You claim to be a Christian and yet you deliberately, knowingly sinned against God. **There is only one way** to **answer the devil when he accuses you:** "You're right, Satan, I did sin. But my salvation does **not rest** on my sinless performance, **but rather on the blood** of Jesus that paid the price for my sin. **I'm trusting in His shed blood** and if His blood isn't adequate to acquit me, I am doomed. **So the Lord rebuke you, Satan!**" (Zech. 3:1-5.)

If you are His child, and I pray you are, **you never need to worry** that **your sin** will ever **outstrip God's super-abounding grace.** Do you ever feel that God has run out of forgiveness or patience with you? Do you ever feel that **your sin is too great** or your progress too slow? **I want you to know** that **you cannot sin** beyond God's grace because he has completely and totally cancelled your sin. I John 1:7 states, "The blood of Jesus Christ His Son **'keeps on cleansing us'** from all sin."

In fact, the cause of redemption is "the riches of his grace." The whole Bible is about God's loving grace for a sinful people. **Let me share with you why Jesus came to this earth.** Grace **planned** it. Grace **provided** it. Grace **performed** it.

Grace **applies** it. Grace **will complete** it (at the final resurrection!). Paul stated, "... that in the ages to come He (Almighty God) might show the exceeding riches of His grace in His kindness toward us in Christ Jesus." (Ephesians 2:7) **Many believers fail to appreciate the riches that they already have.**

The story is told of an aged silver miner who had spent his whole life searching for silver in the **mountains of the Old West.** He had become **so involved** with his search that his **wife and children had left** him. When **he died,** the handful of people who came to **bury him** found in his possessions a **note instructing** them to bury him **under his cabin. As the shovels turned** over the earth, a **lustrous gray material** began to appear. It was the famous **Comstock Silver Vein,** the **richest** in **California history.** That miner had been a **billionaire** all his life, but he **did not know** about the wealth that he had and he had **never claimed it.** He did not realize how rich he really was.

Please pay attention to this: Every **true believer is a spiritual billionaire.** The **Bible says that Christ became poor** (and died for us) **that we** through His poverty might **be rich** (2 Corinthians 8:9). The **believer,** who is a **child** of the King, often goes around **living like** a **pauper** rather than living like a **prince.** God wants us to know how **rich we are because of His matchless grace:** "Blessed be the God and Father of our Lord Jesus Christ, **who hath blessed us with all spiritual blessings** in heavenly places in Christ" (Ephesians 1:3).

Donald Grey Barnhouse, the great Presbyterian pastor/theologian, once **preached** a sermon on the **extent of God's forgiveness. Throughout the sermon** he noticed a **12 year old boy** leaning forward and **listening intently.** When he **came to the end** of his sermon **He summed it up** by putting it all into one sentence. **He said,** "Our sins are forgiven, forgotten, cleansed, pardoned, atoned for, remitted and covered. They have been cast into the depths of the sea—blotted out as with a thick cloud, removed as far as the East is from the West—remembered against us no more and forever cast behind God's back!"

After the sermon the little boy came up to him and **said, "Great sermon Doc, we're sittin' mighty pretty aren't we!"** That boy had understood. The **forgiveness** God gives is complete! **It completely restores us to God** for all time and eternity.

Year after year I find repeatedly **among Christians,** even the **most mature** of them, when God convicts the greatness of their sin, it is very **difficult for them** sometimes to **believe that that sin can really be fully and finally dealt with. Because of that sin,** when they see **how ugly** it is, **how painfully** it has impacted those that we love and those that we know, **how deeply it has grieved** and **offended** our loving Father, **it becomes so real** and so near and so big and so great to us that it becomes very **difficult to believe** that it could be **fully and freely forgiven.** And here is **the Lord God saying** that **His lavish grace** of forgiveness is **far more lavish than our sin. Hallelujah!**

John MacArthur, points out that **Israel's greatest holy day** was **Yom Kippur,** the **Day of Atonement.** The high **Priest** selected **two unblemished sacrificial goats. One goat was killed** and his blood was sprinkled on the altar as sacrifice. The High Priest **placed his hands on the head of other goat** (called the scapegoat), symbolically laying the sins of the people on the animal. The **goat was then taken out deep into the wilderness,** so far that its could **never find** its way back. **In symbol,** the sins of the people went with the goat, never to return to them again.

That of course **did not ultimately save** the people of the OT—the Jews. It did however **point to the ultimate sacrifice of Christ** whose blood was shed and at the same time who became our Scapegoat. **That is what our Redeemer did** to redeem us! **Here is a Savior** who **doesn't put us on a guilt trip,** Oh no, **He sends our guilt on a trip—away!** This reality is **described in verses** like Psalm 103:12, which states, "As far as the East is from the West, so far has He (God) removed our transgressions from us." **And** Micah 7:19 states, "He will again have compassion on us, and will subdue our iniquities. You (Almighty God) will cast all our sins into the depths of the sea." **What a comfort.** What **hope!** What **victory!**

We sing the Hymn, "Grace that is greater than all our sin..." **But did you mean it? Have you seen your sin?** Have you been **able to say** "I'm worse! I'm worse than I appear to be! I'm worse than I ever thought myself to be before, **but God's grace is greater; it's greater than my sin?"**

Pastor Steven Cole tells this story: One night in a **church service** God opened the heart of a **young woman** to respond to His call and believe on Christ as her Lord and Savior. **She had a very rough past,** involving alcohol, drugs, and prostitution. But, **the change in her was evident** as she experienced God's forgiveness. **Over time, she became a**

faithful member of the church, and served by **teaching young** children. It was not long until she **caught the eye and heart of the pastor's son. The relationship grew** and they began making **wedding plans.** But then the problems began. **Many in the church did not think** that a woman with a past such as hers was suitable for a pastor's son. The church began to gossip and argue about this matter.

So, they decided to have a meeting. Emotions heated up, tension increased, and the **meeting was getting out of hand.** The young woman became **very upset** about all of the things being **brought up about her past.** As she **began to cry,** the **pastor's son stood to speak.** He said, "My fiancé's past is not what is on trial here. **What you are questioning** is the ability of the **blood of Jesus to wash away sin. Today you have put the blood of Jesus on trial.** So, does it wash away sin or not?" **The whole church began to weep** as they **realized** that they had been **slandering the blood** of the Lord Jesus Christ. **We sometimes sing** the old hymn, "**What can wash away my sins?** Nothing but the blood of Jesus." **Either that's true or it's not.** Does the blood of Jesus does not wash away all of our sins completely? **Praise the Lord, the answer is YES!**

You see, that's what the Apostle Paul is saying. When you come into the throne room of the heavenly Father, and you **come in to pray** and to **adore Him,** don't you forget to adore Him **for His costly grace** and for **His forgiving grace,** and for this **free,** this **lavish,** this **generous grace** which He has given to us. It's a forgiveness that's more lavish than all our sin.

So today, if you don't know my Lord Jesus, I call upon you to trust the Lord Jesus Christ, our great Redeemer. "I press upon you and myself, my brothers and sisters, the claims of his blood." (1 Corinthians 6:19-20).

> "**Redeemed,** how I love to proclaim it!
> **Redeemed** by the blood of the Lamb;
> **Redeemed** through His infinite mercy,
> **His child** and forever I am."
>
> —Fanny J. Crosby

CHAPTER FOUR

"In Christ" You Are 'Redeemed' by God With an 'Inseparable', 'Inescapable' Love.

Romans 8:38-39 **gives us** a very **positive comment by Paul,** "I am persuaded (very sure) that neither death nor life, nor angels nor principalities (rulers), nor things present nor things to come, nor powers, nor height nor depth, nor any other creature (anything else in all creation), will be able to separate us from the love of God **in Christ Jesus our Lord.**"

This sublime chapter, opened in verse one with a strong declaration of **"there is now no condemnation** to those who are in Christ Jesus." **And, it is fitting** that this passage should close with a declaration equally strong to us, that **there is "no separation** from the love of God to those in Christ Jesus our Lord." **It is one of the great passages** of Scripture relating **the eternal security of the believer.** We must remember: **God's love is unconditional,** and that, my friend, gives me security. **These verses confirm the truth,** that **when one is truly "in Christ,"** the salvation of God which he possesses is secure.

Security is **a critical element in life.** Unfortunately, it's also **very elusive.** Recent **world events in Japan, Iran and Libya demonstrate how insecure our world is. On a personal level,** perhaps you live in insecurity because you have **been the victim** of a crime such as robbery or rape. **Maybe your spouse** has threatened divorce and you lack marital security. **Your children** may be struggling with physical or emotional issues that have deprived you of security. **Perhaps you've lost your job** and your **retirement has plummeted** leaving you feeling hopelessly insecure.

When reflecting on your life, you realize that you have **little or no security** in those areas where you crave it most. In the single area that truly matters most—your **relationship with God**—you can have **ultimate security. The Bible declares** that God offers believers His unconditional love and acceptance. I want you to know that **God's love** for you is perfect and He will never let you go. **He yearns for you** to have **complete assurance** and **security** in Him. This peace and confidence is absolutely critical if you are to experience the Christian life the way God intended. **It is my prayer**

that you can find complete, blessed assurance in this chapter. What is the **solution** to all the world's trouble? **How can I be secure?**

In these verses, **Paul moves into the circumstances of our life** that cause us problems and trouble. **Under the inspiration** of the Holy Spirit, **he tells us** that **what sin could not do,** and what **Satan cannot do,** even among the terrible situations of life, **is take away our security.** In this context, the term **"love of Christ"** refers to **our salvation.** It speaks of **our special relationship** with our God, that the world does not have. **"In Christ,"** speaks of our **security.**

In 1937, the great Golden Gate Bridge was completed. It cost over **$35 million** to build and was completed in two phases: the first slowly and the second rapidly. In **the first stage, no safety devices** were used. As a result, **twenty-three men fell** to their deaths. However, for the **final part** of the project, a **large safety net** was used as a precaution. **At least ten men fell** into the net and **were saved** from certain death. **Once the net was installed** production increased by 25%. Why? Because the **men were assured of their security** and they **were free to wholeheartedly serve** the project. These verses speak of **Christian security at its best!**

I always respect a minister who will quote the Word and **say, "Thus says the Lord."** I get a little disturbed and perturbed, and have very **little respect** for a Bible Teacher who constantly "humms and hawes" around, saying things like: "I think, I suppose, I believe, I hope, I feel, I'm not sure, but, etc." **Paul says emphatically,** "I am persuaded"—**he knows!** What does Paul know? **He states** in these verses **he knows of nothing** that can separate (take away) the redeemed from Christ, once we are under His love.

The price that Jesus paid to **redeem** us was **His own life.** The Bible says about Jesus Christ, "Who gave Himself for our sins, that He might deliver us from this present evil age, according to the will of our God and Father." (Galatians 1:4). Jesus loved us enough, while we were yet in sin, to buy us back by taking our sin upon Himself and dying in our place. **Titus 2:14** adds, that He "gave Himself for us, that He might redeem us from every lawless deed and purify for Himself His own special people."

Redemption is yours when you are 'in Christ.' The **word 'redeem' as we have already studied means,** 'to buy back.' The Bible teaches that we 'sold' ourselves under sin, but Jesus paid the price necessary to 'buy us back.' **In Romans 3:24, Paul states,** that we have "been justified freely by His grace through the redemption that is in Christ Jesus." Sin has separated us from God. Our relationship with the Father has been severed because of that sin (Romans 3:23). But **'in Christ'** that great divide, **that chasm** has now been spanned in order to place us back into fellowship with God. There is now a **bridge** to cross that great divide between God and man. **The cross** of Christ is **that bridge** which spans the great divide. **Jesus gave His life as a ransom to buy us back!**

Let me ask you a question. It is the most important question that I could ever ask you. **Think about it carefully before you answer.** Will you go to Heaven when you die? Before you answer, let me tell you this—**I know I am going to Heaven when I die! Or, I will meet Jesus personally when He returns.**

I'm sure some people believe that it's very **presumptuous** to say that you can be certain about going to heaven. And if my own certainty **were based on anything less** that what it says in verses 38 and 39—and the confidence I have from it that God Himself is "for me," **I would have to agree** that to say that **is** presumptuous. **I believe that those of us** who have placed our trust in Jesus **can be certain of heaven** because of what Paul says in **this passage. My certainty is based** on a **relationship with God** in which He Himself is truly "for us." **If God is for us**, then **we're secure** on the basis of a relationship with the greatest Person that there is. And if that's true, then, as Paul says, **there isn't anyone or anything** that can ever be against us. **A Christian** is under the **covering of the blood** of Jesus.

Even though we are Christians, we **will fail** and **sin against the Lord.** At times we will **mess up big time.** Does that mean that God no longer loves us? **Could we** even **lose** our salvation? Well, the **Bible calls Satan** "the accuser of the brethren" (Revelation 12:10). **When you sin,** Satan will try to accuse you before God, and attack your conscience. He will **remind you of past sins.** He wants to **beat you down,** and **make you doubt** your salvation and **give up** on the Christian life. He wants you to think less of yourself; you're no good, you're to sinful, you're nothing.

You may feel like a nothing. God tells us, "For a nothing sinners, you are really something, and I love you." (Romans 5:8-11). **And if God has already given** us the greatest gift, **Jesus Christ,** can we not trust His love forever? **Once we've answered** that in our own lives, **we can experience the security** of the gospel.

There is a Peanuts cartoon in which **Charlie Brown** is **talking to Linus** and says: "Linus, I can't talk with that little red-haired girl. **She is really something** and **I am nothing**. If I was something and she was nothing I could talk to her **or if** she was something and I was something, **or if** I was nothing and she was nothing. But she's something and I'm nothing." **Linus says:** "Charlie Brown, for a nothing you are really something." **Christian, sometimes** you may feel like a nothing. **God has said** to us, "For a nothing, you really are something."

Notice how **Paul responds in vs. 33-34, He says,** "Who shall bring a charge against God's elect? It is God who justifies. Who is he who condemns?" Since God **Himself has justified us and declared us "not guilty,"** can anyone now bring charges against us to condemn us? No one can! Our **sins and mistakes cannot** separate us from the love of God **What do you and I need to get to heaven?** Certainly nothing we have access to can get us there. **We don't have the means** within our grasp, no matter how self-assured we may be, to get to heaven. **If we trusted in anything we could do,** then we'd have absolutely no right to be sure of heaven.

God Himself has provided everything that is needed. He has **held back nothing** from us that would get us to heaven. There has been **no limit** to what He would give to get us there. **He** "did not spare His own Son, but freely delivered Him up for us all." (Romans 8:32). **God gave up** that which is most dear to His heart, His own precious Son, in order to bring us to Himself. **Please be aware:** if He would give up His own precious Son for us, **we can be sure** that He'll never withhold anything else from us that we need. **He will never allow** any "lack" or "need" to prevail over us that could keep us from heaven. If He gave up His own Son for us, "how shall He not "with Him also freely give us all things?" (Romans 8:32).

There was a wealthy Roman who had a son who **broke his heart.** He also owned had **a slave** who commanded his admiration. And so, the **wealthy man decided** on his deathbed to **disinherit his son** and leave everything to his slave, Marcellus. He drew up the papers and **called in his son to tell him** what he had done. **He said,** "Son, you have **disappointed me** in life, you have **rebelled** against me. Your decisions have **hurt** me. You have **broken my heart.** So, I have decided to **deed everything to my slave** Marcellus. **However, you may choose one item** from my estate for yourself, what will it be?" **"I'll take Marcellus!"** was the son's reply.

Great little story, but I want you to be assured, **according to the Word of God, God will never disinherit you! Never!** I want to tell you that **when you become** a **child of God,** you have it all. That's one of the great themes in Romans 8. Romans 8:31,32. "What, then, shall we say in response to this? If God is for us, who can be against us? He who did not spare his own Son, but gave him up for us all—how will he not also, along with him, graciously give us all things?" **Praise God** for that.

Please realize, His own **sacrifice** for us. Has made it **impossible for any sin** to keep us out of heaven. **No less an accuser** than the **devil himself** is utterly **frustrated** in every charge that he brings against us. **If you have trusted Jesus,** then once again you have great reason to rejoice in the confident hope of heaven. God Himself is for you. Who then can be against you?

Once we are "in Christ," absolutely nothing can separate us from the love of God, which is centered in Jesus Christ. There is no sin in your life that can take you out of being **"in Christ!"** Paul mentions everything: life, death, angels, present circumstances, future situations, whether in space or here on earth, or anything else you want to mention. **Absolutely nothing or no one** can ever separate you from the love of God, centered in Christ. The Christian has **every possible security** for his safety. The **purposes** of God, the **work** of Christ, the **aid** of the Holy Spirit, and the **tendency of all** events under the direction of his Father and Friend, conspire to **secure his welfare and salvation.**

Our identification with belonging to Christ is also **our guarantee** that we can never lose our salvation. **Remember: it's not our job** to **either secure or keep** the salvation which we received from God. It is "not by works of righteousness which we have done, but according to His mercy He saved us, through the washing of regeneration and renewing of the Holy Spirit, Whom He poured out on us abundantly through Jesus (or in Jesus) Christ our Savior., that having been justified because of His grace we should become heirs according to the hope of eternal life." (Titus 3:5-7).

What a powerful, insightful and beautiful scripture that is. Just look at the words: righteousness, mercy, salvation, washing, regeneration, renewing, grace. justification, heirs and eternal life. That's powerful, especially when **we didn't do anything for it. He did it all . . . for us!** If I could do it, work for it, or get it on my own . . . I could lose it. **Listen: God imparted His righteousness to us,** and with that, we are completely forgiven. **The Word of God states that God** has predestined those who are '**In Christ,**' "to become conformed to the image of His Son." (Romans 8:29).

When you get on board one of those **big jet aircraft,** you **relinquish the control** of your life **to that pilot.** Once you get up to a certain altitude, the "fasten seat belts" light goes off. **Is there ever any doubt** in your mind that the **pilot has full** intentions of **delivering you your final destination?**

He's going to do it, or give up his life trying. **He is committed to delivering you to the final destination.** When you give your life to Jesus Christ, and you are **"in Christ,"** you relinquish the control of your life into the hands of Jesus Christ. Do you realize that He is fully committed to deliver you to eternal life? **Roman 8 is the great assurance chapter of the Bible. God will finish** what He **started at the Cross.**

Paul shouts out triumphantly, "Who will bring a charge against God's elect? God is the one who justifies; who is the one who condemns? It is Christ who died, and furthermore is also raised, who is at the right hand of God, who also intercedes for us." (Romans 8:33,34). **It firmly states here** that the Father will never condemn us, and neither will Christ. **Our salvation is secure!** Once in His family, we can never be separated from Him. **What security we have!** What would **you pay** for such security? Do you seek security **in insurance?** Do you seek security in **the government?** Do you seek security in **your savings?** Real **eternal security** can **only be found "in Christ".** Believe it, and you can **experience peace** in the **midst of troubles!**

At the Judgment Seat of Christ, when all **Christians stand** before the Lord and give account of our lives, (II Corinthians 6:10,11), we shall be judged by our life for rewards. (This is **not** the Great White Throne Judgment of Revelation 20 where all non-Christians will be judged). **The apostle Paul stated** in Romans 8:1, "There is therefore now no condemnation to those who are in Christ Jesus, who do not walk according to the flesh, but according to the Spirit."

However, **for those** who **refuse to obey** the Gospel of Jesus Christ, **there is condemnation!** In II Thessalonians 1:8 we are told that **Jesus is going to come** "in flaming fire taking vengeance on those who do not know God, and on those who do not obey the gospel of our Lord Jesus Christ." **The Bible states that** "they will be punished with everlasting destruction from the presence of the Lord and from the glory of His power." (II Thessalonians 1:9).

The Bible consistently teaches us that when a sinner accepts Christ as Savior and Lord, at that very moment in time, **God saves and makes the believer secure "in Christ" forever.** The **Christian** does **not** have to keep on being "born again, and again, and again," over and over. **No! Nothing will ever separate us** from the love of God which is in Christ Jesus our Lord. Not "death or life," that's **physical** opposition; "nor angels nor principalities nor powers," that's **spiritual** opposition; "nor things present, nor things to come," that's **circumstances** outside our control;

"nor height or depth," that's a **limitation** from distance; "nor any other created thing," that includes **everything** except God Himself.

Think about this: Only God Himself can separate us from God; and God has promised that He will never do so. **Do you believe the words of Jesus? Jesus said,** "My sheep hear My voice, and I know them, and they follow Me. And I give them eternal life, and they shall never perish; neither shall anyone snatch them out of My hand. My Father, who has given them to Me, is greater than all; and no one is able to snatch them out of My Father's hand (John 10:27-29). **Salvation once possessed cannot be lost.** This belief in God's merciful and secure salvation is not a license to careless living, but on the contrary is a powerful incentive for godly living. (For more study see: John 10:27-30; Romans 8:38-39; 12:1-2; 1 Corinthians 1:4-9; 12:12; Hebrews 10:14; 12:6-13; 1 Peter 1:3-5).

In Philippians 1:6 the **apostle Paul teaches us,** "For I am confident of this very thing, that He who began a good work in you will perfect it until the day of Christ Jesus." **Has God begun the good work of salvation** in you? **Have you been born again?** Has He put His life in you? **Have you confessed** your sins to Him and put your faith in Jesus Christ as your Savior?

God began a good work of salvation when you believed on Christ, and He will consummate it when Jesus returns. **"Being confident"** is in the perfect tense in Greek indicating the apostle **Paul had come to a settled conviction** earlier about their salvation and he still is confident that it was true. Salvation is the good work of God (Ephesians 2:8-10).

Pastor/Teacher George Matheson was one of the **great hymn writers.** He **fell in love** with a **young lady** and they planned to get married, but one day she came and told Mr. Matheson that **she no longer** was going to go through with their marriage. He was crushed. He went home to gather his thoughts, meditate and pray. He thought about it a great deal. **Finally, picked up his pen** and **wrote** that **great hymn** that we sometimes sing. **The Hymn starts,** "O love that will not let me go, I rest my weary soul in Thee, I give Thee back the life I owe, that in Thine ocean depth its flow, may richer fuller be." **You see,** he realized that **no other love can match the love** of our Heavenly Father in Christ. Unlike an **earthly love,** which you may lose, you will **never lose,** or be loosed from, **God's love.**

The oft-used phrase, "Once Saved—Always Saved" is **not in the Bible!** The **Bible does teach** the "eternal security of the believer," but the trite saying 'once saved, always saved,' has led many to a misunderstand the doctrine of eternal justification. Nowhere, **I repeat, nowhere** does the

Bible teach that a child of God can lose the salvation work that God has done in him through Jesus Christ.

In my personal experience I have found that those who want to argue over the subject of the eternal security of the believer are usually those not living as sold-out disciples of Christ. **Most of them** seem to be holding to their flesh, and their sins while trying to act like a Christian. **Rather than relying** on the **Sovereignty of God**, the **power of Christ**, or the **teaching of the Scriptures**, they want to argue logic, and the "what-if's" of a person's experience. **Since you are not saved by good works**, you **cannot lose it by bad works**, or the bad things you do or say. **We must remember** that **eternal security** doesn't come from our pet doctrines, but from **God's grace alone** that is found in Jesus Christ. **Mark tells us,** "For even the Son of Man (Jesus) did not come to be served, but to serve, and to give His life a ransom for many." (Mark 10:45).

The Scriptures are replete with the fact that Jesus came to redeem us from our sins, and not to leave us in them. **He came** to save us and renew us after God's image, as He told Nicodemus in John, Chapter 3. **He did not come** to provide security in our sinfulness. (Jude 4).

There are scores of Scriptures, that teach, not only a **secure salvation**, but also teach that **"in Christ" the believer is also complete. Paul told** the church at Colosse that, "in Him (Christ) you have been made complete. (2:10). **The Apostle Peter informs us,** "His divine power has granted to us everything pertaining to life and godliness." (II Peter 1:3). **"In Christ,"** we lack nothing!

I know, and you know, that **none of us**, in this flesh, **is perfect. Paul even refers to carnal Christians**, "I could not speak to you as spiritual (people), but as to carnal, as to babes in Christ. I fed you with milk and not with meat (solid food), because you were not able to receive it.... you are still carnal. For where there is envy, strife, and divisions among you.... are you not carnal an behaving like mere men?" (I Corinthians 3:1-3) **In my Texas lingo, let me translate that for you ... he is saying,** "I came to feed you a big Texas size T-Bone steak and you couldn't handle it, because you were still sucking on the bottle." You are yet whining and dining as a baby ... **carnal** in all your lifestyle.

Simply put, 'carnality' means: to be controlled by the flesh, falling into past sins, a picture indicative of spiritual immaturity. **These Corinthian Christians were even fighting** over which preacher to follow (and I'm sure some of you have met some people like that in your church). (I Corinthians 3:1-11). **Carnality not only produces** bad attitudes, but also bad actions. **Paul tells** these careless, fleshly Christians to grow up. **He does not ever—never ever—admonish them to be 'saved' again. When a person** uses the promise of eternal security as a **license to sin it only proves** the deceitfulness of his own heart and **proves** he has never been born again. **It proves he does not understand grace** and has never experienced the radical change of the spiritual birth.

Know this truth: God's love is **an inseparable and inescapable love!** Paul asks the question, "Who shall separate us from the love of Christ? Shall tribulation, or distress, or persecution, or famine, or nakedness, or peril, or sword . . . Yet in all these things we are more than conquerors through Him (Jesus) who loved us." (35, 37)

Here Paul refers to height and depth. If we were to travel to the "highest" or "lowest" points in the universe, or **anywhere** in between, we would **never** arrive at a place where we **could escape** Christ's love. There is nowhere we can go where anyone or anything can take our eternal salvation away from us. Nowhere.

Eternal life is eternal. No one or no thing, at any time or place, **can ever separate** us from God's love.

I am the earthly son of **my mother and daddy.** I am their child . . . forever. Just like we **can't cease** being the children of our earthly parents once we are born, **so too we can't cease** being children of God once we are born again. **We can no more be unborn spiritually** than we can go back and be **unborn physically.** This was what Jesus was teaching Nicodemus in John 3. When we trust in Christ for salvation, **by His grace,** at that very moment we become members of **God's forever family.**

Under the leadership of the Holy Spirit, Paul now pens one of the greatest passages of Scripture in all the Bible. In verses 38 and 39, **Paul enlarges** on the great **keeping power of God** by writing, "For I am persuaded that neither death nor life, nor angels, nor principalities, nor powers, nor things present nor things to come, nor height, nor depth, nor any other created thing, shall be able to separate us from the love of God which is '**in Christ Jesus.**' our Lord."

Question: To finalize this section, let me ask, "Do you believe that God is **Sovereign** (the supreme authority)? Do you believe that God is **Omnipotent** (having complete, universal power and authority)? **Do you believe** that with God, are all things possible? **Do you believe** that God can do anything that is not contrary to His nature? **Then let me share, if He** has redeemed you, then rest assured, **He is able to guard and keep you?**" He will light your way.

There was a man and his small 5 year old son Bobby, that were **going home** and they had to go **through the dark woods** on a cold winter night. The **man held a lantern** in one hand **and held this little boy** with the other hand. Their lantern illuminated the footpath in the pitch black darkness. **Little Bobby said:** "Daddy, I'm scared! The light reaches only very short way!" **The father said:** "I know son, but if we just keep on walking, we will see that the light keeps on shining and it will eventually shine all the way to the end of our path."

God promises to give us all things, but only a step's worth at a time. **You and I are little Bobby's.** We are **not in need** of more light. We simply **need to utilize** the light He has already provided. **God does not give** us a string of **flood lights** shining as far as the eye can see **like an airport landing strip.** No. His heavenly lantern provides light on only **one spot at a time.** Psalm 119:105 states, "Your word is a lamp to my feet and a light to my path." **Just enough** for our feet, **not the whole path.** God will light up the path ahead only as we keep advancing along that path. **There will be vast stretches of the road ahead that we can't see.** We just have to trust the light that we have.

When we are 'in Him' we are **'sealed'** with the Holy Spirit. **Paul states,** "In Him (Jesus) you also trusted, after you heard the word of truth, the gospel of your salvation, in Whom also, having believed, **you were sealed** with the Holy Spirit of promise, who is the **'guarantee'** of our inheritance until the redemption of the purchased possession, to the praise of His glory." (Ephesians 1:13-14).

This verse in Ephesians is one of the most astounding verses in God's Word. **The 'seal' of security** is placed on the believer by God. **The 'sealer'** is God, the **possession 'sealed'** is the believer, and **the 'seal' itself (or Himself)** is none other than the Holy Spirit of God. The **'seal' is "in Christ."**

Verse 14 shows us that **the Holy Spirit's 'seal' is our 'guarantee.'** The word **guarantee** (translated earnest in some versions) **is a legal word. For example:** when **real estate** is purchased, sometimes a **'down-payment' or 'earnest money'** is required to prove the legitimacy of your offer. When accepted, **the seller must hold that property for you.** Sometimes this word is translated 'advance payment,' 'pledge,' 'deposit,' which **means,** that the **final transaction** is to follow. **You may be asking,** "what does this have to do with anything?" **It means God guarantees** that we are His possession . . . forever . . . sealed! **We will always be His child!**

First John 5:13 reads, "These things I have written to you who believe in the name of the Son of God, in order that you may know that you have eternal life." "These are written that you may know," **not just know, but** "to know with a settled intuitive knowledge." **You can have eternal life** by believing in Jesus Christ (John 20:31), **and know that you have it.** As many, through the years, have said, "You can know that you know that you know. The **assurance** of one's salvation **always rests** essentially and satisfactorily **on the direct promises that God** makes to the believer **in His Word.**

One of the greatest, if not the greatest, **motivations to live** for God is absolute **assurance** of eternal life. **The apostle Paul said,** "The love of Christ constrains (compels) us." (2 Corinthians 5:14). **Christ's love compels** us to serve Him. **There are hurting people** in our communities, and they are **watching you and me** to see how we handle life. **Christ should make a difference** in our families, our marriages, our work place, our witness and our church.

We must continue to demonstrate to a lost community **the difference Christ makes in His body.** They'll know we are Christians **by His love working** itself out **in our lives. Pagans** in the first century of Christianity **pointed to** the **Christians and said,** "See how they love one another!" Just knowing that we have **spiritual safety** and **security "in Christ"** should give us a big **spiritual boost** to "not be ashamed of who we are in Christ," (Romans 1:16), and lead us to be real witnesses.

The very reputable **C. T. Studd gave up fame and fortune** to serve God as a **missionary** on three continents in the **wild days** of mid-nineteenth century missions. **What prompted him?** He said, "If Christ be God and died for me, then there is nothing too great that I can do for Him."

There is a strange and very un-biblical teaching circulating today. Actually, it has been around for a long time. **This is the idea** that **a saved person can lose eternal life** by committing some awful sin, or ceasing to practice belief in Christ or by departing into a life of moral impurity. **This teaching is strange** because it is **completely antithetical (opposite), to the Gospel of Grace** and to the clear teachings of Jesus and the Apostles.

There is one passage which I believe **incontrovertibly proves** that once a person becomes a part of the family of God, nothing, **absolutely nothing,** now or forever, **can separate him** from the love of God in Christ. **That passage** is the verses that we are studying here . . . . Romans 8:38-39. **At the end** of Romans 8, **Paul asks, What (or who) can separate**

believers from God's love in Christ? Verses 38 and 39 form the heart of his answer.... **nothing!**

"Nothing shall be **able to separate us** from the love of God which is **"in Christ"** Jesus our Lord." **The word "separate" means** to **"violently tear from,"** to **"completely divide."** Paul says that **nothing** that can happen to us can finally and completely separate us from the love of God. There is **one qualifier** we need to **remember** . . . **"Nothing can separate us."** Who is the **"us"** of verse 38? **The "us" refers to those** who are **"in Christ Jesus"** This **promise applies to believers and only to believers.** It is **not a general statement** describing **everyone** in the world. **Only those** who **know Jesus** Christ through **saving faith** may claim this promise. **They will never be separated** from the love of God.

The Scripture, "God is for us," cannot be interpreted or applied apart from His purpose (8:28). **God is not "for us"** in some **nebulous, undefined way.** We do not have the promise that God will deal with us in any way that we ask or desire. The **prosperity gospelizers** promise a God who is a kind of **magic genie,** as though we **need but inform Him** how **He can serve us.** God is "for us" in a way that produces the "good" He has purposed and prepared for us in eternity past.

Based upon the premise that God is "for us," Paul presses us to consider the implications. "If God is for us (as He most certainly is), who is against us?" **Paul is not suggesting** that we have no opposition. **We all know** that the Christian will have many adversaries. **Paul's question** is designed **to point out the puniness** of any opponent in light of the fact that God is our proponent.

One of my favorite movies, "The Bear," has in the **final scenes a little grizzly cub** being **attacked by a mountain lion.** The life of the **little cub** seems to be in **great danger** as the mountain lion moves in for the kill. **Suddenly, the baby bear rears up** on its hind legs letting out the **fiercest growl** it can muster. **Amazingly, the mountain lion shrinks back!** Then the **camera then slowly pans back** to **reveal** just behind the cub a **massive grizzly,** reared on his **hind legs, delivering a fierce** warning to the mountain lion. **The cub's enemy was great.** But in **the protective shadow of the great grizzly,** that mountain lion was nothing. **With the giant grizzly** as its **protection,** who was this mere mountain lion? **Oh, dear friend,** with **God on our side,** who could possibly be an **opponent** who would cause us to shrink back in fear? **The sovereignty of a God** who is "for us" provides a new perspective on **anyone or anything which threatens to oppose or destroy us.**

Paul writes about "separation," from both our perspective and God's. Popular music and poetry often describe **separation as loneliness. Simon and Garfunkel** began their **song,** "Hello darkness my old friend. I've come to be with you again." **That is the greatest pain** in separation, **being alone,** totally alone. **Psychiatry** describes it as a **dark condition. Helplessness and despair in anxiety** is believing that this **being alone,** being **cut off** from those **people** and **things one loves** and desires, is a **permanent condition** and will never be restored. We know all too well that is **what death is all about,** being separated knowing there will **never be a 'together again'. We all know the fear of separation.** Sometimes it is a vague, undefined uneasiness and sometimes it is a stabbing pain. And in the midst of this fear **God comes to us and says:** "I will never leave you or forsake you." Even if we cannot love ourselves, **God loves us with an everlasting love.**

What does it mean to be **born again? It means** that **God has made us** a **new creation.** It means, as Paul says earlier **in Romans 8,** that we have received the Spirit of God into our lives to carry out His work of renewal. **This describes all Christians**—not just an elite few. **The phrase** "born again Christian" is redundant because **there is no such thing as a Christian** who has not been born again. **If you are a Christian** you have been born again and **if you haven't been born again** you are **not a Christian**—no matter what else you may be.

A correct understanding of what it means for us to be "born-again" is **essential** as we consider an important question in the Christian life. **Now, here is a most important question. Ready?** Is it possible to be "unborn-again?" **If you are "sealed" in the Holy Spirit** (II Corinthians 1:22; Ephesians 4:30), **as Paul says** we are when we come to Christ, **is it possible to be "unsealed"** in the Spirit? Is it **possible for a Christian to lose his or her salvation?** God's Word says, **"No!"**

God made you to love you. God made you to love him. "And we know that for those who love God all things work together for good, for those who are called according to his purpose," (v. 28). **God's purpose for each person** is to love each and every one and for each **to love Him,** to live in that perfect love. None of God's work is an accident. **God does not want you** to be separated from him. **He wants you with Him** each step of life on earth and into life eternal in heaven. **Death and Hell are eternal separations** for those who turn away from him. But **Jesus' declaration**

brings comfort and strength **to each one who hears and believes,** "I am the way and the truth and the life," [John 14:6].

This powerful love of Christ is linked to us. What can we point to in order to know this? **Certainly we have God's Word** that we can point to. Right here in our text, for example, **it tells us how God loves** us powerfully. The place we **ultimately want to point to is the cross.** We are **linked to God's love** through the **cross.** There **His love** was expressed for all people. There was the **one supreme act of love demonstrated** to us through Jesus Christ.

We point to the cross to see God's love at work for us, connected to us. **At the cross,** Christ sacrificed His life to give us eternal life. **Jesus suffered and died** so that **guilt from our sin** would be removed. **He was punished** for our sins. **The cross is** where we point to **see Christ's love.** It is by faith that we receive the benefits of the cross. **Faith is the channel** through which the love comes to each of us personally. **It is by faith** you can know that what Christ did on the cross was for you. You can know that **God has not forgotten you. God sent Jesus** as evidence of this. Whenever **we might think** that God is forgetting us, we only need to ask if Jesus still died on the cross for us. **Whenever we doubt and feel guilty,** we simply point ourselves back to the cross. **Jesus' sacrifice** on the cross **demonstrates God's love** for us for all times.

Contemporary theology, using the term loosely, **tries to make the cross of Christ** the **measure of our worth to God:** "We were worth so much to God that He sent His Son to die for us." **This misses the point altogether.** It turns the **spotlight,** the focus, **from God to man.** The **cross of Calvary is not** the measure of our worth; it is the measure of God's love. That is what Paul wants us to see here. **The cross imputes worth to sinners** who receive the gift of salvation. **The cross is not** the evidence of our worth **but the source** of our worth. **We are worthy because Christ** died for us. **Christ did not die** for us because we were worthy.

For the Christian, Christ doesn't make our lives easy and painless. We live in a sinful world, **and we suffer** the consequences of our sin. But **Christ's love can't be stopped** by this sinful world. **When you're crawling** underneath your pain, **God's love** is not affected. When you feel like there's no way that anyone can help you, **God's love** still gets through. **Above all the things** that may happen to you in this life, **God's love** has got a hold on you. **God's love** will not fail you when you're trapped in the earthquakes of life. **We will not be cut off** from God's love. **He remains strong** even while we are weak, sick, troubled, and dying. **He remains strong** and stretches out **His love to give you comfort,** strength, hope, and faith. **He stretches out** His love to give you **abundant life** here and in the hereafter **through Jesus Christ.**

In Chapter 10 of John's Gospel, Jesus said, "I am the good shepherd; and I know my sheep, and am known by my own... I lay down my life for the sheep... I give to them eternal life, and they shall never perish... no one is able to snatch them out of My Father's hand..." (John 10:14,15,27,28,29) **I John 2:25 states,** "This is the promise that He has promised us—eternal life." **You are 'sealed' in God's hand!**

Remember: It's the **Gospel that affirms you,** not something you do, or don't do. This is **not the gospel of self-esteem.** This is the Gospel of the **esteem that God** gives us through faith in Jesus Christ. **We are redeemed to be, what ... as God's children?** Now pay attention to the **attributes** that God has **given** to His children... The **children** of God, **heirs** of God, and **joint heirs** with Jesus Christ. I'm a **child of the King** (the King of Kings and Lord of Lords). **That's what I am!** Brother, sister—that's what **you are when you know Jesus.** I'm a child of the King. Let me encourage you, **when you finally come to know this fact,** who **cares what anyone else thinks?** I'm a child of the King. **You want assurance?** You want **affirmation? Run to Jesus! Embrace** Him, **enfold** Him in your arms, **and say with Paul,** "Nothing, absolutely nothing, can separate me from the **love of God** which is in **Jesus Christ our Lord." Hallelujah!** And **as the old country preacher once said,** "If that don't set a spark to warm the cockles of your heart, your wood's wet!"

Paul closes Romans 8 by speaking of **his confidence** in his **own security** and in **that of the redeemed.** He tells us that **we can be confident.** He speaks about a **"know-so"** salvation, **not a "hope-so"** salvation. He tells us here that there is nothing from the beginning of our life with God to the end of our life, that will ever be able to separate the believer from the salvation we enjoy in Christ Jesus. **The end result of all this** is the **blessed assurance** that **"in Jesus"** we are forever protected and secure come what may in life or death!

C. H. Spurgeon once shared this story: Somebody said, "That is **Calvinistic doctrine."** If you like to call it so, you may; but **I would rather** that you made the **mistake** of the **good old Christian woman** who did not know much about these things, and who said **that she herself was** "a high Calvarist." She **liked "high Calvary" preaching,** and so do I; and **it is "high Calvary" doctrine** that I find in this passage. **He who hung** on high **Calvary** was such a **lover of the souls** of men that from that **glorious fact** I am brought to the blessed **persuasion of His love.**

I'm afraid that most people just don't understand what Almighty God secured for us on Calvary. When Christ died he secured his own people in **death and in life. Nothing** in life and nothing in death **will undo the triumph** he achieved in the cross and the resurrection. **So Paul says in** Romans 14:9, "For to this end Christ died and lived again, that He might be Lord both of the dead and of the living." **His lordship** over life and death is invincible (cannot be overcome). **So life and death** cannot separate us from the love of God.

Satan always condemns the saints before the throne of grace, and his charges are true because we are sinners. **Satan's job** is continuously to try to **trip us up** with temptations to make us fall. However, **when the prosecution** has finished presenting its case, **Jesus, our Advocate,** stands forth and shows the prints in His hands **and the Righteous Judge cries "Case dismissed!"** The Father declares us **right** in His sight! (read: Job 1 & 2)

With all these scriptures and the teaching of God's Word is added up and all these **truths are digested,** it becomes clear **that "in Jesus"** we have absolute, eternal security. **The believer need never fear** anything coming between himself and God's salvation. **When you are saved,** you are saved forever! Therefore, we **can say with all the assurance** of our souls, "Which hope we have as an anchor of the soul, both sure and steadfast, and which enters into that within the veil." (Hebrews 6:19).

When you are able to weather the storms of conflict, affliction, turmoil and persecution and you want to live for the Jesus, **that is a good sign** that you have the real thing . . . **"in Christ!"** When every thing that comes along **blows you off course,** you had **better check up!** According to this verse, **the love of God enables us** to **persevere** until the end!

A little boy was holding on to his **father's hand** while walking across a field. He **kept falling as he lost his grip.** Time after time the **father patiently helped him up** and on they went again. **Finally the little boy said, "Daddy, if you were to hold my hand** I wouldn't let go and fall." So the **father took his son's hand** in his own and the boy did not fall again. **We are all like that little boy.** When **we hang on** to God we **lose our grip.** But when **He hangs on** to us, **that grip is solid** and **sure** and **nothing can shake us loose.**

Do you remember what Jesus said **about the hand of God?** In John 10:27-30, **Jesus taught,** "My sheep hear my voice, and I know them, and they follow Me. And I give them eternal life, and they shall never perish, neither shall anyone snatch them out of My hand. My Father, who has given them to Me, is greater than all; and no one is able to snatch them out of My Fathers hand. I and My Father are one."

Dr. B. H. Carroll tells this wonderful story about the security of the believer. "**When I was a youth** I was wonderfully stirred by an eloquent sermon preached by **J.R. Graves. He pointed out the fact** that by faith we commit our lives to Jesus. Our life is **hid with Christ in God.** Our life is sealed with the **impression of the Holy Spirit** unto the day of redemption, and then he asked, 'Who can pluck that life out of the hands of God?' **Drawing this vivid picture:** If **Hell** should open her yawning mouth and all of the **demons** of the pit should issue forth like huge **vampires** darkening water and land, could they **break that seal** of God? **Could they soar** to the heights of Heaven? **Could they scale** its battlements? **Could they beat back** the angels that guard its walls? **Could they penetrate** into the presence of the Holy One on His eternal throne, and reach out **their demon-claws and pluck our life** from the bosom of God where **it is hid** with Christ in God?" **What a picturesque description** of the **security of God!**

Question: Is there anything in this universe **greater than God?** Is there any one greater than He? **No!** Indeed not. **If this be true,** then there is **nothing** that can ever **take us or separate us from the love of God.** Our salvation, our sanctification, **is as secure** as the God of heaven is strong. It is **with this confidence** that we may live out our Christian responsibilities, **knowing that God** is the source of our salvation and our sanctification, and, therefore, **it is sure.**

When everything is added up and all these truths are digested, **it becomes clear** that 'in Jesus' we have absolute, eternal security. **The believer need never fear** anything coming between himself and God's salvation. **If you are saved,** you are **saved forever!** Therefore, **we can say** with all the assurance of our souls, "Which hope we have as an anchor of the soul, both sure and steadfast, and which enters into that within the veil." (Hebrews 6:19 One of the **great benefits of being "in Christ,** is that you can **have an intimate relationship** with God through His Son Jesus Christ.

"When peace like a river attends my way,
When sorrows like sea billows roll;

Whatever my lot, You have taught me to say, It is well,
it is well with my soul.

Tho Satan should buffet, tho trials should come,
Let this blessed assurance control,
Christ has regarded my helpless estate,
and has shed His own blood for my soul.

My sin, oh the bliss of this glorious thought,
my sin, not in part, but the whole;
Is nailed to the cross, I bear it no more, praise the Lord,
praise the Lord O my soul.

It is well with my soul, it is well with my soul, it is well with my soul."

—Horatio G. Spafford

CHAPTER FIVE

"In Christ" You Are 'Justified' Before God, and the 'Righteousness' of God in Christ is 'Imputed' to You.

God's Word states in II Corinthians 5:21, "For our sake God made Christ to be sin who knew no sin, so that **in him (in Christ)** we might become the righteousness of God."

Whenever you minister the Word of God, whether it be through preaching and/or writing, **you are going to have to walk by faith** and not by sight. **Faith has the eyes** that **see that the Spirit is working,** and God is sovereign, in whatever is happening. That is why, no one should ever study God's Word **without prayer** and meditation. **Anyone can read** the Bible, but **only those** who are **in tune with God,** the Holy Spirit will be given truths that are hidden from the unbelievers. I ask you to pause a moment now and ask God to help you in this study.

How important is this verse? Miss this and you've missed the **truth of God.** If you get this right, you can be wrong in a lot of other places and still go to heaven. In **these days of rampant theological confusion,** it is **vitally important** that the church of Jesus Christ **be firmly settled** on the gospel message. **That is,** after all, **our only message.** God has **not committed** to us a message **about political power** or **military might. We are not called to right** all the wrongs in the world or to **pass judgment** on every passing trend. **The church** has been given **one major task,** to preach the gospel to **every person** on earth (Mark 16:15).

What we couldn't do for ourselves, Almighty God stepped in and did for us. **We are spiritually dead** in the eyes of God and remain so **until we receive spiritual** regeneration through the presence and power of the Holy Spirit, when we are placed "in Christ." Let me repeat: **We are spiritually dead** until we are born again. (John 3). **He was sinless;** we are guilty sinners. **We stand condemned** in the presence of a righteous God. Ezekiel 18:4 **says,** "The soul that sins will surely die." Where there is no salvation, the person who sins is exposed to the fierce wrath of God.

The above verse states that, **Almighty God made Christ to be sin** for us the sinners. God regarded or treated **Christ, who was sinless,** as a sinner. God regarded our sins, i.e. the believers as if our sin belonged to Christ. **God made Jesus sin** by imputing to Him our sin. **Our sins were charged** to the account of Jesus Christ.

God is the author of our salvation. He charged Christ with our sins. **Peter declared** "this Man, delivered over by the predetermined plan and foreknowledge of God, you nailed to a cross by the hands of godless men and put Him to death" (Acts 2:23). How did he do this?

Jesus had no sin. This means that, **unlike us sinners,** He was not under the dominion of sin and death. **Remember Adam and Eve** in the Garden. They were told not to eat of the tree of the knowledge of good and evil, "for when you eat of it you will surely die" (Genesis 2:17). **Well, man disobeyed God and ate.** Since then every person has come under the dominion of sin and death. **But not Christ.** He had **no guilt.** Unlike us, He had **no need for confession.** Unlike us, he had **no sin to repent of.** Unlike us, He had **no need for sin offerings** or guilt offerings. Unlike us, He had **no need for a Savior.** He was **not in the grip of sin and Satan.** Many of us have experienced the painful grip of sin in our life. Like a **sex addict** to his perverted ways, or **an alcoholic** enslaved to his drink, or a **druggie hooked** on his drugs, **we sinners are in bondage** to sin and Satan. **But not Jesus.**

In becoming sin for us, Christ became our substitute. **The apostle Peter wrote:** "knowing that you were not redeemed with perishable things like silver or gold from your futile way of life inherited from your forefathers, but with precious blood, as of a lamb unblemished and spotless, the blood of Christ" (1 Peter 1:18-19). **Jesus was the Lamb of God** who was slain for sinners (John 1:29). It was for our sins that He died. **Our sins, which separated us from God,** have all been removed. **Now God can accept us** based upon the sacrifice of Christ. Based upon that atoning sacrifice, **God drops all charges** against us, and declares us acquitted, and dresses us in His righteousness.

The Scriptures teach that He was made to be our sin bearer, or sin offering (Matthew 27:45-46). **Jesus experienced the abandonment** and despair of being separated from God as punishment for the **sins He bore for everyone else,** not because **He was made to be sin** Himself (Isaiah 53:5-6, 11; 1 Corinthians 5:7; Galatians 3:13; Ephesians 5:2). **Jesus on the cross was the sin bearer** for all mankind (John 1:29; Romans 3:25; 1 John 2:2; 4:9-10). **The sin offerings** in the **Old Testament foreshadowed** what Jesus would become in the New Testament (Exodus 29:10-14; Leviticus 16:1-22, 27; Numbers 19:1-9; Hebrews 9:6—10:9).

Friend, **The supreme expression of God's love** for sinners is the death of Christ on their behalf. **Their salvation results from** the fact that their sins are paid for and God's justice has been satisfied at the cross of Christ. **As repentant sinners** they have **peace with God,** and **His wrath,** which will fall upon unrepentant sinners, no longer threatens them. **They are accepted "in Christ"** and can stand in the presence of God free from guilt and condemnation, and righteous in a righteousness which God accepts, the Lord Jesus Christ. This is what being made the righteousness of God in Christ means (Romans 4:1-3, 20-25; 5:1-2, 6-11; 8:1-4)

Verse 17 says, God took the punishment that was due us, and put it on Jesus, even though He was completely sinless. **In addition, God took** all the **righteousness of Jesus** and placed it upon us. **Jesus spent thirty-three years** on planet earth living a life of righteousness, a life of doing the right things. **During that time,** He healed people, raised the dead, fed the hungry, released the demon-possessed, made the blind to see, the deaf to hear, and many, many other things. **Those good deeds were His "righteousness."** Not only did God put the punishment for our sins upon Jesus, but God also took the credit for all the good things that Jesus ever did and gave the credit to us!

We find in this verse that Jesus Christ was the **target** of **God's punishment** for sinners. God has imputed the sin of all humankind to Him (Romans 8:3; and 1st Corinthians 15:3). Now **God makes us the targets** of His righteousness and imputes that to us as well. (1 Corinthians 1:30; Philippians 3:9). The effect of God imputing righteousness to believers is that now God sees us as He sees His righteous Son, namely, fully acceptable to Him.

Paul uses striking and in-depth language in this exceptional wording, "made sin for us" in order to emphasize the **"sweet exchange," or the "great exchange,"** whereby **sinners are given** a **righteous status** before God through the righteous One who absorbed their sin (and its judgment) in Himself." **The identification of the sinless Christ** with the **sin of the sinner,** is so complete, including its **dire guilt** and its **dread consequence** of separation from God, that Paul could say profoundly, "God made him . . . to be sin for us."

Jesus was made to be sin. This means that He was treated as if He had He had defaced the image of God. **This means** that He was treated as if He was under the dominion of sin and death. **This means** that He was treated as if He was guilty.

This means that He was treated as if He was in the grip of Satan. **This means** that God's wrath and anger against sin was placed upon Him.

Jesus took the sinner's place (my place and yours). So, what happens to the sinner? "In Him we . . . become the righteousness of God" (2 Corinthians 5:21). **Christ's righteousness, His perfect righteousness was transferred** to us. **This means what?** Meaning: as **if I have never sinned** nor been a sinner. Meaning it is **as if I had been perfectly obedient.** Meaning I am treated **as if I am as righteous** as Christ Himself, that is, perfectly righteous, without sin, without guilt, without shame, without separation from God.

The NKJV says He "knew no sin"; the NIV translates this "had no sin." Jesus knew all **about** sin, but He **never committed** a sin. **Peter tells us** in 1 Peter 2:22, "He committed no sin, neither was deceit found in his mouth." **What does this mean?** What would a sinless man look like? **We tend to think** in terms of **gross, obvious sins:** We think a sinless man would be someone who never robbed a bank, never committed adultery, and was always kind to others. **But Jesus tells us** that these gross, **outward sins are the fruit of sinful hearts.** A sinless man must have a sinless heart. So this means that Jesus: 1) never desired someone else's possessions, 2) never lusted after a woman, 3) never was greedy for money. **Jesus had no sin!**

Furthermore, **He always and continuously fulfilled** the purpose of man's creation: **Every moment of every day He delighted in God, and glorified Him in thought and deed.** Every moment of every day **He loved the Lord His God** with all His heart, soul, mind, and strength. Jesus was sinless, and thus Jesus was the **only** man, ever, who did **not** deserve punishment.

Donald Grey Barnhouse, the eloquent pastor/theologian of the Presbyterian church wrote, "He (Barabbas) was **the only man** in the world **who could say** that Jesus Christ **took his physical place. But I can say** that Jesus Christ **took my spiritual** place. **For it was I** who **deserved** to die. It was I who **deserved** that the wrath of God should be poured on me. **I deserved** the eternal punishment of the lake of fire. **He was delivered** up for my offenses. **He was handed over** to judgment because of my sins. **Christ was my substitute.** He was **satisfying the debt** of divine justice and holiness. **That is why I say** that Christianity can be expressed in the **three phrases:** 1) I deserved hell; 2) Jesus took my hell; 3) there is nothing left for me but His heaven."

"He [God] **made Him** [Jesus Christ] who knew no sin to be sin on our behalf, so that we might become the righteousness of God in Him" (2 Corinthians 5:21). **Jesus became in a judicial,** legal way the representative for sin and died in our place. **He paid** my sin debt in full. **He took my place** because I am a condemned sinner and **He died** for me. **He paid** my death penalty. I deserved to die; **He died** my death. Christ died for the sins of everyone past, present, and future. **He became sin on our** behalf. **Because of that great fact,** God imputes the righteousness of Christ to the believer. It is **"in Christ"** our Righteousness that the sinner is made the righteousness of God. **This righteousness** is that which **justifies,** or **satisfies** the demands of the law. **The believing sinner** stands **justified** (innocent) in the sight of the law. The law or **justice is satisfied by the sacrifice of Christ** on behalf of the sinner. The believer has a new legal standing before God. **Hallelujah!**

God cannot be made sin, but He who **is God,** and eternally **was with God** and was God, His **eternal Son,** took our nature for that purpose; **that purpose being that He might** be **made sin.** In order that the **Father** might deal with sin in our nature, not in our own persons. In our nature united to the divine nature in the Person of Immanuel, this **justice of God,** and the **grace** of God, and the **love** of God, and the **mercy** of God was necessary in pursuit of **God's purpose—which was to save.** Sin cannot go absolved by default. It cannot be commuted and disregarded by God. When **sin has been committed,** it **must be dealt with by God.**

Every sin we commit, every **sinful thought** we entertain, and our very sin nature must be dealt with by God, **either in** His **vindictive justice** in condemning us eternally to perdition, in banishment from Him in Hell under the curse, **or be dealt with by God in the Person of a Substitute.** In His infinite wisdom, mercy, and grace, **God concieved the plan** to permit and **provide** such a **Substitute** as should be able to **receive, by divine imputation,** all the sins of His chosen people. It was for this purpose **the Son of God took human nature. Remember: For us!**

We must never forget, **God is responsible for our eternal salvation,** "namely, that **God was in Christ** reconciling the world to Himself, not counting their trespasses against them, and He has committed to us the word of reconciliation" (2 Corinthians 5:19). **God caused a double transfer** to be made. **Our sins** were imputed to Christ, and **His perfect righteousness** is imputed to us. He bore our sins; we are clothed in His righteousness. **All of our sins** were placed on Christ. **He was punished** for our sins. **All our guilt** was placed on Him and He died in our place.

Christ's righteousness was imputed to us, the believing sinners, in order that we might be accepted by Him. **God acquits the guilty sinner** who believes in the atoning sacrifice of Jesus Christ for his sins.

The first false gospel tells us, "Do good, so that your good deeds will outweigh your bad deeds!" I was taught that **as a boy, in Catechism** in the Roman Catholic Church. I can **still remember the golden scales** on the teacher's (Nuns) desk, and her explanation, that our good deeds must weight the scales down or we will go to hell. **This false teaching recognizes the truth** that we will **all** be judged, we **all** must **give an account** before God. **But this false teaching fails** to understand the **depth of the sin** that every one of us commits. **We can never do enough good** to balance the accounts. **We are always violating** the command to love the Lord our God with all our hearts. "All have sinned and **fallen short** of the glory of God." (Romans 3:23)

The only true good we can do results from the miracle of a new life that God gives us. Apart from that, we are without hope. **We may look ok** when we compare ourselves to other humans. But before God, **our sins will always far, far outweigh** whatever good we do. **We can never balance accounts** between the good and the bad. **This is a false gospel.** It is not good news at all.

An early church father wrote, "Christ was called what we are, in order to call us to be what He is." Jesus took our sins upon Himself, so that we can be transformed. **We become holy and without blemish** in His sight, and we are free from accusation.

The unfathomable mystery of the cross is that Jesus, the One without sin, was our substitute. **Scripture tells us** that God both planned and executed this substitution (Colossians 1:13-20; 1 Peter 2:24; Romans 5:10). **God was pleased** with the work of the cross, despite the fact that on the cross Jesus was **separated from Him.** The intimacy that Jesus had with His Father turned into **abandonment and isolation.** That is why Jesus cried from the cross, "My God, my God, why have You forsaken me?" **Jesus is able to relate to our predicament** because he too has experienced alienation.

Now this means that the Lord Jesus Christ stood in the place of the **election of grace,** stood in our **law-place,** God imputing to Him the sins against His law that His people had committed. **In Isaiah 53,** that **wonderful portrait** as it were of a **suffering Savior, it is said :** "All we like sheep have gone astray; we have turned every one to his own way; and the Lord hath laid on Him the iniquity of us all."

I have written most of this during the winter months of 2012. It is about **Easter time,** and sure enough, here they come . . . **Every year, with no exception, around Easter,** some of the **major news** magazines, Newsweek or Time, run a **front page article on "Jesus."** They are often taken from a **humanistic, liberal perspective,** which denies the inerrancy of the Bible. As such, **Jesus is often displayed** as a "good human teacher" as if He was on the level of Budha or Ghandi, or others.

Listen, Christian friend, everything in you must cry against that. Because **if Jesus** was simply another human teacher, He would have been **a sinner.** And **if Jesus** was a sinner, His sacrifice upon the cross wasn't a pure sacrifice. And **if His sacrifice** upon the cross wasn't a pure sacrifice, **God could not accept** such a sacrifice. **And if God cannot** accept such a sacrifice, then **we** are still **dead in our sins!** So, when someone says, "Oh, Jesus was just a good, human teacher, it is **as if they were taking out an axe** and hacking away at the root of the tree called Christianity." **Well,** in the April 9, 2012 issue of **Newsweek,** the Editor-in-Chief, Tina Brown, wrote an **article entitled "Holy Smoke! God save us from the godly."** It is so irreligious and political and confrontational, you'd think she'd know better. Then inside, there is a several page article on, **"The Forgotten Jesus."** With a few good points and facts, it then turns into a liberal, left-wing, critical attack on everyone who believes in traditional Christianity.

The new believer acts upon new principles, by new rules, with new ends, and in new company. **The believer is created anew;** his heart is not merely set right, but a new heart is given him. **He is the workmanship of God,** created in Christ Jesus unto good works. Though the same as a man, **he is changed** in his character and conduct. These words must and do mean more than an outward reformation.

The man who formerly saw no beauty in the Savior that he should desire him, **now loves him** above all things. **The heart of the unregenerate** is filled with enmity against God, and God is justly offended with him. Yet there may be reconciliation. Our offended God has reconciled us to Himself by Jesus Christ.

The apostle John declares, "He who believes in the Son has eternal life; but who does not believe the Son shall not see life, but the wrath of God abides on him." (John 3:36). "We were by nature children of wrath." (Ephesians 2:3). **We are guilty because we are guilty.** "For all have sinned and come short of the glory of God." (Romans 3:23). The result is "The wages of sin is death..." (Rom. 6:23). "The soul that sins will die" (Ezekiel 18:4).

The Bible teaches that God declares the believing sinner righteous based upon the sinner putting his faith and trust in the death Jesus Christ to cover all his sins. **Justification does not mean** that God makes us righteous; that is the doctrine of progressive sanctification. **The sinner is declared righteous.** The key word is "declared." **By the free gift of God's grace** we are declared to be right with Him through Jesus Christ who died to set us free.

The Scriptures that specifically deal with the question of sinful man's acceptance before God are clearly used in the **forensic sense** (formal/legal argument). This is also true when using the word **"condemnation"** (Romans 5:16; 8:33, 34; Psalm 32:1; 142:2; Romans 2:2, 15; 8:33; 14:10; 1 John 2:1). **A justified person** is brought into a **changed judicial relation** to God (Rom. 4:3, 6-8; 2 Cor. 5:19, 30).

God sees the believing person as constituted righteous in Christ, and accepting him "in the Beloved," **He pronounces him** to be what he is—**"in Christ."** It is only a "righteous" man who can be declared righteous or "acquitted" on account of the righteousness of God in Christ Jesus.

I was down here on this earth... a sinner... lying, cheating, stealing, yes, committing all sorts of sins. **Then Jesus came down here.** He who knew no sin (Jesus was sinless), **came** that I (a sinner) might be made the righteousness of God in Him. (**He took** my sin. **He took** my Hell in order that I might have Heaven).

We know the **Word of God states of Jesus that:** "He is the same yesterday, today, and forever." **He loved you before** He saved you, and He loves you now, and He will love you forever. We know He "came to seek and to save those who are lost (that is all of us)." (Luke 19:10). He came to seek you, to save you, and to bless you. **So, the real question now is,** "What are you doing to let the world know this truth?"

Being **"in Christ"** means you have a **spiritual identity** with Christ. When God sees you, He sees His Son. That's **why God** can **"impute" righteousness to you** and **forgive your sins,** because He sees you 'in Christ.' This is **why Paul** could **teach us that we are** "fellow heirs with Christ." (Romans 8:17). Our union **"In Christ,"** is the reason that all our spiritual blessings are ours. "Blessed by the God and Father of our Lord Jesus Christ, who has blessed us with every spiritual blessing in the heavenly places in Christ." (Ephesians 1:3).

I'm always running into **people who discuss** the idea that they believe they "cannot be saved," because of certain sins in their life. **OR,** they believe that because of certain sins in their life they "are "lost again." In other words, what they are saying is, "they can lose their salvation, get it back, lose it, get it back, ad nauseam."

God's righteousness is given to us by **imputation.** Though misunderstood by most, this **act of God** is abundantly plain in many Scriptures. **For example, Paul wrote to the church at Rome stating,** "Just as David also describes the blessedness of the man to whom God imputes righteousness apart from works." (4:6). **Speaking of Abraham (and us), Paul wrote,** "Now it was not written for his sake alone that it was imputed to him, but also for us. It shall be imputed to us who believe in Him who raised up Jesus our lord from the dead." (6:24,25). You may be asking yourself, "Where, when and how was this done?" Great question!

As we examine the word, "righteousness," it is a glorious, magnificent term. **Every desire** you have for beauty, wholeness, value, purity; every time your heart calls to you to be something worth being, **you are longing for the righteousness** of God. **Jesus said,** "Blessed are those who hunger and thirst for righteousness, for they shall be satisfied." (Matthew 5:6).

Our bodies were made for **physical sustenance** and call out for it when deprived even for a short time. **Our souls** were made to **know righteousness,** and a sensitive conscience implores us to be made right with God. **"Be all that you can be,"** says **the Army** recruiting slogan, referring, of course, **to this life.** In some ways (on a much more profound level) **this is the message of the Bible:** "Be all that you can be." **Be the righteousness of God** himself **"in Christ".** Jesus became sin so that we might become in Him the righteousness of God. What a fantastic truth!

Righteousness imputed to us is grounded on the **actual imputation** of our sins unto Him: "The Lord has laid on Him the iniquity of us all." (Isaiah 53:6). **This verse could be called the 'blessed exchange,'** the exchange of places between Christ and His people. **What do I mean? Hallelujah,** this was when He took our sin and unrighteousness, that they might be exchanged for the white robe of His righteousness. "He was made sin for us, who knew no sin; that we might be made the righteousness of God in him." (II Corinthians 5:21).

He made Him who knew no sin to be sin for us. Under the inspiration of the Holy Spirit, Paul carefully chooses his words. **He does not say Jesus was made to be a sinner.** Jesus never became a sinner, but **He did become sin for us.** Even His becoming sin **was a righteous act of love,** not an act of sin. **Jesus was not a sinner,** even on the cross. But on the cross, the **Father treated Him** as if He were a sinner. All the while, sin was "outside" of Jesus, not "inside" Him, and a part of His nature (as it is with us).

Christ was not guilty of sin, and could not be made guilty; **but He was treated** as if he were guilty, **because He willed** to stand in the place of the guilty. He was not only treated as a sinner, but **He was treated** as if He had been sin itself in the abstract. This is an amazing utterance. The sinless One was made to be sin.

"He that spared not His own Son, but delivered Him up for us all." **He was not spared,** notwithstanding the dignity of His Person, **the holiness of His human nature, nor the perfection** of His obedience. **He was not spared** from the unmitigated wrath of outraged justice in the law. **He was made sin** so really, that He stood in the exact place in which His people stood as sinners, and **received** in His holy Person the **solemn vindictive wrath** due to their sins.

Please be sure, it is beyond our imagination, but if we get a little sacred manifestation of this in our hearts, **it will embitter sin to us,** and make the grace of God wonderful, **and give us to see** as nothing else will, how a sinner deserving eternal damnation can be saved. **But the great point** in our experience concerning this substitution was as Isaac Watts penned it, "Was it for crimes that I had done He groaned upon the tree? Amazing pity! Grace unknown! And love beyond degree."

"**What Jesus endured** rendered to the **justice of God a vindication of His law** more clear and more effectual than would have been rendered to it by the damnation of sinners for whom He died," **stated Charles Spurgeon.** "We obviously stand at the brink of a great mystery and our understanding of it can only be minimal."

Do you know how ridiculous it would be for us to **even think** we could somehow **pay for our salvation.** Just imagine that **you are taking a walk down the street** and **a $500,000 Rolls Royce** pulls up to the curb. The **man in the back seat jumps** out and says, "**Young man,** I appreciate you so much **I'm going to give you** this car!" He **hands you the keys and the title** while the **chauffeur gets out** and **holds the door open** for you. You are absolutely astonished! **You are so grateful** that you **thrust your hand into your pocket** and begin to fish around for some money.

Finally you find an old beat up penny. You **hold it up** proudly **before the owner** of the Rolls **and say,** "I appreciate this Rolls so much **I'd like to give you this penny** as a **token of my appreciation."** Can you **imagine how this man would feel?** Well, that's **the same thing** as our **presuming**

to somehow **earn the salvation** God provides **with our feeble,** sinful attempts at goodness.

Not only does the believer receive from God a right standing before Him on the basis of faith in Jesus (Philippians 3:9), **but here Paul says** that **"in Christ"** the believer in some sense **actually shares the righteousness** that characterizes God Himself. ". . . that I may **gain Christ,** and be found **"in Him,"** not having my own righteousness, which is from the law, but that which is through faith **"in Christ,"** the righteousness which is from God by faith, **that I may know Him** in the power of His resurrection, and the fellowship of His sufferings, being conformed to His death, if, by any means, **I may attain** to the resurrection from the dead." (Philippians 3:8-11).

When we are united to Christ in salvation, the white robe of the Mediator's righteousness is spread over us, through His blood, **and we once-for-all,** are **freed from condemnation**, and are ever known as righteous in the sight of God: **Paul wrote,** "But of Him you are in Christ Jesus, who became for us wisdom from God—and righteousness and sanctification and redemption—that as it was written, 'He who glories, let him glory in the Lord.'" (I Corinthians 1:30,31).

"**In Him (Jesus)** we have redemption through His blood, the forgiveness of sins, according to the riches of His grace." (Ephesians 1:7). **And Paul wrote to the Romans,** "there is therefore now no condemnation to those who are in Christ Jesus." (8:1). **Earlier in his epistle, Paul told them,** "Being justified freely (without any cost) by His grace through the redemption that is in Christ Jesus, Whom God set forth as a propitiation by His blood, through faith, to demonstrate His righteousness, because in His forbearance God had passed over the sins that were previously committed." (Romans 3:24, 24).

The story is told of a girl in Gary, Indiana, **terribly burned** in a flash **fire, and** lingering between life and death. **A delicate and extensive skin graft** offered the only hope for her restoration. When **the hospital issued a call** for volunteer skin donors, a **young boy responded.** During the **surgery, complications set in** and the **boy died.** But **through his sacrifice** he made it **possible** for that **young girl** to be completely **restored.**

Nothing in our Lord's life called for His death. **He was free** from sin's fatal infection. Yet, **He willingly offered Himself to die** in our place. **Someone wrote:**

> "He suffered in our stead,
> He saved His people thus;

The curse that fell upon His head,
Was due by right to us."

Dr. John MacArthur stated, "When Jesus was put to death on the cross, **God treated Him** as if He had committed every sin of every person who would ever believe. **He bore the punishment** for our sin, though He was guilty of none of it. Furthermore, since Jesus died such a death, **God treats those** who believe in Jesus as if they were as righteous and holy and blameless as Jesus Christ. **Though guilty** of all of our sin, we bear the punishment for none of it. **This is the gospel.** This is **Christ crucified.** This is **Christ raised** from the dead. This is what happened at the cross of Christ. You have been reminded."

This is a work of divine grace, a work of **divine wisdom.** It is the effect of **divine love,** and it embraces the exercise of **divine justice.** Only God who is the Creator, and Law-giver, and Judge, can deal with sin and sinners. From His high and holy throne in heaven God could eternally deal with sin and sinners in condemning them.

We who are "in Christ," having been restored to God's favor by the sacrifice of His Son, should lift our hearts in praise to our sinless Substitute. **For you who are "in Christ,"** the Scriptures teach that **you are perfectly safe. How?** You are **freed** from the law; you have the **indwelling** of the life giving Holy Spirit; you are one of the children of God; you are **chosen, called, and justified** according to the divine purpose of Almighty God; and you are the **subjects** of His unchanging love.

Justification is the gracious act of God whereby He declares a believing sinner righteous because of the finished saving work of Jesus Christ. **According to Paul in II** Corinthians 5:21, God puts to our account the righteousness of His Son. "He [God] made Him [Jesus] who knew no sin to be sin on our behalf, so that we might become the righteousness of God in Him." **Justification** (being justified) **also refers to a change in the legal status** of the believer in Jesus Christ. **God legally declares righteous** the sinner who puts his trust in Jesus Christ.

The Old Testament sacrifices illustrate the work of Christ's substitutionary atonement. **The sinner brought his animal to sacrifice** at the altar and laid his hands on the head of the animal and confessed his guilt. **The animal** had done no wrong. **The animal died in the place** of the sinner. **The sinner, by faith,** comes and puts his hands on Christ's head, confessing all his sins. They have all been imputed to Christ who died in the sinner's place. **Christ was punished** as if He were the guilty sinner.

Think for a moment of **every evil thought** that has gone through your mind, **every evil deed** or behavior you have ever done, every sinful imagination that flashed upon your mind, every **evil desire** you have fulfilled, and place them all on Christ. **What a seething mass of iniquity.** He died for you. **Think of every believer** for whom Christ died the world over, down through the millennia. Christ died bearing all of that load of sin. "He [God] made Him [Jesus Christ] who knew no sin to be sin on our behalf, so that we might become the righteousness of God in Him." (2 Corinthians 5:21).

Jesus became in a judicial, legal way the representative for sin and died in our place. **He paid** my sin debt in full. Because of that great fact, **God imputes** the **righteousness of Christ** to the believer. It is in Christ, our Righteousness, that the sinner is made the righteousness of God.

Let me attempt one more time to **explain the phrase,** "the righteousness of God," **Not merely righteous,** but **righteousness** itself; not merely righteousness, but the **righteousness of God,** because Christ is God. "What He is we are," (1John 4:17), **and He is** "made of God unto us righteousness." **As our sin** is made over to Him, so **His righteousness** to us is made over to us, in His having fulfilled **all the righteousness of the law** for us all, as our representative, (Jeremiah 23:6; 1 Corinthians 1:30). **The innocent was punished voluntarily** as if guilty, **that the guilty** might be gratuitously rewarded as if innocent (1Peter 2:24). Such are we in the sight of God the Father, as is the very Son of God himself.

As a result of that great exchange, "Therefore there is now no condemnation for those who are in Christ Jesus" (Romans 8:1), and because of our acceptance of the death of Jesus Christ, God forgets that we are sinners. **Hallelujah! "In Christ" we become** the righteousness of God. The total, complete, perfect, righteousness of Christ is the righteousness which is **imputed to the believing sinner.**

We must grasp the fact that we are "justified freely by His grace," and **not** by anything we can possibly do. **We are sinners who are unworthy** and cannot merit God's favor. Since I have been "justified" by God, it must be by the **pure grace** of God alone. **Our salvation** was **rendered certain** in the eternal covenant of grace.

I spent almost 9 years in a fast growing Baptist church in East Texas. **One Sunday a lady** came to join the church from another nearby Baptist church. The **main emphasis** of here church was training Christians. **I asked her** if she knew the Lord and was saved? She said, "Yes, I confess my sins and take the Lord's Supper (Communion) every month." **The**

only time her pastor mentioned the **doctrine of the atonement** was after people confessed their sins in prayer **before the monthly Lord's Supper service.** As a result, **this lady, a long-time Baptist,** had no better understanding of **Christ's substitution** than a lost Roman Catholic. **The pastor of** her church had spent more than **twenty-five years teaching** the congregation to live **the Christian life,** and all that time this **was a lost person,** going to Hell! You, if without Christ, are unable to live the Christian life. You cannot do it yourself.

Salvation is God's work, from start to finish. **It is not my work or yours! I heard one preacher say,** "God is sovereign over everything except salvation." **He was dead wrong.** God is sovereign over everything, **especially salvation!** He **Planned It.** He **Purchased** It. He **Performs** It. He **Preserves** It. And He will **have the Praise** of It. Thank God, salvation does not depend on your will or mine! Salvation is accomplished by God's will! (Romans 9:16, Psalm 110:3)

Righteousness is not only our unchanging standing before a holy God; it is also our present state whenever we are walking in the Spirit. **The cross,** therefore, is forever **the ground of Satan's defeat.** It was the **ace up God's sleeve** (if you'll pardon the analogy), which Satan could not have anticipated. **The great accuser, Satan,** can never find any ground by which he can turn a righteous God against us, for **all our evil was forever cut off from us in the cross,** and we now have a totally new identity. **We are one spirit** with Jesus himself. "But he who unites himself with the Lord is one with him in spirit." (1 Corinthians 6:17).

No wonder Paul shouts in Romans 8:31: "If God is for us, who can be against us?" **The inevitable outcome** of righteousness is freedom. **The righteous man** is at rest; all his internal tensions and problems are solved. **He is not anxious** about himself but is **free to give his attention to others.** That is the glory of the new covenant. "So if the Son sets you free, you will be free indeed." (John 8:36).

Someone once said, "The only thing of my very own which I can contribute to my redemption **is the sin** from which I need to be redeemed." **Now, the eternal question is: What is the foundation** (from God's perspective) for the **pardon from sin** and the acceptance of a person into righteousness? It isn't anything that we can do, anything that we experience, anything that we can feel. It is a work that is accomplished by God Himself!

Since you are God's workmanship, go ahead and let God finish the job. **Yield to His leading** in your personal life. Make yourself available to

Him. Don't try to coach from the sidelines. **Let Him be the boss (Lord)** of your life. He knows what is best for you. Why would you want to settle for second best by choosing to be your own master? **We are His workmanship** and that means He always gives us His very best. What is there that God cannot do for you far better than you can ever do for yourself?

"In Christ," since you are God's workmanship it is time to get busy. There is **no better time** to make yourself available to all of God's availability to you than **right now**. Let God take you and do **in and through you** only that which He can do. Look around you this week and see **where God is working** and **make yourself available** to Him and get busy.

You must stand firm on the conviction of the Bible that you are justified by grace alone through faith alone because of Christ's atoning sacrifice alone. **Christ's righteousness is imputed to you** as the only possible satisfaction of God, with His perfect righteousness. "For whosoever is born of God overcomes the world. And this is the victory that has overcome the world—our faith." **(I John 5:4)**.

A man was greatly disturbed about his sin, so he **wrote to Martin Luther.** The reformer, who had agonized much over his own shortcomings, **Luther replied,** "Learn to know Christ and Him crucified. Learn to sing to Him and say, Lord Jesus, You are my righteousness. You took on You what was mine; You set on me what was Yours. You became what You were, that I might become what I was not."

Men can do nothing to gain their salvation; salvation is received as a **free gift from God,** by faith. **Faith believes God's evaluation** that we are sinners, deserving of His eternal wrath. **Faith understands** that we cannot do anything to earn God's favor or blessings. **Faith not only believes** that Jesus Christ was the Son of God, **but trusts** in His death, burial, and resurrection for the forgiveness of sins and the gift of eternal life. **Saving faith entrusts oneself** to the person and work of Jesus Christ. **Saving faith** does not just give mental assent to the gospel. **Saving faith** clings to the gospel, and acts upon it. **Saving faith** is entered into once for all, but it is practiced daily, **as we live** out the gospel by the grace and power of God, dying daily, and daily experiencing and expressing the resurrection power of Christ.

As you can see, Romans 8:21 is one of the most amazing verses found in the Word of God. **The results** of this verse are **mysterious and life-changing** when there is a response to it's message. **An early church father,** Theodorit of Cyprus, **wrote,** "Christ was called what we are, in order to call us to be what He is."

Jesus took our sins upon himself so that we can be transformed. **We become holy** and **without blemish** in His sight, and **we are free** from accusation. This is the **unfathomable mystery** of the cross, in that Jesus, the One without sin, was our substitute. **Scripture tells us** that **God both planned and executed** this substitution (Colossians 1:13-20; 1 Peter 2:24; Romans 5:10). **Almighty God was pleased** with the work of the cross, despite the fact that on the cross Jesus was **separated** from Him. **The intimacy** that Jesus had with His Father **turned into abandonment** and isolation. That is **why Jesus cried from the cross,** "My God, my God, why have you forsaken me?" **Jesus is able** to relate to our predicament because he too has experienced alienation.

Martin Luther struggled to **understand Jesus' words** when he was preparing a sermon on Psalm 22, the psalm from which Jesus quoted. He said, "The beloved of the Father forsaken. It is beyond human understanding!" **He said that the mystery** was too deep. How could Jesus become sin, and be abandoned by the Father? **But it is Jesus' willingness to suffer** abandonment and die sacrificially, which results in the miracle of each one of us being given the righteousness of Christ Himself. **Through Christ we are forgiven,** accepted, and restored. **"In Christ"** we can become everything that God requires us to be. **"In Christ"** we can be everything that we have always wanted to be. **That is the good news of the gospel!**

When God saves a man, He does **more than pardon** that sinner of his guilt; He also **completely erases** the old offenses from the "books," **clears** the penitent's name, and **bestows upon him** the perfect righteousness of the Savior. For that reason **believers** may justly be **called "saints,"** for they **stand perfect "in Christ!"**

Dr. Harry A. Ironside used to tell of an experience he had while he was the **guest** of a **western sheep herder.** One morning **he saw** an **old ewe** lope across the field **followed** by the **strangest looking lamb** he had ever seen. It apparently had six legs! The last two seemed to be torn from the body and were just dangling there. **The shepherd caught the odd lambkin** and brought it to Dr. Ironside for examination. **Closer inspection** showed that the **skin from another lamb** had been stretched over its body. **The shepherd explained** that this little one had been orphaned, and none of the ewes would adopt it. **However, a day or two later** a **rattlesnake killed** another young lamb. Its **bereaved mother** could not be consoled. She also stoutly **rejected this orphaned animal** when it was offered to her as a substitute. However, when they **skinned** her own dead lambkin and draped its wooly coat over the orphaned one, **she immediately accepted it,** because it smelled right to her.

Ironside was much impressed, and **said: "What a beautiful picture of substitutionary atonement. We too were once orphans—spiritual outcasts**—without hope of Heaven. We were **not acceptable to God** because of our sin. **However, the lovely Lamb of God** took the sting of the 'old serpent' and died upon the cross for a lost world. **Now by receiving Him** through **faith we are redeemed** and made ready for Heaven because His righteousness has been applied to our account." **Sinner,** have you been made acceptable to God "in the Beloved?"

Remember: There is no other religion in the world teaches this great truth. All other religions are working to get a right relationship with God. **God's Word teaches that in grace,** God takes the perfect righteousness of His Son and places it on (covers) the believing sinner as a perfect robe. **The believing sinner stands** in the presence of a holy God robed in the pure righteousness of Jesus Christ. **The righteousness God** manifested is through faith in Christ for all who believe. There is no place for self-righteousness at the foot of the cross.

There are no self-made Christians. All **true** Christians are **Christ-made.** We are made "the righteousness of God in Him." **Sinners must glory in Christ** alone because our trespasses were reckoned to Christ and the absolute spotless perfect righteousness of Christ is reckoned to us. **As Paul recorded,** "For by grace you have been saved through faith; and that not of yourselves, it is the gift of God; not as a result of works, so that no one may boast. For we are His workmanship, created in Christ Jesus for good works, which God prepared beforehand so that we would walk in them." (Ephesians 2:8-10).

His righteousness is that which justifies, or **satisfies the demands** of the law. The believing sinner stands just in the sight of the law. **The law or justice** is satisfied by the sacrifice of Christ on behalf of the sinner. **The believer has a new legal standing before God.** This is not our inward moral state because we are still sinners. **We are now saved sinners** with a legal standing before God. **In the eyes of a Holy God** we are accepted as righteous, and treated as righteous by God based on the saving work of Christ. Christ was made "sin" and we are made "righteous."

Paul stated to the Romans, "For as through the one man's disobedience the many were made sinners, even so through the obedience of the One the many will be made righteous." (Romans 5:19). **Christ is the head** of our family. **Adam** is no longer the head of our family. **Adam**

was the representative of the fallen humanity. **Christ is the head** and representative of all who are members of His family of believers. **God made Christ to be sin for us** (II Corinthians 5:21); He makes us righteous. God the Father **sees us "in Christ"** and declares us righteous. Everything that Christ is was credited to our account.

Believing sinners are **treated** by a **righteous God as righteous** through their union with Christ. They are saved and justified. **God sees us "in Christ." Christ's righteousness is given freely** to all who believe in the atoning sacrifice of Jesus Christ. **Christ presents us before the Father clothed** in His perfect righteousness. **We are clothed** with His robes of pure righteousness. **It is** "the righteousness of God through faith in Jesus Christ for all those who believe." (Romans 3:22; Romans 4:6-8; 10:3-4, 6-10). **We are justified freely** by God's free grace through the redemption that is provided by Christ Jesus.

The atoning sacrificial death of Christ is sufficient **for every person** in the world, but it is efficient **only for all who believe** on Him. **Every individual must decide** what He will do with that sacrifice. **Only those who appropriate** Christ's death through faith receive His forgiveness and righteousness standing before God. **Christ died for all who believe** on Him. **Your personal faith** is an essential element in your salvation. Only the individual **who places his trust** in Christ receives eternal life and reconciliation with God. Have you ever wondered why God went through all this trouble?

A.W. Tozer writes: "If our greatest need had been **information,** God would have sent an educator. If our greatest need had been **technology,** God would have sent us a scientist. If our greatest need had been **money,** God would have sent us an economist. If our greatest need had been **pleasure,** God would have sent us an entertainer. **Our greatest need was for forgiveness, so God sent us a Savior!**"

If you are reading this today, and you've **never believed in or trusted in** the Lord Jesus Christ, as an ambassador of Him, **I say to you** what Paul said to the men of his day, **"Be reconciled to God."** "Believe in the Lord Jesus Christ and you shall be saved." (Acts 16:31). **Faith alone justifies,** but not the faith that is alone.

I'd like to close this chapter with a **short story** about a **little Johnny** who was **visiting his grandparents on their farm.** He was **given a slingshot** to play with out in the woods. The only rule the grandparents gave was—**don't shoot the animals** or **birds. He practiced,** but he could never hit the target, and so, getting a **little discouraged,** he **headed back**

for lunch. But as he was walking back, **he saw his grandmother's pet duck**, you know this story will not end well!

He saw the duck, and just **out of instinct he let that rock fly, hit the duck square** in the head and **killed it.** He **couldn't believe** what he had done—he was **shocked** and **sad,** and so in panic he **hid the dead duck** in the **woodpile,** only to see his **sister watching.** Sally had **seen it all** but said nothing. After lunch that day, Grandma said, **"Sally, let's wash the dishes."** But Sally said, **"Grandma, Johnny told me he wanted to help in the kitchen."** Then, she whispered to her brother, **"Remember the duck!"** So, the young man helped his grandmother do the dishes.

Later that day, **Grandpa asked if the kids** wanted to go **fishing,** and Grandma said, **"I'm sorry, but I need Sally to help make supper."** But the **little girl** just smiled and said, **"Well that's all right because Johnny told me he wanted to help."** She whispered again, **"Remember the duck!"** So the little **girl went fishing** and the young man stayed to help.

After several days of the **boy** doing **every single chore,** he finally couldn't stand it any more. **He went to his grandmother** and just spilled it—he **told her** exactly what had happened. And at that point the **grandmother knelt down,** gave him a big hug and said, **"Sweetheart, I know. You see, I was standing at the window and I saw the whole thing. Because I love you, I forgave you. I was just wondering how long you would let your sister make a slave of you."** Face it, sin has made many a man and woman **a slave to their sins.**

All of us should embrace God's forgiveness. When God forgives **He sees you** as though your sin never happened. **Can you forgive like that?** You never will, until you realize that change **won't happen** through 'trying harder' but only through **encountering the radical grace of God.** There is **so much in your future** but you've got to leave the past behind you! **You need to bury the past,** what could've been, what should've been, and how justice must be served in the life of that individual who has hurt you. "Be kind and compassionate to one another, forgiving each other, just as in Christ God forgave you." (Ephesians 4:32).

Christians sometime believe in a theology of grace, but not a lifestyle of grace. **Grace abounds** when we take on the heart of Jesus. **Grace-filled people** are joy-filled people. **Grace-givers are fun** to be around. They're the people you want at your party. **In fact, they know how to party! Don't miss this:** Jesus is saying the kingdom of God is like a party. **It's a feast!** And **why is it that so many Christians are unhappy,** tight, grumpy, and solemn?! They have never truly embraced God's grace. **Because grace-filled people are** constantly overwhelmed by the grace they've received from God—so much so, **they want you to experience** as well—so they **show you what grace looks like.** You can spot grace-givers. Are you one?

The evidences that you **have truly believed "in Christ,"** includes such things as the presence of the Holy Spirit. He that has not the spirit of Christ is none of His. **The evidence of a transformed life** is a fundamental difference in our existence. **My prayer for you** is that God may, in His marvelous grace, reach out to your heart, and bring you to the **experience of a right relationship** with God, and the enjoyment of the righteousness of God in our the Lord Jesus Christ.

Jesus was and is called Savior, Messiah and Lord. God invaded this planet in the fragile form of a **little baby.** He had to become like us **so we could relate to Him.**

John 1:14 **says,** "The Word (God) became flesh and dwelt among us." **If God wanted** to relate to **birds,** He would have become a bird. If God had wanted to communicate to **cows,** He would have become a cow. If He wanted to communicate to **dogs,** He would have become a dog. **God wanted to relate to you and to me,** so He became like us, **a human being. Jesus is very God and very man!**

It's like the little girl who was afraid of the dark and called out, "Daddy, come in here and be with me." **Her father said,** "Just hug your teddy bear." The little girl said, **"No, Daddy, I want somebody with skin on it." Jesus is God with skin on.** You can know Him as much as He knows you. This is what happened **according to** Philippians 2:5-7: "Your attitude should be the same as that of Christ Jesus, who being in very nature God, did not consider equality with God something to be grasped, but made Himself nothing, taking the very nature of a servant, being made in human likeness."

Jesus compares our lives to a **house** in Revelation 3:20, **and says,** "Here I am! I stand at the door and knock. **If anyone hears My voice** and **opens** the door, I will **come in** and eat with Him and Him with Me." **Isn't that wonderful?** The Lord **Jesus knocks at the doors of our lives. He will not gatecrash** or **force His way** in, but will come in **only at our invitation.** So, **we must respond** to His knocking by **opening the door of our heart and life** in order to become a

Christian. **Will you open the door** of your heart and life and **ask Jesus to come in** today?

> "I heard an old, old story, how a Savior came from glory,
> How He gave His life on Calvary to save a wretch like me.
> I heard about His groaning, of His precious blood atoning,
> Then I repented of my sins and won the victory.
> O victory in Jesus, my Savior forever!
> He sought me and bought me with His redeeming blood.
> He loved me before I knew Him, And all my love is due Him.
> He plunged me to victory beneath the cleansing flood.
>
> Eugene M. Bartlett

CHAPTER SIX

"In Christ," You Have 'Assurance' That You Are a 'New Creation' and a 'Child of God!'

II Corinthians 5:17 **states,** "If anyone is **in Christ,** he is a new creature (creation). The old (person) has passed away; behold, the new (person) has come."

What a tremendous statement! The Amplified Version puts it like this: "Therefore if any person is (ingrafted) **in Christ** (the Messiah) he is a new creation (a new creature altogether); the old (previous moral and spiritual condition) has passed away. Behold, the fresh and new has come!" **Paul states in** Galatians 3:26, "**In Christ Jesus** you are all sons of God, through faith."

Question: Do you know who you are? I'm serious! This world is filled with people who have an identity crisis. **A psychologist named Erik Erikson** was the first person to use the **phrase identity crisis** in 1950. Since then, almost everybody in our culture has had an identity crisis. **People talk** all the time about **not knowing who they are** . . . trying to **find themselves** . . . the never ending **search** for **self discovery.** You've probably **seen the great T-Shirt** that summarizes an identity crisis. **It says,** "I'm lost. I've gone to find myself. If I should get back before I return, please ask me to wait."

Now brother, that's an identity crisis! Most of us can identify with that to some degree. At one time or another, almost all of us ask the question, **"Who am I?"** What is it that **defines me?** Where is my **identity found?** Where am I **going. How will I know** when I get there? Those are serious, huge questions. **People have been asking** the question, **"Who am I?" for thousands of years.** And our **Scriptures today address** that very question.

And in these verses above, Paul speaks directly to **the issue of our identity.** Who are we? What defines us? Where is our identity found? **The answer** to those questions is at the **very heart of Christianity.**

Christianity is Christ. The Christian life is **Christ living His life in and through the believer.** The life of Christ is reproduced in the child of God by the power of the Holy Spirit. **Therefore, it is a new life** with new relationships. It **has a new source—Jesus Christ. The Apostle Paul wrote,** "Christ . . . is our life" (Colossians 3:4). **Jesus told His disciples,** "Abide in Me, and I in you . . . I am the vine, you are **the branches" (John 15:5). God wants to reproduce the life of Jesus Christ in you. God is glorified** when people see Christ in us.

The Christians in Galatia were trying to find their life **in themselves.** Basically, the Galatians were having an identity crisis. **They were being tempted** to find their identity **in themselves** and **in their own legalistic self-effort instead** of finding their identity in Jesus Christ. And still today, so **many of us face** that same crisis. Do you find your identity in your performance, in your **attempt to impress God**, in your **self-righteousness**, in your religious behavior? **Or do** you find your **identity in Jesus Christ** and His great work on the cross?

We, who are Christians, a follower of Jesus, our identity is found in Jesus Christ alone. That is **what it means** to be a **follower of Jesus.** Your self-worth, your value, your purpose, your identity is **not found in yourself** or in your performance, **but in Jesus Christ** and what He has done for you and what He is doing in you. **Your entire life is now defined** by your **relationship with Jesus.**

The moment we believed on Christ we were brought into a saving relationship with Him. **Faith is the means** by which this vital union with Christ is established and maintained. **Our salvation,** life and blessings all come from Christ. They **become ours only** as we **are identified** with Him by faith. **The apostle Paul declared** "Christ who our life" (Colossians 3:4) lives in us and we in Him.

We had a couple in our church in California. They had several children, and thought they weren't having any more, but after a few years, **another child came along.** This particular **dad, with a smile on his face,** said regarding the child's late arrival, **"Well, he wasn't planned, but he was welcome."** That's a great attitude, and when **we are adopted into the family of God** and made **His children,** in God's view **we are both planned and welcome,** which means everything.

The believer is "in Christ," in the sight of God and is therefore **judged** and **acquitted** as clothed with His righteousness. That is **our standing** with God based upon the righteousness of Christ. "There is therefore now no condemnation for those who are in Christ Jesus" (Romans 8:1). **A. T.**

Pierson wrote, "The believer counts God able to make him alive with His own life and holy with His own holiness. God in turn counts the sinner now dead in sin to be dead to sin and alive to God, counts him as righteous, and then proceeds to make him what he at first only reckons him to be." (Romans 4:4-8, 17, 21, 22).

Let me repeat: **God sees every Christian as being "in Christ."** We have this **new position "in Christ"** because of our justification by faith. We are **in union with Christ** and identified with Him in His death, burial, resurrection and exaltation. **This new relationship** with God applies to all believers.

How many of you know who **Ty Pennington** is? He is the loud and enthusiastic host of the **popular TV** show **Extreme Makeover: Home Edition. Each week** Ty, his co hosts and a host of community volunteers **demolish and then rebuild** the home of a needy family. **No matter how much** of a bad-tempered person you might be, **the story is so told so as** to deliberately **strike** a deep **chord within your heart,** so you know that there will **always be a lot of tears shed** in the telling of the story.

Well, you know something? Extreme makeovers are God's business as well. In fact, **God** is the **best extreme makeover** that one could ever experience. **Because His desire** is to **transform your life** and **mine.** But here is the big difference. **God's makeover is not focused** on the **external** like Ty Pennington. God's **makeover** is **an internal job** where he **makes us a new person** from the **inside out.** And **nowhere in all the Bible** is that more clearly stated than in **II Corinthians 5:17,** "Therefore if any one be **in Christ** he is a new creation. The old has passed away and the new has come." And **that is the good news** I want to **share with you** in this Chapter.

Do you ever wish you could have a fresh start? There are **many reasons** for wanting a fresh start. Many **suffering relationships** would be salvageable if they could only find a fresh start. People who have **betrayed a trust** wish they could find a fresh start. People who are weighed down by problems, guilt, addictions, ruts, debt, or habits, **wish they could find a fresh start.**

I want you to know that people **need more than a fresh start,** or simply a new day. **If you say to them,** "Come now, today is the first day of the rest of your life." **That doesn't help.** They may reply, "Yeah, so what, it is still me. Nothing has changed!" People **need more than change of scenery.** A **parent** may pull a **child** out of one school because of **bad relationships** to help their child get a fresh start, but in a few months they have **found worse friends** in the new school or new neighborhood. **New scenery is not what is needed,** but some kind of radical internal change. **People with problems** need more than a change of scenery, or the hope of a brand new day. People need the internally transforming, radical fresh start offered through Jesus Christ. How is this done?

"If anyone be **in Christ,** he is a new creation, old things are gone." We are a **new creations.** We are **radically changed** by God. This means, no change, no Christian! This is **not a minor modification,** it is a major overhaul. **You do not evolve** into a Christian. Yes you should grow in your walk, your behavior, in your maturity. With-out a change, you are no more a Christian today than you were yesterday. Why? **Because the change isn't up to you.** You don't change yourself, you are changed. This is an 'inside job' done by God, Himself.

A man was selling an old warehouse. The building had been **empty for months** and needed repairs. **Gangs had damaged** the doors, smashed the windows, and thrown trash everywhere. As he **showed a prospective buyer** the property, the **realtor took pains** to say that he would replace the broken windows, bring in a crew to correct any structural damage, and clean out the garbage.

"Forget about the repairs," the buyer said. "**When I buy this place,** I'm going to **build something completely different.** I don't want **this building;** I want the **site.**

Compare this with the renovation God has in mind. Our efforts to improve our own lives **are as trivial** as sweeping a warehouse that is slated for the wrecking ball. **When we become God's,** the old life is over, He has **bought us** with a price. (I Corinthians 6:20). He makes all things new. **All he wants is the site** and the **permission to build.**

Please notice the phrase **"in Christ"** in verse 17 **and** in verse 19. **Paul uses** this phrase **"In Christ"** over and over again. **A quick search** of the phrase **"in Christ"** in Paul's epistles brought up a **list of 84 verses** where Paul used this phrase. **I want to ask you a question** of spatial logic. **Are Christians** in Christ **or** is Christ in Christians? **Paul speaks of both.** (Galatians 2:20; 2 Corinthians 13:5).

Now, let's look at the phrase **"In Christ"** relationally. **If we are "in Christ,"** we are in a **'relationship'** with Christ. **To be "in Christ"** was one of **Paul's favorite expressions.** He used it often and to him it meant the very fact of being a Christian. **To be "In Christ"** is to have a close, intimate, real, relationship with Him.

In verse 17, the striking phrase—"In Christ"—which the Apostle uses signifies nothing else but to be saved out of a life of which the self is the centre and to enter into a life of which Love, **the Love of Christ is the centre.** To be **"in Christ"** then, means **deliverance from** selfishness in all its forms **into** the Love in all its forms. **In other words** it is a spiritual process of decreasing the "I" in us, and **allowing Christ to increase** within us.

The believer "in Christ" Jesus who comes to see his eternal **Christ-centered** position in the Lord Jesus begins to **experience the benefit** of all that he is **"in Christ." We become like** the person with whom we associate. **And the greatest characteristic** of the New Testament teaching is that **it demands not** a new pattern of society, **but a new creation** of everyone by living in Christ. "If Christ is not born in you, He is born in vain", **is a form of Christmas greeting** which drives home the fact that **without receiving Christ in us,** we cannot be Christians. **Without Christ** there can be **no real transformation** in us.

When a person is "in Christ," the whole world around him vibrates with a new challenge, and a new suggestion. **Everything has a new look** about it, which has a new meaning. **For it is a well known fact** that when you change a man's outlook, you change the whole world in which he lives, whether it be a cottage or a palace. **He begins to look at everything with new eyes.**—Old Things Are **passed Away**—All Things Have **Become New!**

This is a great and amazing truth. It is also a hard truth for us to live out. You see, **the world** and our own self-centered, **sinful nature tempt us** to find our identity in **100 things other than Jesus,** to **find our identity** in our **money** or material **possessions,** to find our identity in **our looks** or our **intelligence** or the way we **dress,** to find our identity in our **grades** at school, or our **popularity,** in **sports,** or a **dating** relationship, or **impressing** other people, or **pleasing** our parents, to find our **identity in our job** or our successful **business,** to find our identity in our **children,** to find our identity in our **political affiliation,** or even to find our identity in our **church affiliation** and our religious practices. **The Bible declares** over and over, "Find your identity in Jesus Christ alone. None of those other things define who you are. **They cannot fulfill you.** You are defined by your relationship with Jesus."

"Therefore if any man is 'in Christ,' he is a new creature." **Do you know** what that **word "new"** is? It is the same word used for new covenant, New Testament. It is the Greek word which **means absolutely, qualitatively brand new,** never seen before. What did you use to do? You lived in darkness. You hid your sin under darkness. **Now, "in Christ,"** that has changed! **The scriptures are telling us** about a completely new and improved you. **You are not the same** as you were. **Old parts are not hidden** but each part of **your life is made new.**

Charles G. Trumbull speaks vividly of this new life in Christ: "The resources of the Christian life, my friends, are just—Jesus Christ. I realized for the first time the many references to Christ in you, you in Christ, Christ our life, and abiding in Christ are literal, actual, blessed fact, and not figures of speech… **Jesus Christ does not want** to be our helper; He wants to be our life. **He does not want** us to work for Him. **He wants** us to let Him do His work through us, using us as we use a pencil to write with, better still, using us as one of the fingers of His hand."

Have you ever watched a child come in from playing and they are **absolutely covered** from **head to toe in mud?** You tell them to go **take a bath** and sure enough for once they listen to you and do. **But as soon** as they get out of the shower they **put the same clothes back** on and then wonder why you're upset. **People are just like that.** They ask God to change them and then go back to wearing the same old clothes. **God doesn't clean the outer half,** He **doesn't reshape** it or even enhance what is already there, **He works from the inside** out to re-create. **God's number one purpose** in your life is to make you like Jesus Christ. **The Spirit of God** uses the **Word of God** to make the **child of God** more like the **Son of God.**

Let me ask you, if you have given your life to Christ, how do you see yourself? **You are not merely** reformed, rehabilitated, or reeducated— **you have been re-created** (new creations). **A living vital union with Christ** has literally made you a different kind of spiritual being. **This is not turning over a new leaf,** but starting a new life. It is **life under new management!** Under **a new Master.** Old things have gone. **Do we really believe this?** Since we constantly review the past, it is often difficult to accept that God puts our past in the past. **The new has come.** Do we **really believe** this? We **don't always look new,** but where it counts we are.

This is only possible because we are **in Christ.** He is the only one with the power to make us new. When you truly believe this, the practical implications are amazing.

Perhaps someone is reading this today, and you're haunted by the **mistakes** of **your past.** You're weighed down by the **guilt and the baggage** of things you can't change or undo. And **when you think of yourself, there's a label** that always comes to mind: Drug Addict, Gambler, Thief,

Liar, Adulterer, Divorced, Aborted a Child. I want you to know **God will rip that label off** of you today and tear it into a million pieces and burn those pieces. **When you trust** Jesus Christ, **God wipes away** your sin and **puts all new labels** on you: Forgiven, Righteous, Cleansed, Holy, Sanctified, Set Free, Child of God.

When you trust Jesus, you're not defined by your **failures.** And when you trust Jesus, **you're not defined** your accomplishments. When you trust Jesus, you're **defined by the work of Jesus** in your life. **Your identity in Christ** is based upon **your faith in Jesus.**

Someone told the story of Augustine of Hippo who lived a life of dissipation prior to his conversion. After **God changed his life,** he was **noticed** on the street by a **prostitute** he had previously frequented. **She called to him,** "Augustine, it is I." **He ignored her** while **she continued,** "Augustine, it is I." **Finally he replied,** "Yes, but **it is no longer I."** How about you? **Unlike Augustine, there are many who refuse to face their sins with honesty.**

Remember this? After 14 years of denials, **Pete Rose finally admitted** he bet on baseball games. **According to** U. S. News & World Report, **He wrote:** "I'm sure I'm supposed to act all sorry or sad or guilty. Let's leave it at this: I'm sorry it happened, and I'm sorry for all the people, fans, and family it hurt. Let's move on."

Though he was a great player, he was **not great** in relationships and personal responsibility. **Rose fails** to understand that **the enmity created** by his betting on games and **then his denial** of **it cannot be removed** by a simple, "let's move on." **Unfortunately,** some want to **treat their relationship** to God like this. **Rather than facing their enmity** and their **need for reconciliation,** they skip that, move on to attend church or do some kind of **religious penance,** and essentially **say to God,** "Let's move on." It doesn't work like that!

What happened when light came into your life? **You exposed yourself to the light,** you were exposed to the light, the light exposed you and you saw yourself as a sinner. You came out of the darkness. **Ephesians says you were once darkness,** now you have been made light. How can a person who has been made light go back and consistently live habitually in darkness? John is saying you can't do that.

"**Well,**" **you might say,** "if that is the case, there are a **lot of people** who have joined the church **who aren't saved."** That is what I am saying. **Yes, salvation is by grace,** but you've got to understand grace. I think when you stay in the book of 1 John all the way through you are going to see he is **drawing a contrast** between those who know Christ and those who don't know Christ. That is the whole reason for writing, remember. **I John 5:13 says,** "These things I have written . . . that you may **know** that you have eternal life."

I passed a store in Stuart, Florida the other day that had a **big, really big banner hanging** on the outside front of the store. **People were busy** going in and out of the store. The **sign simply read: "UNDER NEW MANAGEMENT!"** These words, 'In Christ,' far **surpasses** any other expression given for salvation. It not only encompasses the **Christian's forgiveness of sins** paid for by the **substitutionary death** of Jesus on the cross, **but indicates that what is ahead** in the new creation life is far superior. Oh, yes, evil and sin are still present, but the believer sees them in a new perspective . . . and, they no longer control him. **The CHRISTIAN is under: "NEW MANAGEMENT!"**

I hope you understand what this means. I've heard **some say** things like, "I have **given up** my bad habits (and they list them), and **they think** that the change in their habits is a fulfillment of this verse. **Not so! Being "In Christ"** simply **defines** every saint's eternal, permanent, spiritual location, the spiritual "address" and the "spiritual atmosphere" as it were in which we now live and breathe and have our being. **"In Christ"** describes every believer's new position and new sphere of existence. Before we were born again into the Kingdom of God (John 3:3,5), **our existence was** in Adam (1 Corinthians 15:22, Romans 5:12) **We were spiritually dead** and under the dominion (supreme authority, control, absolute ownership) of the "sin virus" we inherited from Adam.

Christianity only makes this statement that Christians are "In Christ." **Dr. John MacArthur** states that **a Buddhist** does not speak of himself as in Buddha, **nor does a Muslim** speak of himself as in Mohammed. **A Christian Scientist** is not in Mary Baker Eddy **or a Mormon** in Joseph Smith or Brigham Young. **They may faithfully follow** the teaching and example of their religious leaders, **but they are not in them! Only Christians** can **claim to be in** their Lord, because they **have been made spiritually one** with Him.

When God makes us "new creations," He is speaking of a **total change** in our life. **For too many people,** this change never takes place. When we trust Christ, we are **no longer identified** with Adam. We are **no longer identified with this world's systems . . . which may include the fact that old relationships** are passed away.

When you are a follower of Jesus, your identity is found in Jesus Christ alone. **Your worth and your value** are not found in who you have been or what you have done, neither in your successes or failures. **Your worth and your value** are found in Jesus and Jesus alone. I pray that God will use the power of that truth to transform your life.

But you say, Pastor: "I joined the church." "I got baptized." "I took communion (the Lord's Supper)." "I give my money . . . . I even tithe." "I attend church faithfully." You may ask, **"What else does Jesus want?"** **He wants YOU! Don't base** your confidence on "doing things." **Don't base** your confidence on "experiences or feelings." **Don't base** your eternal future on teachings of some Priest or Minister, and what they told you. **You are a new creation because Jesus says so. How do I know? Because of the Word of God! Base your decision on** "thus says the Lord!" **Salvation is not** turning over a **new** leaf, but **receiving a new life** (life in Christ). Salvation not only **requires** change, it **demands** change.

In his book, Mere Christianity, C. S. Lewis—who **was changed radically** by his experience with Jesus Christ—has a marvelous story of how you come in heart first, then your head straightens it out later. He **tells the story** that you can **take a horse out** into the field and **teach** the horse to jump a fence. You can **train** a horse, take it to shows, and **win prizes** with it. But essentially, **the horse is still a horse. But the Bible says** that **if the horse grew wings,** started **flying** around and doing **acrobatics** in the sky, it **wouldn't be** a new and improved horse. It would be an **entirely new creature** on the face of this earth. **When we come to Christ, we have been changed** and we are **completely new creatures "in Christ."**

It has been my privilege to teach in Public Schools in 4 different states. While serving as a Southern Baptist **pioneer missionary** in the **Pacific Northwest** in the late **1950's,** I was a **coach** and taught **history and biology.** As a teacher, I learned that **the Bible's word** and the **biology word "metamorphosis,"** was the same word in origin. It comes from a Greek word **"metamorpheto" meaning "to be transformed".** It's the word you **learned about the ugly little caterpillar** turning into **a beautiful butterfly.** And you look at that little **squiggly worm** and you ask yourself, how in the world did it ever sprout wings? I don't know. **When I saw a butterfly,** as a boy, I didn't make the connection to the caterpillar. **I didn't figure** that out until I studied biology. My teacher said, "This is where that comes from, because they are so **radically different."**

That is what the **Bible is talking about.** The Bible is **not talking** about **moral rearmament** or a new year's **resolution** but the Bible is talking about making new people out of us, which would change the story. **If you want to rewrite your story** and get out of the victim mode, then the way to do it is just take the risk and make a decision to meet and follow Christ. This verse speaks of a **new life "in Christ."**

"If any man is **in Christ,** he is a new creature (creation). Behold, all things (old) have passed away." **When you look at the life of a Christian** who has been **transformed** by the grace of God, **this text comes to life.** Behold, all things have become new. **Isn't that remarkable?** I mean, that **is among the greatest things ever said** to humanity. **We have the chance to just simply be totally, completely, transformed. The old, he says,** has passed away.

As we think of this **miraculous change,** we see **many in the Bible who,** after they met Christ, **they were never the same again. In Luke 19 we see Zacchaeus.** He was a vacuous, selfish, money-grubbing, rich tax collector. Walking down the street, **Jesus said,** "Come down, Zacchaeus. This day I'm going to have lunch at your house . . . This day you are a son of Abraham. You are restored to your roots. Your story is restored." **Zacchaeus said,** "If I have defrauded any man, I will restore to him fourfold. I will take half of my money and give to the poor." **You know he was converted and changed!** Jesus touched his life. That's why, if you want to hang it on something, **you can hang it on** "if a man be **in Christ,** he is a new creature."

This word **"new"** is a word that **means** . . . it is **gone** and it is permanent and it is over and it is removed, and it can't be dredged up. It's that image from the Old Testament. **That our sins** have been **buried** in the **depths of the deepest sea.** (Micah 7:19). That they have been **removed** from us, as far as the East is from the West (Psalm 103:12). You can look for them forever and you will never find them because **when God forgives you, they are gone.** Do not be a **gravedigger,** always trying to dig them up. **When you are "in Christ," they are gone!**

According to John Wesley, we not only lose our sins, we gain new things. **Wesley states,** "He has new life, new senses, new faculties, new affections, new appetites, new ideas and conceptions. **His whole tenor of action and conversation** is new, and he lives, as it were, in a new world. God, men, the whole creation, heaven, earth, and all therein, appear in a new light, and stand related to him in a new manner, since he was created anew in Christ Jesus."

Verse 17 states that we have another chance. **The life we once lived in sin** no longer exists. It has been wiped from the memory of God, and He says our sins will no longer be held against us. **Before becoming a Christian,** we were dead in sin. "All of us have sinned." (Romans 3:23) "There is not a just man who does good and does not sin." (Ecclesiastes 7:20). **All of us,** in our life were dead in sin and destined to a sinners doom. **Hallelujah! Now the good news** . . . "But God be thanked that though you were slaves of sin, yet you obeyed from the heart that form of doctrine (teaching) to which you were delivered." (Romans 6:17).

While ministering in California in the mid 1960's, one Sunday a young man attended the a.m. service. He continued to come for several weeks, before he asked to speak to me. **He told me** that he'd like to join our church, but he was afraid the people would not accept him. **To make it short,** he had just gotten out of **Huntsville Penitentiary** in Texas. **Originally from Long Beach,** he was with a group of young people **traveling,** when they ran out of money. They decided to "knock-off" a Liquor Store. He **was arrested, convicted and served two years** before release. **While in Prison he was saved.** As a prisoner he took and graduated the **Schofield Bible Class** from Moody Bible Institute. **To keep this short,** he joined our church and worked with me in reaching other youth for Christ. Later, he **became the Young People's Bible** Class **teacher. Today,** after earning his Phd from U.S.C., he is now a Christian Doctor and Psychiatrist.

This man's sins were wiped out by virtue of his union with Jesus Christ in His death, burial, and resurrection. **We dare not** view him as a second-class Christian.

What we were before our salvation—no matter how good or great it may appear to men—**means nothing** in regard to our status in Christ. **Every Christian is** on the same footing before God, and that footing is the work of Jesus Christ in His death, burial, and resurrection in the sinner's place. **There is absolutely no basis for pride** in Christ, for **what we are in Christ** is **due solely to His work** on our behalf. **Whatever we are,** whatever we **have,** or whatever we **do** as new creations **in Christ** is the **result of His grace.** We dare not take credit for it as though it were our doing.

Unfortunately, there may be frauds in the fellowship of the **local church, but Christians are definitely brand-new people on the inside.** It's a "heart and soul" thing. The **Holy Spirit gives them new life,** and they are not the same any more. **We are not** reformed, rehabilitated, or reeducated . . . **we are new creations,** living in vital union with Christ. "As you therefore have received Christ Jesus the Lord, so walk in Him." (Colossians 2:6). We are **not** merely turning over a **new leaf;** we are beginning a new life under a new Master. **Those who do not have this transformation . . . are not saved.** They are **not God's children—redeemed!**

Let me emphasize...**regeneration** (salvation) is very, very **much more** than simply shedding a **few tears** because of some **temporary remorse** over sin. It is **far more** than **changing our course** of life, the **leaving off** of bad habits and the substituting of good ones. It is **something different** than just practicing of noble ideals. It goes infinitely **deeper** than **coming forward in a church service** to take some popular pastor or evangelist by the hand, **signing a pledge-card,** or **"joining the church."**

The new birth is no mere turning over a new leaf, but is the beginning and reception of a new life! It is **no mere reformation,** but a radical **transformation.** In short, **the new birth is a miracle**—the result of the supernatural operation of God. It is radical, revolutionary, lasting! Have you had this experience? If not, why?

C. H. Spurgeon challenges us with these words: Common, ordinary, church-going religion is nature **gilded over** with a thin layer of what is thought to be grace. **Sinners have polished** themselves up, and **brushed off** the worst of the rust and the filth, and they think their old nature is as good as new. **This touching-up and repairing** of the 'Old Man' is all very well; **but it falls short** of what is needed. **You may wash the face and hands** of Ishmael as much as you please, but you cannot make him into Isaac. **You may improve nature,** and the more you do so the better for certain temporary purposes; **but you cannot raise** it into grace. **There is a distinction** at the very fountain-head between the stream which rises in the bog of fallen humanity, and the river which proceeds from the throne of God.

There are two worlds we Christians live in . . . the **old world** before conversion and the **new world** we become citizens of when we are born again into His kingdom. In this world mankind is divided into two groups. **Those outside** of Christ, and those that are **'in Christ.' By our first birth** we are "in Adam." (I Corinthians 15:22), and he is a part of the **old creation** that was spoiled by the fall of mankind into sin. **With man's second birth** (John 3) he is **"in Christ."** (I Corinthians 15:22), and part of the **new creation. Remember: You are in Him, only when you are 'In Christ." PERIOD!**

Being "In Christ" | 109

Let me illustrate: You are **walking through the woods.** In a distance you see an **old house.** The closer you get the worse it looks. It is a very old, **dilapidated, falling down shack.** As you look at it, it's not much to look at. Many of the **shingles** are missing on the roof. The old **screen door** has been blown off and is lying on the ground. Some of the **windows** have broken glass. There are **potholes** in the cluttered driveway. Inside, there is **grease and garbage** everywhere. And **bugs,** they are everywhere. It is almost ruined, and is decaying. **What a tragedy!**

One year later, while hiking, you come upon the place once again. **WOW! what a change.** The place has been **cleaned up.** The shingles are repaired. The house has been painted, the potholes filled, and new glass in the windows. **LISTEN: This is the same old shack, Restored and under NEW OWNERSHIP. God is in the business of the old shack// new shack ex-change!**

One of the greatest changes I have ever seen in my lifetime is the late Chuck Colson. He was the **Watergate conspirator,** and he spent time in **federal prison.** He **met Christ** through the **ministry of Billy Graham.** God **touched** him, and **changed** his life. **He spent the rest of his life** trying to bring some kind of redemption into the prison systems of the world. I read recently **he has visited 6,000 prisons.** He is the one who popularized what the Bible says when something happens to us—he was "born again," changed by the power of God.

Listen to what the Lord Jesus said, "Truly I say unto you, He that hears my Word and believes on Him that sent Me, has eternal life (present tense), and shall not come into condemnation (judgment); but is passed from death unto life" John 5:24.

What assurance this verse should give us! And Paul wrote, "The Spirit Himself bears witness with our spirit, that we are the children of God, and if children, then heirs—heirs of God and joint heirs with Christ, if indeed we suffer with Him, that we may also be glorified together." (Romans 8:16-17). **God is teaching us here that** God the Holy Spirit, **confirms the validity** of our **adoption,** not by some strange happenings or mystical voices, but **by the fruit** He produces in us, (Galatians 5:22,23), **and the power** He provides for spiritual service. (Acts 1:8).

Christians can know with **absolute assurance** that God answers prayer when they approach the throne of Grace. "Now this is the confidence (assurance) that we have **in Him** (in Jesus), that if we ask anything according to His will, He hears us. (I John 5:14). **While teaching us about assurance and confidence,** we also have a very strategic key to answered prayer ... **to pray according to God's will.** This is to pray in accord with what He would want, according to our needs, and **not** according to what we desire or to fulfill our selfish, fleshly desires. (John 14:13,14).

Let me illustrate with a hypothetical story, by asking you a question: What if I died tonight and **stood before the Lord God** who is the **Supreme Judge** of the Universe? No doubt **He would ask me,** "Glen Clifton, why should I let you into my heaven? You are a guilty sinner. How do you plead?"

My response would be, "I plead guilty, Your Honor." **My advocate (lawyer), Jesus Christ,** who is standing there beside me **speaks up for me.** He says, "Your Honor. It is true that **Glen Clifton is a grievous sinner.** He is guilty. However, Father, I died for him on the cross and rose from the dead. Glen Clifton **has put his faith and trust in Me** and all that I have done for Him on the Cross. He is a believer. I died for him, and he has accepted Me as his substitute." **The Lord God turns to me** and says, "Is that true?" **"Yes, Your Honor,"** is my answer.

The Lord God responds: "Acquitted!" By **order of this court,** "I command that you be set free. **The price has been paid in full by My Son."** Furthermore, I even get to go home and live with the Judge! **WOW! Of course, that illustration couldn't really happen that way but,** because of the **blood of Jesus,** I have already, **now,** been acquitted! **Praise the Lord!**

Paul assures us, "For if, when we were God's enemies, we were reconciled to Him through the death of his Son, how much more, having been reconciled, shall we be saved through His life!" (Romans 5:10), **and,** "For in the gospel a righteousness from God is revealed, a righteousness that is by faith from first to last, just as it is written: 'The righteous will live by faith.'" (Romans 1:17).

I can hear someone say, "Oh, but Brother Glen, when you are **inside Jesus** that's one thing. He **holds on to you,** but you can choose to walk outside of Him." **Hold it. Hold it. Whoever** in the world **told you** that the Holy Spirit inside of you would allow you to make that choice? **You know there is Someone** now who **lives in you** that didn't live in you before.

And He's in you, the book of Philippians says, **to will and to work.** He even works in your desires. **Many people who don't believe in eternal security** and can't understand this truth are people who have been raised and taught that **salvation is a gift.** Let's just say that **you have a handful of change.** I stand up in front of you and **say, "I have a gift** for whoever wants this gift. If you want it you run up here and get it." If you've **got it now I can't take it back.** Why? Because it's a gift, and it's always your gift.

If you grow up thinking salvation is nothing more than you receiving a gift from God, **it's no wonder you believe** you can lose your salvation. **That's not what salvation is.** In the **words** of our **Lord Jesus Himself** in John chapter 3, He said **salvation is a birth,** something takes place. You are a brand new creature. II Corinthians 5:17 says, "Therefore if anyone is in Christ, he is a new creature; the old things passed away; behold, new things have come."

The Spirit of God has entered into man's spirit, and they have become mysteriously related together. **For instance: Take the ingredients of bread.** You put in the **flour,** and you put in **yeast.** You put in the rest of the ingredients. You put it all together, **stir it up** and make **dough** out of it. You put it on the **pan.** You put into the stove. **You cook it,** and when you take it out, **there's bread.**

Listen: No scientist in this world has **ever been able** to go back into that loaf of bread and **take out the ingredients.** They can't do it. **They are mysteriously blended** together. You can **never rip** them apart. **Answer this question:** How do you **take God's Spirit out** of a **man's spirit?** There's no possible way. It's an entrance of God into a person's life, a cleansing, and that is **for all of eternity.**

Who are you? Race, nationality, gender, success, failure, religious traditions, social status, economic status, human relationships? **None of these are the sum total of your life.** Your life does not rise and fall on any of those things. **Your life rises and falls on Jesus Christ.** Jesus is your life, and everything else is to be seen in relation to Him. **Your entire life is to be radically Christ-centered.** You are wrapped up **in Jesus.** You are obsessed with Jesus. You are immersed in Jesus. Your whole life is for Jesus. **And your whole life is about Jesus.**

Dr. William James, Harvard University's famous professor of philosophy and psychology, once **stated that after age 30** we become set like plaster and never change. **He was wrong.!** We can and do change. Let me give you **one example.**

John D. Rockefeller had become the **world's first and only billionaire.** But he **was a miserable man** who couldn't sleep, who was unloved, and who needed bodyguards. **At age 53 he was stricken** with a **rare disease.** He lost all his hair, and his body became shrunken. He was **given a year** or so to live. **Rockefeller started thinking about eternal issues,** and suddenly he began to change. He **gave away his money** to help **churches and the poor.** He established the Rockefeller Foundation, which has underwritten critical health research. **His health improved,** and contrary to the doctor's prediction, he **lived to be 98.**

If a man could undergo such a physical and emotional change, **how can we doubt** that **God, by His grace** and **power,** can transform us spiritually? **The Bible says** that anyone who believes in Jesus Christ and His sin-atoning, guilt-cleansing death will **become a new creation.**

Stuart Hamblin wrote country and western songs. Before he got saved he wrote a song titled, "I won't go hunting with you Jake but I'll go chasing women" **Stuart got saved** and **John Wayne, his good friend, made a bet Stuart** wouldn't last six months. Sometime **after the six months** Stuart saw **Wayne** who said **"you cost me some money,** Stuart, I bet you wouldn't last six months." **Stuart said** "It's no secret what God can do." **John Wayne said,** that sounds like a **good song title** and so **Stuart went home** that night and **wrote the song** "It is no secret what God can do."

"The chimes of time ring out the news another day is through,
Someone slipped and fell, was that someone you?
You may have longed for added strength, your courage to renew,
Do not be disheartened, for I bring hope for you.
It is no secret what God can do, what He's done for others, He'll do for you.
With arms wide open, He'll pardon you, It is no secret, what God can do!"

Have you really trusted and accepted Jesus as your Lord and Savior? **He assures you** in these verses, that you have (present tense) eternal life now and you cannot go to hell . . . because you have passed from death unto life. **LISTEN: You are not subject to judgment and death—because you are a new creation. Hallelujah!**

You may be asking, "I know that is a wonderful verse, **but how may I know** absolutely that I am a new creation in Christ?" **Listen to what the Lord Jesus said:** "Verily, verily, I say unto you, He that hears my word, and believes on him that sent me, has everlasting life, and shall not come into condemnation; but is passed from death unto life" (John 5:24). **Have you believed in the Lord Jesus** Christ? **Do you trust Him to save you?** If you do, **He assures you** that you have **eternal life** and will not come into judgment; you have passed from death unto life. **This makes you a new creation,** no longer subject to judgment and death. You have passed into life.

Are you "in Christ"? Because if you're **"in Christ," you're new,** and when you finish reading this, you can walk away, just as excited as you can be about life, **so free** of what you used to be. If you're not **"in Christ,"** then

I don't know what else to tell you, **but to do** what this text says, **ASAP! The real question is: Who do you serve?** Are you still serving **self?** Are you serving **self and selfish desires? OR,** are you serving the **Savior, Jesus?** Every person is a slave (a servant) of something or someone. There is a sense in which no person is free. **You can choose to be a slave** (servant) **to sin** or you can choose to be a **slave** (servant) **to God. There is no middle ground.**

Bob Dylan (musician and song writer) actually **had it correct** in his song, **"Gotta Serve Somebody,"** in 1979,

> "You may be an ambassador to England or to France;
> You may like to gamble, you might like to dance;
> You may be the heavy-weight champion of the world;
> You may be a socialite with a long string of pearls;
> But you're gonna have to serve somebody.
> Yes indeed you're gonna have to serve somebody.
> Well it may be the devil or it may be the Lord,
> but **you're gonna have to serve somebody."**

I ask you, "will it be Jesus?"
Many of us feel like Nicodemus who was **told by Jesus** that he "must be born again." (John 3). **He asked,** "How can we be reborn?" We can't see beyond ourselves. We can't see beyond the portrait the world has painted for us. **We must believe that it is possible. The world must learn** what Johnny learned at Sunday School. **A little boy came home** from Sunday School and his **mother asked,** "What did you learn at Sunday School today, Johnny?" **Johnny replied,** "Today I learned that I have **two dogs inside me,** a **black** dog and a **white** dog, and they are **always fighting!"** His **mother was quick to realize** the lesson being taught, so she went on to ask, **"And which dog is going to win?"** Little Johnny answered, **"It depends on which one I feed!"**

Not everyone who comes to Christ will have the same **salvation or conversion experience. Some are adults** who have a **history of sordid sins** they are ashamed of, and are living in Christ's forgiveness and cleansing. **Some of you** (who are reading this book), **don't** have a **laundry list of sins** that you committed before surrendering your life to Christ. **In fact,** there are people who are reading this that can not **remember a time they didn't love Jesus.** They, perhaps, **grew up in a loving Christian family** who worshipped, prayed and studied God's

Word together. **That does not change the fact** that there **was a point** at which they stopped being a **slave to sin** and **started being a slave to God.** If you are a Christian, there was a **certain point in time** when you were set free. **Can you point back to a time** (does not have to be a specific date), **when God started the process** of making you into His likeness? I am **not talking about church stuff,** catechism, joining the church, or baptism. **When was the change in your life obvious** to those around you?

How do you feel about God? Does the **thought of God** make you uncomfortable? Is God a Being to be **avoided?** Do you feel the eyes of God judging you even as you sit in God's house? **Are you ridden with guilt** because you feel **you are letting God down?**

Did you see the story in the newspapers of a young fellow named **William,** who was a **fugitive from the police.** William had **run away with his girlfriend** because her parents had been trying to break them up. **What William didn't know** was that the **police were seeking him** for another reason. Just before his disappearance he had **seen a doctor.** The **diagnosis** had come in that **he had cancer.** William was doing his best to **elude the police,** lest **he lose his love,** while **they were** doing their best to find him, lest **he lose his life.** He thought they were after him **to punish him;** they were really after him to **save him.** The writer of this story concludes: **"William is representative of every (person),** whose guilt tells him God is after him to straightjacket him in this life and torture him forever."

How do you feel about God? Your sense of identity will affect your perception of God. **Who are you, really? Paul tells us** who we are in our lesson from Galatians: "For now we are all children of God through faith in Jesus Christ..."

Jeff Williams tells a story that I also relate to: I grew up watching **a dare-devil motorcyclist** who tried to jump lines of buses, boxes of mountain lions, and even the Snake River Canyon. **His name is Evel Knievel.** Evel was **known for his wild, sinful lifestyle** as much as he was known for his death-defying stunts. **Evel came to faith in Jesus Christ.** He said that "he always believed in God but **he refused** to **accept Jesus Christ as Lord** because he couldn't walk away from the gold and gambling and the booze and the women."

Speaking at a large church in California on April 1, 2007, **Evel** said, "All of a sudden, I just believed in Jesus Christ. I did, I believed in him! **One day I rose up in bed** and, I was **by myself,** and **I said,** 'Devil, Devil... you get away from me. I cast you out of my life.'... **I just got on**

my knees and prayed that God would put his arms around me and never, ever, ever let me go."

After sharing his testimony and then being baptized, 'Christianity Today' Magazine reported, "In a spontaneous response described by some worshipers as one of the most spiritually significant events they had ever experienced, an estimated **500 to 800 people came forward** for baptism and **to commit** or **rededicate** their lives to God." **Evel was transformed** by God's grace and it has affected others. **Changed lives, change lives!**

II Corinthians 5: 20 says this, "We **beg you** (implore or urge), be reconciled to God." If you're **not "in Christ", I literally beg you not** to wait. **Don't put this major decision off any longer.** I just **want you to experience newness.** Becoming new is a really good thing, **there are some folks who could say "amen" to that.**

> "**Blessed assurance** Jesus is mine!
> O what a foretaste of glory divine!
> **Heir of salvation,** purchase of God,
> Born of His Spirit, washed in His blood.
> **This is my story,** this is my song,
> Praising my Savior all the day long;
> **This is my story,** this is my song,
> Praising my Savior all the day long."
>
> —Fanny J. Crosby

CHAPTER SEVEN

"In Christ" You Have Been 'Seated in the Heavenly Places,' Even While You Live On Earth.

Ephesians 2:4-6, states, "But God, who is rich in mercy, because of His great love with which He loved us, even when we were dead in sins, (God) has quickened us (made us alive) together with Christ, by grace you are saved; and (God) has raised us up with Christ and seated us with Him in the heavenly places '**in Christ Jesus.**'"

Having lived in Colorado for about 15 years, my children and I have hiked and hunted high in the Rocky Mountains. **I have been in valleys** that are several thousand feet **below the peaks** that I am hiking up to. There is **nothing as daunting** as to be in a deep valley **looking up at a snow-capped peak** and realize that you have to scale that mountain, sometimes in the dark with temperatures near zero.

Likewise, there is no greater ecstasy than to reach the **top of a high peak,** and **look out** over the other **snow capped peaks and see hundreds of miles,** and feel **the surge of excitement** that you made it. If not a hiker, you can drive up to the top of **Pikes Peak** and survey the beauty. The **majestic views** and the magnificent feeling are indescribable! **Our study in this chapter** takes us on a similar journey. We will see from **our lowly valleys** to the **heights of God's** love and grace.

The major truth of Christianity is stated right here: **We are made alive** together with Christ. Notice that **Paul says 'with' or 'in' Christ three times:** We are **made alive** with Christ. We are **raised up** with Christ. We are **made to sit** with Him. He has come to live in us, and He has joined himself to us, and **we are one person with Him.** That is the **most important fact** upon which to build all the rest of Christian faith and experience, **this great, tremendous statement** that we are made alive with Jesus Christ.

You may not think this is **appropriate,** but I would like to began Chapter 7 with **a cute story. I read this prayer** recently. **It was prayed** by a **little boy of about 8 years old** . . . "**Dear God,** please take care of my daddy and my mommy and my sister and my brother and my doggy and my kitty, and me. Oh, and please take care of yourself, God. Cuz if anything happens to you, we're gonna be in a big mess."

I'm glad that God does take care of Himself. How do I know? Because **God's activity** in the plan of salvation **provides** some of the **richest blessings** a human being could ever experience. Not only is **salvation** an act of God that **rescues us** from the realm of sin, but it **also has** some other **intricate parts** that need to be appreciated, it is done by love; it's work is done for life; with a purpose; through faith, and for good works.

Pastor Bob Deffinbaugh relates this story: **It isn't often** that one finds **good theology written** on the back end of an **18 wheeler.** The truck was one of those long **dump trucks,** belonging to a demolition company. The truck passed **me quickly, and I had a chance** to read the signs painted on the tailgate. The **first sign was** written in large letters, and it read: **"We Could Wreck The World."** The **second sign** was on the bottom of the tailgate, written in smaller letters. **It read: "Jesus Saves."**

He says he couldn't believe his eyes. **Did the owner of the truck** intend for these **two signs to be read** and understood separately, or were they meant to be understood together? **Men could wreck** the world, and **only Jesus** can save it. **The Apostle Paul's theology** is **not** written on the back of an **18 wheeler,** it is **recorded** in the **New Testament** epistles which he wrote. In Ephesians, chapter two, **Paul summarized** the condition of mankind, the kindness of God, and the nature of the salvation which He has provided for lost men in Christ.

Our study in this chapter is based around **three words** in our text. The words mercy, love and grace. What a melodious trio they are! Mercy, love and grace. **We who have been touched** by that mercy need to shout the adjectives. **rich** mercy, **great** love, and **saving** grace; available **"in Christ."**

God's love (v. 4), is not a response, **but a cause. God's mercy** (v. 4), is **not** prompted by our potential or by any qualities we think we possess, **but by our own pathetic, sinful condition. Divine grace was not bestowed** on us because we were so worthy, **or** because God found anything good in us, but **because of the goodness** which is **in God Himself. The goodness is in the giver, not the recipient.** This states, "But God, being rich in mercy, because of His great love with which He loved us..." **God's mercy is richly given** to us, **because He loves us** so much.

A little boy in Sunday School was asked to tell the **difference between kindness and loving-kindness,** because Scripture uses both those words. **He answered this way:** "If I ask my mother for a slice of bread and butter, and she gives it to me, that is kindness. But if she puts jam on it, that is loving-kindness!" **What a great answer!** That is **great theological insight!** That is a beautiful **illustration** of the difference between these terms. And there is a **difference between mercy and grace.** It is true that God's grace reaches out to man also, but it does so for a different reason than His mercy does. I wonder if you know the difference?

It is the guilt of man which draws forth the grace of God. When **God** looks at us and **sees us as guilty,** as actually having made choices and done things which were deliberately wrong when we knew them to be wrong, it calls forth His compassion, expressed in grace. Even **though we deserve it,** he still doesn't want to leave us in our guilt. **But it is our misery** which calls forth **His mercy.** That is what Paul says has awakened the mercy of God, the misery of man. **God's mercy touches his love,** and love is active: "God, who is rich in mercy, out of His great love with which he loved us . . ." (Ephesians 2:4). What the **apostle has in mind here is the cross,** and, behind it, the whole story of Jesus' coming to Earth. **That is the sign** of the love of God. How do we know that God loved us? Well, because "God so loved the world that he gave . . ." (John 3:16a). This is **always the mark of love.**

We must remember that we can't do anything to make ourselves loveable and we have done a great deal to make ourselves **despicable. But God loves us anyway!** The God who could never love us because of what we are, **loves us in spite** of what we are. **Donna Summer sings** a very **confusing song** that says, "Give me that unconditional love, the kind that I deserve." **Unconditional love** is precisely what we **don't deserve.** It may be what we **need,** but not what we dead sinners deserve. It is when I was dead in sin that **God did love me anyway.** Romans 5:8 states, "But God demonstrates His own love toward us, in that while we were yet sinners, Christ died for us." Although you were formerly alienated and hostile in mind, engaged in evil deeds, yet He has now reconciled you in His fleshly body through death." (Colossians 1:21, 22a).

Mercy is that tender attribute which looks with compassion on the wretched, and hastens to their relief. **Who is more completely wretched** than man in his natural condition? **He is ignorant of God,** and he knows no real lasting enjoyment. **As a slave of the Devil** (even though he may not know it, or won't admit it), he toils throughout all his days in the vilest drudgery; and the **wages at the end is** the blackness of darkness forever. This is real wretchedness! This is the state which mercy flies to alleviate.

Mercy ceases to be mercy, if no efforts are made to rescue these sufferers from perishing. **But our** "God is rich in mercy, because of His great love ... made us alive together with Christ (by grace ...." (Ephesians 2:4, 5).

Remember: A radical disease requires a radical remedy. Because we are "dead in sin," our only hope is the radical remedy of God raising the dead. We know that **apart from Christ** not only are we spiritually dead but we are shackled in sin.

Stay with me now. Let's say that you are **drowning in the ocean.** The **water** is cold, the **wind** is ferocious, the high **waves** keep knocking you under. You have **no hope** of survival. **You are so weak** that you **cannot swim** toward **an approaching rescue boat,** or reach up and **grab the rescue ladder** on the boat. **Your only hope** of survival is that **someone takes a lifejacket** and throws it directly into your hand. **And, spiritually,** that is the **activity of God.** God sends the Savior, but whether you are saved or not is **up to you,** you still have to curl **your fingers around** the rescue. **You can refuse help.** It's up to you to curl your fingers ... that's faith!

Mercy will not leave us in our low **abyss of misery!** It cannot be. **See God sparing not His own Son,** but delivering Him up for us all; putting Him to shame and grief, being pleased in bruising Him, sheathing the sword of vengeance in His heart; taking of Him the full payment of our countless iniquities; and say, has not God's tender mercy moved over us to help us? **God is rich in mercy!** Where we abound in sin, He far more abounds in mercy. **Let believers put all their trust in God,** "looking for the mercy of our Lord Jesus Christ unto eternal life." (Jude 21b).

When we were dead (in sin), and were **absolutely hopeless,** then **God did** something. This is **what the apostle wants us to see.** God took action. God broke through. **What happened** when you believed? **What did God do** which has broken this pattern, and how does it work? I don't hesitate to say that **if we don't understand** this clearly we will **never be able** to enter into the riches that are ours in Jesus Christ. **We will always be groveling** around, **trying** to live a good Christian life, **struggling** and discovering a few helpful things here and there, but **watching others go on into freedom** and liberty and joyfulness and beauty of character, **while we** ourselves never seem able to discover the secret. We must understand thoroughly what has happened to us.

A poor woman from the slums of London was invited to go with a group of people for a **holiday at the ocean.** She had never seen the ocean before, and when she saw it, **she burst into tears.** Those around her

thought it was strange that she **should cry** when such a lovely holiday had been given her. They asked her, "Why in the world are you crying?" **Pointing to the ocean** she answered, "This is the only thing I have ever seen that there was enough of." **My friend never forget,** God has **oceans of mercy.** There is enough mercy for all. **He saves us by His grace.**

Because of what God is doing in these verses, it has been called by some, "**The Great Makeover.**" If a plastic surgeon called you, offering you **free cosmetic surgery,** so that he could use you for advertising, **you should feel grateful,** but not proud. **He did not choose you** because you were **so attractive,** but because you **were so ugly,** and could demonstrate the marvelous skills he has as a plastic surgeon.

That's the way it is with God's **grace. God sent Jesus Christ** to the world, to suffer and to die in the sinner's place. **He did this because** we were in such terrible shape because of sin. **He did this in order to demonstrate His grace,** and His power in **transforming a "dead" man** or woman into a living sacrifice, a **living testimony** of His grace and power. **God's motivation** in saving us should not flatter us, but it does glorify Himself. **In verse 5 Paul states,** "when we were dead in trespasses, (God) made us alive together with Christ."

God has chosen me, redeemed me, regenerated me, adopted me, sanctified me, and called me, so that **He could point to me and say,** "Look at what my grace can do. Look at how great my grace is. I can even save and change this guy!" You see, we appreciate grace all the more **when we understand the nature of the raw material** it begins with. When we talk about **great coaches in sports** we typically look for the men who could **mold winners** out of **mediocre talent.** The **great coach** is the man who can **do a lot with a little.**

That great preacher, Dwight L. Moody once said, "Some day you will read in the papers that D. L. Moody, of East Northfield, is dead. **Don't you believe a word** of it! At that moment **I shall be more alive** than I am now. I shall have gone up higher, that is all-out of this old clay tenement into a house that is immortal; a body that death cannot touch, that sin cannot taint, a body fashioned like unto his glorious body. I was born of the flesh in 1837. I was born of the Spirit in 1856. **That which is** born of the **flesh may die. That which is born of the Spirit will live forever.**"

Friend, Moody wasn't talking about something that is still to come, the resurrection at the end of time. **He actually meant** he would survive his own death. In fact, he wasn't going to ever be dead. **There would be no lag time,** no down time between life on earth and life in heaven.

What Paul is telling us in verse 5, is that when you have salvation through Jesus Christ, you will not die, **you will live forever,** don't miss the impact of that significant statement, "Made us alive with Christ." **That's what Jesus meant** when He said these incredible words in . . . John 8:51, "I tell you the truth, if anyone keeps my word, he will never see death."

"In Christ," all men are equal as well. Because it is **not of our doing,** but of God's doing, there is **no privileged class** in the body of Christ. The **only basis** for boasting is in the work of Christ. And so **the gospel destroys the myth** that Jews are better than Gentiles. This is the teaching of the Apostle Paul in Romans.

On account of our sin we were spiritually dead. **"In Christ"** we are made spiritually alive (verse 5). Though we were **formerly dead,** we have been **raised up** in Him (verse 6). **And although we were formerly enslaved** to our own passions, to the world, and to Satan, **in Christ** we are seated in the heavenly places, now free from all heavenly and earthly powers that oppose God, and have become enslaved to Him who by love **delivered us** from our bondage to sin and to death.

An illiterate couple had just been saved. They met with a **group of believers** who **dressed alike. The men wore red shirts** while engaged in a certain project, so the **woman made one** for her husband. He came home after the meeting, however, with a **look of disappointment** on his face because the **others had a message printed** on their shirts but he did not. **His wife, undaunted** by her inability to read, **sewed three words** on his shirt, which she **copied from a sign** in a store window across the street. **He wore it to the next meeting** and came home **bubbling with joy.** He said **all of the men really liked** the inscription because it so aptly described the wonderful change they had seen in his life. It turned out that his **wife had written, "UNDER NEW MANAGEMENT."**

This brother knew he was different and so did everyone around him. **That's what Jesus does!** He makes a difference in all those who come to Him. **The truth is,** man is a sinner, lost and undone, **separated from God** by a wide chasm of sin. He **needs something** done in his life that he will **never be able to do for himself.** He **needs what Jesus and Jesus alone can do.** It is Jesus who makes the difference in the lives of fallen men.

Unfortunately, most Christians have never been taught what they have received from God in salvation. **It is a life no longer dominated and controlled by sin** but one lived in union and fellowship with Christ for His honor, glory and purposes.

When we come to Christ we receive a new nature, a new will, a new mind, a new heart, a new power, a new knowledge, a new wisdom, a new perception, a new understanding, a new life, a new inheritance, a new relationship with God, a new righteousness, a new love, a new desire, and a new citizenship. **When we realize this,** the more faithfully we walk in the Spirit the more evident our life will be. The more **our life will be characterized** by holiness, purity and a passion for the things of God like the Word of God, prayer, worship, service, witnessing, etc.

Paul tells us in Ephesians 2:6 NIV, "God raised us up with Christ and seated us with him in the heavenly realms in Christ Jesus." **This is the source of our strength** to live the Christian life. "Blessed be the God and Father of our Lord Jesus Christ, who has blessed us with every spiritual blessing in the heavenly places in Christ" (Ephesians 1:3). **We dwell within the very source** of every spiritual blessing with which the Father has blessed us.

Jesus Himself taught that, "I am the vine; you are the branches" (John 15:5a). Can you tell **where the branch ends and the vine starts?** No. They are **one plant,** sharing one life together. From here on **our identity is no longer in Adam** but it is **"in Christ."** We are no longer just ordinary human beings. **We are new creations,** begun again, born again, linked with the life of Jesus Christ.

Paul says God, "seated us with him in the heavenly places in Christ Jesus" (v. 6). **This refers to Christ's reign** in power, seated in heaven at the right hand of God the Father. **Believers partake** of this and its effects become real in our present experience. **Following the contrast** with verses 1-3, we see that this corresponds to our **condemnation** in sin as "children of wrath."

"In Christ", we are no longer condemned, but are seated with him in the presence of God. **The opposite of condemnation** and **judgment** is **not just acquittal** or forgiveness. We aspire to too little if we think this is all we want from God. **The opposite of condemnation** is **acceptance** into **God's inner circle,** adoption into **His family,** and embrace close to his side, **to be seated** at his right hand together with Christ. God has "seated us with him in the heavenly places in Christ Jesus." **As one 'ole country boy said,** "If that don't light your fire, **your wood's wet."** Hallelujah!

One more thing along that line, in olden days, a king would take someone into his favor and allow the man or woman to ride next to him while traveling. **The favored person** would have intimate fellowship with the king, sharing his thoughts and observations. **He would be blessed**

with the king's attention and affection. **This is what it means for us,** who **were condemned** in our guilt, to be **made alive** with Christ, **raised up** with him, and then **seated with Him** in the heavenly places. Some of us, who are near the "great transfer," **should feel** comfort by these words, **Amen?**

This reminds me of the **apostle John seated next** to the **Lord Jesus** at the **Last Supper,** resting his head upon Jesus' breast. **When we celebrate** the Lord's Supper, we **should realize** that we likewise have been **seated at the table of Christ's fellowship,** to partake of the glorious grace of God. **It is expressed wonderfully** in the **hymn** by C. Austin Miles.

> "He walks with me, and he talks with me,
> And he tells me that I am his own;
> And the joys we share as we tarry there,
> None other has ever known."

This complete standing belongs to every believer. God **sees us as perfected** in His Son. It is not the bestowing of righteousness. **It is a declared righteous.** We are **judged righteous** by God based upon the perfect righteousness of Christ. **The believing sinner becomes righteous** in God's sight when placed **"in Christ".**

The late Chuck Colson was one of the **most powerful men in America.** He was one of the top **political figures** in the country. He worked directly under the leadership of **President Richard Nixon.** But the **Watergate Scandal** brought down the kingdom Chuck Colson had built. **Soon, he was just another inmate** in just another prison. **He had been caught** in this sordid act, convicted and sentenced. However, this man was set free from the spiritual imprisonment of his soul. **As he read a book written** by the **Christian apologist C. S. Lewis,** and with the help of **Billy Graham,** he came to know **Jesus Christ as his Savior.** After becoming a Christian, **Chuck Colson no longer sought** power over other men. **He not only spread the gospel,** but also lead the fight for prison reform throughout the world. **What a change of heart and mind and action!**

We are justified by God freely. This righteousness from God is possessed on a faith principle in Christ. It belongs to all who receive Christ as Savior and Lord. **We, who believe, are all** "being justified freely." We do not come into possession of it by being good. It is freely of God's grace through faith in Christ. **God is Himself just and righteous** in His dealing with us who do no more than believe on Jesus. **Our justification rests solely** on the redeeming death of Jesus Christ. **The believer** is '**declared righteous**' because he is "**in Christ."** **This 'declared righteousness'** is the result of a '**new birth**', as Jesus said to Nicodemus in John 3.

A **Supreme Court Judge** was at church one Sunday, and went forward to kneel at the communion altar. **Kneeling next to him** was a man who had been arrested and convicted of burglary. This **Judge had sentenced him** to 7 years in prison. In prison the man gave his life to the Lord. **He served his time** and was now out of prison.

After the service the **judge was walking out** with the pastor and said **did you notice** who was next to me!" The Pastor said, "yes." **The Judge replied** "what a miracle!" The **Pastor said,** "It sure is. His life was so messed up and now he is doing great." The **judge replied back,** "I wasn't talking about him, I was talking about me!" **The pastor said,** "I don't understand." The **Judge said,** "It was natural for that man to get saved, he had nothing but a history of crime behind him. His life was a mess!"

The Judge continued, "**When he saw Jesus as his Savior** he knew that he needed help! Thank God for that. **But, in my case,** my life was set, I had education, money, position, power; I went to Oxford, earned 2 degrees, I have a great family. But I was just as lost as he was, **and God reached out to me!"** Friend, this is a good reminder that it doesn't matter. You may be a moral sinner or rotten sinner. We have all missed the mark. We, without Jesus, are all dead in sin. We must be born again!!! **Remember:** this is **not a suggestion!** It is a **command!**

What could be more expressive than when . . . "we were dead in sins." Neither the **unattractiveness** of a **"dead"** man, **or** the **weakness** of the **"natural"** man who continually turns his back on God, **God loves us anyway. Paul cried out to the Romans,** "God commended (demonstrated before the world) His own love toward us, that even while we were yet sinners, Christ died for us." (Romans 5:8).

LISTEN: We must all understand that **mankind is divided into two groups:** those who are **resurrected from** the dead, and those who **are still dead.** You also need to know that when you become a Christian, **God lifts us up out of a spiritual graveyard.** If you **are not "in Christ,"** you are without Christ and **are spiritually dead.** The **Bible says** that you are "dead in trespasses and sins."

If this Scripture does not prove to you that within every un-regenerated person there is a **potential spiritual garbage can,** hear this: "The heart is deceitful above all things, and desperately wicked: who can know it?"

Being "In Christ" | 125

(Jeremiah 17:9). "There is none righteous, no not one." (Romans 3:10). **Every unregenerate person** reading these lines has within his bosom a heart that is capable of manufacturing, producing, and delivering any one of the evils listed in Mark 7:21-23.

The only way to guarantee yourself that you will not practice these evils is **to submit your heart to God** and let Him remove that heart by the work of the Holy Spirit and put a **brand new heart** in its place! **Is that possible?** We will look in our Textbook (the Bible) to find out: "A new heart also will I give you, and a new Spirit will I put within you: and I will take away the stony heart out of your flesh, and I will give you a heart of flesh." (Ezekiel 36:26).

While serving a church in Texas, I was out **visiting "door-to-door,"** and came across the raunchiest, dirtiest, meanest, old bearded Hell's Angel I had ever met. **He screamed, "What do you want?" When I told him** who I was, **he screamed again,** "Get off my porch!" **Without trying to sound holy,** I don't know what possessed me, except the Holy Spirit ... **I just sat down** on the bottom step of his porch. **I turned to look back**, as I heard the screen door bang open, and I saw this mountain of a man standing in the door, **exhorting me to leave his property.**

I did stay long enough to speak to him, and give him a gospel tract. **I wish I could tell you** that I led him to Christ, but I didn't.

A few weeks later, he died when he ran his Harley underneath an 18 wheeler. I rode with the undertaker in the hearse on the way to the funeral/burial at the cemetery **His coffin** was being carried in a hearse to the cemetery. **He and his mourners passed** some of the honky-tonks, dance halls and other places of ill—repute he had formerly frequented. **First** they **drove by a tavern** where he had spent much time and squandered many a paycheck, but the old temptation to indulge in alcohol no longer enticed him. A few blocks down the street **they came to a racetrack** where he had lost thousands of dollars "on the horses," but the urge to gamble was no longer felt. A little farther on, the procession **went by an "adult theater"** he had often attended, **but the vulgar titles** on the marquee and the suggestive pictures plastered around the entrance **had no effect** on him now. **None of these vices** and **allurements** could attract him, **for he was dead** to them all.

We were all **"dead in trespasses,"** but **God has** "made us alive together with Christ." **We were uninterested** in the things of God; now we find them exciting and important. **We were unresponsive** to God's promptings and repulsed by the Bible, **but now** we find ourselves being molded by God's Word and eager to learn more of the Bible's teaching. **We never used to pray,** except out of desperation; now we talk with God all the time. **What has happened?** Just as God raised Jesus from the dead, he has made us spiritually alive. **We were living** as if God did not exist, or, like Adam and Eve after their sin, we were trying to escape from God. Now we **not only know** that God is there, but we trust Him as our Lord and Savior.

"**In Christ,**" **we are dead . . . no longer! No one** can crawl out of a casket! **Until** you are "**made alive in Christ,**" you are dead (spiritually). **It is Christ who** "**makes us alive**" and "**raises us up**" from our spiritual grave. (Ephesians 2:5; Colossians 2:13). **A living person** has no business in a casket. **A living person** cannot walk and go forward when wrapped in grave clothes in a casket.

We all know that physically, we are still resident here. **But spiritually,** we have already been introduced into a new realm, made citizens of a new kingdom. **We still reside** in this world physically, **but spiritually** we are no longer a part of it. One of the **first things** a person who has truly become **a Christian becomes aware** of is that he **does not fit** or belong in this fallen and corrupted system of human society any more. **He has a new outlook,** different priorities, new desires, goals, loyalties, tastes, commitments, purposes. **He just does not fit** with those who still have the old ones. **Why?** Because he is now **a citizen of a different country,** the kingdom of heaven. He lives under its laws now. We are a colony, an outpost of that kingdom in an alien landscape. **Our purpose now is to invite others** to become citizens of that kingdom as well. And though we are homesick for our new country, being physically still resident in this one, **we already can enjoy foretastes** and earnests of what life there will be like. **Why?** Because in **the person of Christ, our Head,** we are already there; we have been seated there already with our Savior Jesus Christ.

Spiritual death is more than this lack of moral reasoning ability. **Just as physical death** is marked by the **inability to respond** to **external** stimuli, **spiritual death** is marked by a growing **failure to respond** to **spiritual** stimuli. Let me put it this way. **Send a live person** to an exciting football game; send him to a stimulating movie; give him a dramatic book; expose him to a beautiful sunset, **and he responds.** He is moved. **But, put a dead person** in the same places and **what does he do? Nothing!** Why? **Because, being dead,** he is no longer able to respond to external stimuli. **A corpse does not hear** the **conversation** going on **in the funeral parlor.** It has **no appetite** for food or drink. **It feels no pain** because—**it is dead.**

That's how it is with the **person who is spiritually dead.** When it comes to spiritual matters. They tend to be non-responsive. **As Jesus said** in Matthew 13:13, "Seeing they see not . . . hearing they hear not." **For example,** put a person who is spiritually alive in a moving worship service; expose him to a need he can meet in Christ; let him have an hour with his Bible; **do these things and he'll respond** . . . he'll be moved. **Put a spiritually dead person** in the same places; give him the same opportunities and what does he do? **Usually he will do nothing**, because by being spiritually dead, **he is not able to respond** to spiritual stimuli the way you and I can. Understand. **This means that non-Christians are not sick.** In a very real sense **they are dead.** Are dead men valuable and loved by God?

If you are "in Christ," if you have long since **believed on Jesus** and called upon His name, **then start receiving by faith** the riches that He proclaims to you from this text. **You are no longer dead,** so start living to God. You are **no longer a slave** to sin, but a citizen of heaven. **Start living for things** that will never fade away, **and you are nearer** to the heart of God than you ever imagined, seated with him in Christ. **Give him your heart** and take His in return. **Partake of his glory** and then start **reflecting His light** into a world that is dead in sin, **so that others** might be **saved by the same grace** that gave this matchless gift to you.

Years ago a drunk in Chicago headed toward **Lake Michigan to drown himself.** As he stumbled past the **Pacific Garden Mission,** someone helped him through the open door. **He collapsed** in front of the preacher and fell asleep. **The** superintendent cared for him, gave him a bed, and **explained the Gospel to him** the next morning.

That day Harry Monroe was transformed by the grace of God. **Later he was to preach the Gospel** from that same platform where once he had slept in a drunken stupor. Monroe **became superintendent** of the mission, where literally thousands of men and women were changed by the Lord. **When he died,** it took all day for people to pay their respects. **A Chicago newspaper editorial** described him as **one of the most useful men** in Chicago. **A preacher** then raised this **penetrating question: "What made the difference?** The world would not have missed the **penniless derelict** if he had jumped into the lake, **but God saw great** value in him!"

Paul says the true Christian "has been raised up together with Christ." There is **no other way** to serve and worship God. We cannot look up and down at the same time. We cannot serve both God and the world, or its money. We cannot live for this present life and also store up treasures in heaven. **Jesus said,** "Where your treasure is, there your heart will be also" (Mt. 6:21). **We can live** as if this present life is our ultimate destination, seeking to enrich and fill ourselves with everything we desire, as if there is no God and as if eternity is but a mirage.

The Bible says to such a person, **"You fool!"** (Luke 12:20). **Or we can believe the Bible's teaching** that this life is **not** our destination, **but only preparation** for eternity to come. **The Christian's destination** is in eternity, in heaven, **and we must live now** as those whose hopes have been raised there together with Christ.

Please remember: God is not daunted by death and dead men and women. **God is in the resurrection business.** The **resurrection** of Jesus is the **key. Jesus** went to the cross. **On that cross,** our sin debt was cancelled. **Our sin penalty** was **paid in full! Jesus lifts us up out of the pit of sin!** It is Christ, and Christ alone, Who is able to give us **everlasting life.**

As Christ died on the cross, we were accepted as having died to sin. And just **as He was made alive again** after the cross, we are given new life in him. **Death** is barren, impotent, immobile; **life** is active, powerful, energetic. We who were morally and spiritually dead are now **made alive** in Christ (Gal. 2:20). This is called **regeneration,** the New Birth. **It means** that what you could not do before, being spiritually dead; now you can—love God, trust in Christ, understand the Bible, resist the devil, and overcome both the world and your own sinful nature.

This is hard to explain, but I'll try. Think of another analogy. **Imagine a man who is totally colorblind.** To him, **the rainbow** is just a shape. He is **dead to color.** And **then suppose** that by some **miracle his eyes are opened.** He **becomes alive** for **the first time** in his life to the colors of the rainbow, alive for the first time to the **delicate tints** in his **girlfriend's cheek** as she blushes when he tells her that he loves her, **alive for the first time** to dogwoods and azaleas and mountain laurel and sunsets. Would he not be overflowing with color? Would he be able to keep quiet about it? **He would probably not be able to talk of anything else.**

When a sinner comes to Jesus, he is **baptized spiritually** into the Body of Christ. **Paul writes in 1 Corinthians 12:13,** "For by one Spirit, we are all baptized into one body—whether Jews or Greek, whether slaves or free—and have all been made to drink of one Spirit." **At that same instant, Jesus,** through the Person of the Holy Spirit, enters the new Christian, **Colossians 1:27 states,** "To them God willed to make known what are the riches of the glory of this mystery among the Gentiles: which is Christ in you, the hope of glory." **The saints of God (Christians) are as**

good for Heaven as though they **were already there!** In fact, **every time God looks** to His right and sees the Son, **He also sees you and me. Praise the Lord! He sees His saints** and in the mind of God, **we are reckoned** to be home, even though we are still here! Now, that's a blessing!

Resurrection is followed by **exaltation. Paul states** in this verse 6, believers are "to be seated with Christ in the heavenlies." **What does that mean?** Although we now physically live **'positionally'** in the earth now, we also have a spiritual position in the "heavenly places" with Christ. **What does that mean?** He has **lifted us up out of a spiritual graveyard of death** ... to give us a life eternal ... beginning now. **Now** we **can walk**, we can **run**, we can **sing! Dead men cannot do these things.**

In the Billy Graham Center on the campus of **Wheaton College**, there is a letter which **Charles Fuller wrote** to his wife **the night** he decided to **accept Jesus** as his Savior and Lord. **Fuller wrote,** "There has been a complete change in my life. Sunday I went up to Los Angeles and **heard Paul Rader** preach. I never heard such a sermon in all my life. Now my whole life and aims and ambitions are changed. I feel now that I want to serve God if He can use me instead of making the goal of life the making of money." **Charles Fuller experienced a spiritual resurrection** that night. He eventually **became a great evangelist.** But **that night he was reborn**, from death to life and **countless millions of formerly dead people** down through the ages can say the same thing. **"In Christ"** we who were dead, are given new life!

In "being seated with Christ," **Christians have full assurance** of salvation. God receives us with the **promise of his gospel:** "For I will forgive their iniquities, and I will remember their sins no more" (Hebrews 8:12). **Jesus adds,** "Come to me, all who labor and are heavy laden, and I will give you rest" (Matthew 11:28). **God's Word asks us,** seated as we are **in Christ,** "Who shall bring any charge against God's elect? It is God who justifies. Who is to condemn? Christ Jesus is the one who died, more than that, who was raised, who is at the right hand of God, who indeed is interceding for us. Who shall separate us from the love of Christ?" (Romans 8:33-35). **Because we rest** on Christ's finished work, safe and secure, **Paul concludes,** "We are more than conquerors through him who loved us." (Romans 8:37).

When we are "in Christ," our old sin nature no longer has to have control over us. **We are dead** to its hold over us. We no longer have to obey it. **We can say "no** thank you" **We have a new master.** We are **delivered** through the death of Christ. We are no longer under obligation to obey the commands of our sin nature. We have **been resurrected** and **set free. We may choose to obey** the old sin nature, **but we** are not under obligation to do so. We are **no longer slaves** to that old nature. It is now a matter of choice. **Christ now is free to live His life through us.**

Theologian Charles Hodge wrote: "All that the Scriptures teach concerning the union between the believer and Christ, and concerning the indwelling of the Holy Spirit, **proves** the **supernatural character of our sanctification. Men do not make themselves holy;** their holiness and their growth in grace are **not due to their own fidelity,** or firmness of purpose, or watchfulness and diligence, although all these are required, **but to the divine influence** by which they are rendered thus faithful, watchful, and diligent and which produces in them the fruits of righteousness." **Jesus said,** "Without me, you can do nothing" (John 15:5). "As the branch cannot bear fruit of itself, except it abide in the vine; no more can you, except you abide in Me" (v. 4). **The hand is not more dependent** on the head for the continuance of its vitality **than is the believer** on Christ for the continuance of spiritual life in the soul.

Many people, who are not Christians, think that **living the Christian life** is a **difficult proposition,** but they are wrong! What many people have **failed to grasp** is that the **true Christian life** is **not lived out,** it is **lived through! Really,** it is **not me doing my best** for Jesus. **Rather,** it is me simply **yielding to Him and allowing Him to live His life through me,** (John 15:1-8). **When I learn** but to abide **in Christ, He will send and live His life** through me and **glorify God** by producing His fruit through my life!

The Amplified version of Ephesians 6:10 reads, "Be strong in the Lord, be **empowered** through your union with Him; draw your strength from Him." This speaks of our drawing our daily strength form our position before the throne of God. **We grow spiritually** as we abide **"in Christ."** When we are abiding **in Christ** we are drawing from our Christ—centered position. Our "life is hid with Christ in God." (Colossians 3:3).

We abide when we "reckon" on Christ. Paul said it this way, "In the same way, (count, consider, reckon) yourselves indeed dead to sin, but alive to God in Christ Jesus" (Romans 6:11). Another translation says, "Be constantly counting upon the fact that you are dead to sin, but alive to God in Christ Jesus." **We are to rest our faith** on these great positional truths. **We appropriate God's power 'by faith' in Christ.** We exchange our weakness for His strength.

Being "In Christ" | 131

In verse 8, Now when he says **"though faith,"** he's talking about the receiving of our salvation. **Faith is simply the means** by which we take him. **Augustine said,** "qui creeawit te sin a te, non sinawit, te sin a te." **which means** "He who created you without you will not save you without you." **And what he meant** in the context was that **our part in salvation,** is simply **to receive** the **salvation by faith.** We do believe, God doesn't believe. We believe. But that response, Augustine goes on to say, is something created in us by God. We do believe. By grace are ye saved through the **instrumentality of faith.**

Paul states, "But we all, with unveiled face beholding as in a mirror the glory of the Lord, are being transformed into the same image from glory to glory, just as from the Lord, the Spirit" (II Corinthians 3:18). **We are gradually conformed** to His image, Who is Himself the "express image of His (God's) person" (Hebrews 1:3). **When Christ returns** we will be just like Him (1 John 3:2).

You can always tell when Paul has something burdening his mind, because he simply **cannot hold it in.** Here, **it slips out** at the end of **verse 5:** "By grace you have been saved." **I really feel that Paul gets excited** when he remembers **who he was,** and now, **who he is,** and who he's yet to be, and who **we are "in Christ."** We were **dead,** but God has made us alive. We were **slaves** to sin, but God **liberated** us to live in righteousness, peace and joy. We were **condemned** in our guilt, **but God elevated us** to the inner circle of **His intimate fellowship,** to rest and be assured of eternal blessing and life.

The story is told by William Barclay, of a Scottish woman who was living in **poverty** and **squalor** in the **cellar** of her large house. Shortly after the arrival of **the new pastor** of her church, a man stopped by to find that she now lived in the bedroom on the **top floor** and that all was neat and clean. **The visitor commented** on the change, **and she replied,** "Ay, you canna hear the preacher preach and live in a cellar." So it is with Paul's teaching here. **Are you living in the cellar** of the salvation **God has provided** to you in Christ? **Then move up** into the **rooms** God has long since **prepared for you** and begin to live the life he has made possible for you in Jesus Christ.

The world may not know you. In fact, outside of **your little circle** of family and friends, there may be very few who know and care for you . . . **but, hear me, the world may not care** if you live or die, **but Jesus cares** for you! **He died** to save you from sin and **He lives** to make you free!

Question: Are you "in Christ"? And, if so, are you **appropriating spiritual food and resources** from your position **in Christ?** This is the active side of abiding **in Christ.** We abide **in Christ by resting our faith** in these great biblical facts. I abide in my position **"in Christ."** God the Father has provided everything we need in the Christian life **in Christ.** He is constantly removing our false security to cause us to trust in Him alone.

Have you ever been to Death Valley? It is the hottest, driest, sandiest, place I have ever been. Starting from Yuma, Arizona to Palm Springs, California, years ago, many who were stranded in the desert, didn't live. In the 1940's and '50's I made many a trip with my family back and forth to California. This was **before car air conditioning.** We would wet towels, hold them in the breeze, then put them on us just to cool off. **Without Jesus you are in Death Valley,** already under the judgment of God, and awaiting the Final Judgment at the Great White Throne. (Revelation 20).

When you are "in Christ," God brought you **out of spiritual Death Valley** to the highest heights spiritually, all in one day. **From the deepest darkest** valley of death to brightest highest glory, **from the lowest place** to the highest place in the universe, far **beyond Mt. Whitney** to the peak of the presence of an exalted Christ, **from deepest sin** to the heights of grace! **From earth** to heaven, **from the tomb** to God's throne, **from the grave** to the sky, **Lord we lift your name on high! Amen!**

In an **article in Fortune** magazine, David Whitford wrote of the **shocking discovery prior to his father's death** that **his dad** had amassed **a six-figure debt** on high-interest credit cards. **There had been clues** that his father was having **financial problems,** but when Whitford had **tried to talk** about it his father immediately **changed the subject.** "At one point," Whitford writes, "he put his hands over his ears and made a humming noise." Yet **two days after his father's death,** Whitford found **these words scrawled** on his father's desk: **"Help me. I'm drowning."** Whitford's story illustrates a **tragic reality. There is little we can do** for those who **refuse our help.**

In this study and in this passage of Scripture it is crucial for us to bear in mind that we have been **describing the Christian life.** It **begins with a spiritual birth. If you are not bearing fruit** it may be because you have never been born again. That is where this kind of life begins. **I am always ready to help** you put your faith and trust in Jesus Christ as your personal Savior.

A diamond is found in the ground. It is rough and ugly, but **in the hands** of a **master diamond cutter,** that rough, **ugly stone is transformed** into a thing of tremendous **value and beauty.** It may adorn a **queen** or hang around the neck of **someone famous. Listen:** That is the **same thing the Lord does** in our lives! He takes old **rough sinners and transforms them** by His grace and His patient work in their lives, **then He puts them on display** where they bring **glory** and **honor** to His name!

Are you a car buff, an old-car collector? **Have you** ever attended an **classic car show** or been in an **antique car parade? A car show** is where a group of car owners **bring their 'show cars'** together and they show them off to each other. Often, the **cars** have **been rebuilt. A piece of junk** was bought and then **lovingly restored.** The owner puts it in a show to let everyone see what he's done to the car.

The other day I saw a news story about a **collector** who maintains a **museum** of all sorts of things, including **180 cars** of various types and ages. And **the unique thing** about his museum is that everything works. **All the cars** are drivable. That's more **like the kind of 'car show' that God** will have. **We won't be gutted old shells** that can't function. **We will be living,** functioning, show-pieces of God's grace. **God won't have a 'car show'** in heaven. **He'll have a 'saint show."** He'll be showing you and I off to the angels. They'll be absolutely amazed at **how God has restored us.**

So, who is your master? Is it **sin?** If so, **the wages** of your service to him (Satan) are death and Hell. But, I am happy that I can tell you, that in Christ, **you have the opportunity to change** masters right now! **Is your master Jesus?** If so, then **rejoice!** For **in Him,** you have **found life and liberty.** You should each day be finding **peace and purpose in your life.** "In Christ," you have found **all you need.**

Jesus said, "Truly, truly, I say to you, he who hears My word, and believes Him who sent Me, has eternal life, and does not come into judgment, but has passed out of death into life. Truly, truly, I say to you, an hour is coming and now is, when the dead shall hear the voice of the Son of God; and those who hear shall live." (John 5:24, 25). **Let me ask you this question:** Have you heard the voice of Jesus Christ today, calling you out of death and into life? **God says in** Deuteronomy 30:19 ". . . I have set before you life and death . . . So choose life in order that you may live . . ."

J. D. Bran tells this story: Church had been a major part of **Les Richards'** life from his early childhood. As an adult he **taught Sunday school.** Anyone looking at this friendly, **clean-living churchgoer** would have labeled Les a Christian. **After he retired, Les met Ruby.** Both of them had been widowed, and they struck up a friendship. **One day Ruby said to Les,** "I know where I'm going to spend eternity. How about you?" Although **he had attended church for 70 years,** Les replied, **"I'm not sure."** He had always **hoped** that **God would accept him** because he did more **good deeds** than bad, but he knew he couldn't count on that.

When Ruby told Les, "You'd better get sure!" he agreed. Her pastor shared Romans 10:9-10 and Ephesians 2:8-9 with him. Les was surprised to know that he could be sure of his salvation. **He prayed and asked Jesus Christ** to forgive him and be his Lord and Savior. **Now Les and Ruby** Richards **celebrate his salvation every day. Seventy years** of **good works** and **church attendance** could **never** get Les into heaven. **Only faith in Jesus Christ could!**

All human religions are about **what man does to find favor with God.** But **Christianity** is about what **God has done** to confer favor on man. **The blessings of salvation are not the attainment** of a long life of penitence, service, and self-denial; they are **an immense privilege** conferred as a **free gift** on those who put their trust in Jesus Christ. Such people are already made alive, raised, and seated as surely as Jesus has been made alive, raised, and seated, **because** Jesus has been made alive, raised, and seated.

They are like a sailor rescued from a **sinking ship.** He has **already been rescued.** He is now on the Coast Guard cutter, **but he is not yet in port.** But because he is off the wreck and on the cutter, he is already as good as there. **Listen: we are already seated** in heaven. We are as good as there, and more: we **actually are there** in the person of **our Head and Representative Jesus Christ.**

Perhaps when you started reading this today, you were spiritually dead. **Dead in trespasses and sins.** And **you knew** that God's wrath would one day come because of your **rebellion against Him.** But today you **have been reading** the Word of Christ. Every time I've read the Bible, I gain a little more understanding and faith. **Now, you may be thinking,** "I believe that God loves me, in spite of my sin! I believe that I'm coming out of death and into life!" **In a moment,** at the end of this chapter, I'm going to give you an **opportunity to confirm that faith** in Christ. **To solidify** your new-found faith.

If you are not a Christian, you are dead in trespasses, alienated from God and his love, held fast in the bitter chains of a loveless, cruel and evil world. **Whether you know it or not** you stand condemned in the courts of God's eternal judgment. **Here's good news, if you will confess** your

Being "In Christ" | 135

sin and look to Jesus Christ for salvation, **if you will cry** to heaven, where Jesus is seated with God, you will not only be **completely forgiven,** but completely saved. **You will be transformed** and renewed, liberated from the bondage of your old, rotten life and granted a **share in the eternal inheritance of glory.**

Let me share this story: **A man came from a distant country** to visit a wealthy queen. When he **arrived at her royalty's court** he asked the queen if he might be privileged to have a **look at her most cherished jewels.** The **queen agreed** and with a smile she called for her jewels. Moments later, in walked two handsome young men, **the sons** of the queen. She introduced them to the visitor and explained that these **her sons were her finest jewels,** the grandest adornment that she had ever worn. **Oh, dear friend,** that is what **our gracious Heavenly Father** says of us, who now belong to Him. We are His joy, His glory, His crown of exultation. We are trophies of His grace. That is **why I call you to rise and shine** and give God glory. In Matthew 5:16, **Jesus said,** "Let your light shine before men in such a way that they may see your good works, and glorify your Father who is in heaven." **That should be our goal.** Live so that **our Father can point** to us and say, "Look at what I made out of that ugly, crippled child of wrath!" **That is what I long for.** I want my life's message to say that, "God's grace is every bit as marvelous as my Bible says it is."

If you desire to choose life today, I'm going to ask you to bow your head and read and repeat out loud this simple **prayer.** "**Dear Lord Jesus, I believe** you are the Son of God who came and died for me. Lord, **I repent** of my sins and **I trust** you as my Lord and Savior. Cleanse me, and wash me of my sins, and make me your child. **I thank you** for hearing my prayer and changing me. In Jesus name, Amen!"

Do you know that our youth will not read this story in the **Public School History** books, but **Patrick Henry,** a distinguished statesman from Virginia, and the man **who said those immortal words,** "Give me liberty, or give me death . . ." **was a well-to-do man. Before he died,** he left **a will** in which he left all of his material **wealth to his** children. However, **Mr. Henry concluded his will** with these **thought provoking words:** "There is one more thing I wish I could leave you all, the salvation of Jesus Christ. With this, though you had nothing else, you could be happy. Without this, though you had all things, you could never be happy!"

Know this: for all eternity, you and those of us who have received eternal life, will be a demonstration of God's grace.

"Blessed assurance, Jesus is mine;
O what a foretaste of glory divine!
Heir of salvation, purchase of God,
Born of His Spirit, washed in His blood.
This is my story, this is my song,
Praising my Savior all the day long;
This is my story this is my song,
Praising my Savior all the day long.

—Fanny J. Crosby

CHAPTER EIGHT

"In Christ" You Are Being 'Sanctified' and Made 'Holy'.

I Corinthians 1:1, 2 says, "Paul, called to be an apostle of Jesus Christ, by the will of God, and Sosthenes our brother, To the church of God that is at Corinth, to those who are sanctified (set apart) **"in Christ" Jesus**, called to be saints, with all who in every place call on the name of Jesus Christ our Lord . . ."

In the 1960's, I was **pastor** of a **Baptist church** in downtown Long Beach, CA. The bell bottomed trousers, tie-dyed shirts, the hippie generation roamed the streets and college campuses. **It was the days of Timothy Leary** with his philosophical religion of pot, heroin, and other psychedelic mind altering drugs. **This Harvard educated psychologist** "nut-job" led many youth down the road to dissipation by getting them "hooked on drugs." **He popularized such phrases as:** "Turn On, Tune In and Drop Out." And believe me, the youth, by the thousands, did just that. **I took our church youth to** hand out **Gospel tracts and witness** on some of the Southern California campuses where he was speaking.

It was also the days when it was cool to espouse the **"God-Is-Dead"** movement. I went with our youth to **Sunset Strip** and passed out Gospel tracts, with and near **Arthur Blissett's** place. It was a time of crazy and mixed-up youth. **I will say this,** as **Dr. John Bisagno,** of the **First Baptist Church of Houston said,** "these youth were searching for something, but when they came to our churches, we turned them away, because they looked different and asking too many questions. We didn't want anything to do with them and we lost that generation." **Oh, do you realize that that generation** is now leading our country?

Oh, when the discussions from society said, '**God is dead**', I immediately changed our **large church sign in front of the church** to say,

> "Our God is NOT Dead,
> Sorry About Yours!"
> Check Inside."

The Youth of the '60's were not bashful: "Jesus, yes! The church, no!" That was a popular **slogan in the 60s. It seems to be a revived notion today** as many are put off by **organized religion. This book is being written** because that **church was in serious trouble** with many disgusting things.

The late Dr. W. A. Criswell of the First Baptist Church of Dallas, TX said that the first four chapters of 1st Corinthians were about divisions in the church. **One group** is over here, and **another group** is over there, and **another group** is over there. **Paul is writing** to the church **concerning those divisions** in the church, church fusses, church fights, dividing up. "I am for the preacher." And "I am a'gin him." "I am for none of 'em." It was a real power struggle.

The church at Corinth was gifted. It was a church that **grew against all odds.** They had people in that church that could do all sorts of things. People who **could preach** and **teach** and **lead** inspiring services. There were **healers** and people with the ability to **discern spirits,** to know if something was right or wrong. There were **wealthy** people and **intelligent** people. There was a **diversity of cultures** and backgrounds and languages represented among the members of that congregation.

With their successes, their **problems increased.** One problem was they **got puffed up** about it. Sure the Corinthians were gifted, but **they came to think too much of themselves.** As you read through the books of 1st and 2nd Corinthians you see that over and over again. The people who could preach **thought themselves better** then those who couldn't. Over and over again the Corinthians **failed to acknowledge** that truth, and instead they **thought themselves to be great.** They said "Look at what we have done and what we can do." **The danger** was that they would stop trusting in God's grace all together. They would very **ungracefully fall flat** on their faces. **They did stop trusting in God** and trusted in their pride of accomplishment, and they did fall. This church became powerless and useless, just going through the motions. **And Paul** took them to task over these sins.

The church at Corinth, as noted, was a **church in disarray.** It was not a "Church on the Rock," (of Jesus), but became a **"Church on the Rocks."** This **church was not doing** all that they were supposed to be doing. There **were some in the church** that were really **hurting it.** In fact they were allowing the devil to use them to destroy the church. Corinth was a **defiled church,** full of **sexual drunkenness and immorality** Some lived very worldly, taking God's grace and forgiveness very lightly. It was also a **divided church** with differing **cliques and factions** vying for leadership.

This church was also a **disgraced church.** Not only were they **not glorifying God,** they were **hindering** the progress of **the gospel** all around. **This church** was a "Church on the Rocks". **This church was not doing** all that they were supposed to be doing. There were **some in the church** that were really hurting it. In fact they were **allowing the devil** to use them to **destroy the church.**

Caution! In many of our churches today, we have people who can **act and sing** and **teach and lead....** And many churches have a leadership that is creative and energetic. **In most churches the phrase,** "We've never done it this way before" **means:** "We never will do that." **This stubbornness** has derailed many a good idea. "We've never done that before" **should mean:** "Well, let's try it!"

In many churches there is a **"clique" problem.** A group (usually a few—that grows) has **taken over the leadership** of the church and is **unwilling to "bend"** to new ideas. And many who are in **leadership have taken a "blind eye"** to those in the congregation who are **living in outright sin.** We are who we are, and should **not continue to keep our blinders on,** when this causes distractions from spiritual things. Having said that, **we are to remember** that "those who are spiritual" **should act in love and grace** "to restore the one who has fallen in a spirit of gentleness, considering yourself lest you also be tempted." (Galatians 6:1).

We must remember that the church is not ours to do what we want with. We are **not at liberty** to do with the church what we want, to **manipulate the church** in the direction that we want it to go. **The church is not mine, it is not yours.** The church is **not a platform** for personal advancement, it is **not a platform** for the personal achievement or advancement of your or **my own agendas. The church is His. The church belongs only to Jesus Christ.**

The Corinthian church was **never Paul's** and he knew that quite well. **So often, some in the church** can feel that the church is in some sense theirs. **I have known rich people** in the church who have felt a **sense of entitlement** because of the great amount of money and time they had invested into the church. **The church does not become 'your baby'** the longer you are here and it does not become 'your baby' the more you give. **If you have been here since the beginning** and if you have **invested much** of your time, talents, and treasure to the church, **God bless you,** your **reward will be great in heaven;** however, your great commitment and investment **gives you no special favors** before God. However, it must be asserted that **Paul did** exhort the church to **give special honor** to those who evidenced an incredible sacrificial commitment to serving the body of Christ (1 Corinthians 16:15-18). We just **need to remember** the fact that the "called-out ones" are His.

Let me share with you something about 'sanctification' and 'security.' In spite of their sin **they were still sanctified in Christ** and **called to be saints**. **Verse 2 states,** "church of God which is at Corinth to them that are sanctified in Christ Jesus, called to be saints'. **Question:** could you say that these people were holy? **Practically,** were they holy people? **Of course they weren't!** But **Paul was saying:** "You are sanctified," **so positionally** he's talking about, **they're "in Christ".** They've been **set apart for Christ** and **to Christ,** and they needed many things in their life, but they were **set apart for God and for His glory.** If you are truly a born-again child of God, you are saints by divine calling, **it's not something** that you're going to try and attain to, **it's not something** that is **only for dead Christians** who did a great thing in their life, and hundreds of years later **the church of Rome decides to canonize you** and make you into saints... **that is certainly not Biblical!** It's something that is in your life, **that is a living reality** where **you realize** that you are a saint, and you've been called to that reality.

Listen: none of us is perfect, actually very far from it. **We cannot be sinless** but remember, **we can sin less.** If you knew me like I know myself, you might not listen to me. But hold on, because if I knew you like you know yourself, I might not want to talk to you! **I want you never to forget that our enemy, Satan, wants to kill the church**, and he'll use people to carry out the dirty deed. **He wants to use you!** Sardis was a **dead church.** (Revelation 3). They had a name of being alive, **but they were dead! Did you know that some die** and close their doors, but **others continue** to have meetings even though they **are dead spiritually.**

As much as any society in the Bible, the church in **Corinth represents** many modern day churches in America. **Many churches today, unfortunately,** are filled with decadent, disagreeable, drunken, materialistic, prideful, affluent and immoral people who claim to know the Lord. **The Corinthians struggled** with hyper stimulation from the culture and living a holy, separated life seemed to be their greatest hurdle.

While America still falls short of **temple prostitution,** no doubt **there is much** in America that would **have made** even **the Corinthians blush.** In the same manner that the **word "corinthianize"** became **synonymous** with immorality and extremes. **"Western culture"** holds the same negativity for many in our world today. **To embrace modern American ideas** is to invite moral decline, decadence and rabid individualism. **Set against this backdrop of sensuality and materialism,** the Corinthian church was forged.

The tendency toward spiritual decline in our churches is not limited to the early 1st century church. **It has happened again and again** down through the centuries, and has been **especially evident** when **Christians prospered** and enjoyed **freedom from persecution.** It's a danger we must all be aware of. **Jesus gave us the antidote** for this **disorder.** He said, "Remember therefore from where you have fallen; repent and do the first works" (Rev. 2:5). **This prescription** will prevent the spiritual regression that brings so much harm to us individually and to our churches.

When jewelers show forth their jewelry, the diamonds and **rings** and **watches** they always put them **on a black background** and **shine bright lights** upon them. This is done so the **attention will be brought** to the jewelry and not to the background. **They want the jewelry to shine** and **sparkle** in every way possible. They **want their potential customers** to be so **enamored at the beauty** of their jewelry that they feel almost compelled to purchase it. **We are the black background.** There is **nothing in us that is good** whatsoever to be looked at. **God's grace is the jewel. "In Christ,"** the grace of God shines forth in all of its brilliance. These verses reveal the grace of God to you so that when you finish this study you will feel sanctified (set-apart) for His service.

Question: Have you ever remodeled your home? Many of you have experienced this: living in the house you are remodeling. **You know how dirty** everything gets, how **complicated,** how **inhospitable** your own home becomes. **Dust** everywhere, **cold air** rushing in from holes in the wall where windows used to be, **bare floors** and **covered furniture, plastic hanging** over doorways, **tools** everywhere. **Well, this is a picture of the Christian life** and of **God's renewing work** in his children. And that is the **picture we have in 1 Corinthians. These Christians were in disarray.** They were disorganized spiritually and morally.

Several years ago in East Texas, I was **preaching** from the **sixth chapter of Corinthians beginning** in **Verse 9** where the **apostle says,** "Do you not know that the unrighteous will not inherit the kingdom of God? Do not be deceived; neither the immoral, nor idolaters, nor adulterers, nor homosexuals, nor thieves, nor the greedy, nor drunkards, nor revilers, nor robbers will inherit the kingdom of God. And such were some of you." (1 Corinthians 6:9-11)

I remember **I was so struck** by those **words, "such were some of you,"** that I stopped and **said to the congregation,** "This was the make-up of the church at Corinth. **These people had come out** of this sordid background. **Many of them,** perhaps, still **were struggling** with much of the aftermath in their lives of these evil things. **I am curious** as to how many of you here have some similar things in your past?" **And here,** I then did a **rather bold thing,** something I seldom do. **I said,** "If any of you have **anything like this** in your background I'd like to **ask you to stand** where you are, quietly, for a moment that **we might know how much we're** like the church at Corinth."

I did not know it, at the time, but a **young man I had witnessed to** was **present** with us that morning **who had never been in church before.** He told me afterwards that he had been **converted at a recent Billy Graham Crusade,** and he **came here with fear and trembling,** not knowing what he was getting into. **He said he heard me** make that announcement, and **he looked around** to see if anyone would stand. **At first no one did,** but then a **little old lady** right on the aisle **got up.** **Others** then began to stand, **and soon two-thirds** of the congregation was standing. **This young man** looked around the crowd and **he said to himself, "These are my kind of people ... honest!"** That day, he came **forward** professing Christ and seeking baptism.

The problems you read about in Corinth, **the problems that Paul** will deal with one by one in his letter, **are the problems** that are typical of times of the Spirit's powerful working. There were people who began, in their enthusiasms to follow men instead of Christ himself. **There has never been a revival** in which these problems did not come along behind it. **Was there an unhealthy interest** in spiritual phenomena, especially of the more dramatic type?

Someone has said, "the way we see ourselves as Christians determines how we behave." **And, I'm sure you've heard the phrase,** "A picture is not only worth a thousand words, it is **the parent** of a thousand deeds." **Question: Are you really "in Christ?"** In other words, **are you really a Christian?** If you answer "yes," then, **"how do you see yourself as a soldier** in God's army? A **sister or a brother** in faith's extended family? A **learner** in the school of Christ? A **traveler** along the Christian way? **Each of these metaphors** has served Christians well. **One of the major metaphors** used in the New Testament for **Christians is, being "in Christ."**

William Booth, founder of the Salvation Army, used the **military metaphor** with great effect; slum dwellers of nineteenth-century London found the **discipline of a soldier** to be strong armor against the pull of a former life. **The New Testament** is not limited to the images of soldier, sibling, scholar, or sojourner. **It offers** such **metaphors** of the Christian life as "ambassador for Christ," and "citizen of God's commonwealth." Then there is the "disciple," "the member of Christ's body," "the friend of Jesus," and of course, being **"in Christ."**

Growing up on the outskirts of town, when I was a boy, playing hide-and-seek as the sun went down on a summer evening, inevitably our **side door would open** and my **mother's voice** would **call,** "Glen, time to come in!" I would go on with hide-and-seek, making my way to the house. To anybody passing by, I'm sure I looked no different from my playmates. **But I *was* different; I moved in a different direction. Why?** Because **I had been "called in."** Everything had changed. In a similar way **Christians,** who may appear no different from others, have ringing in their ears **God's summons to believe** and to obey. **Henry Thoreau said** that some march to a different drummer. **Christians** do not hear a different drumbeat; **they hear Jesus' distant but clear voice saying, "Come, follow me."**

Paul states that he was an apostle (one sent) of Jesus Christ "by the will of God." (Ephesians 1:1). There is **no higher authority** than that! **Paul was delegated by God** to speak and write. Although today we are not apostles, it makes **no difference where** you are, or **how** you are, or **what** your circumstances may be, **when you are "in the will of God,"** you are in an obedient, wonderful, glorious place of blessing.

As I have commented so many times **to begin a service ...** "If you're glad you're here, say, Amen! Aren't you glad you're here in this service, rather than the **best Hospital** in town? Amen?" **Let's face it dear friends, sometimes** it's necessary to be in the best Hospital in town . . . . but, we'd all rather be with our friends in the warm, caring fellowship of God's people . . . in worship. Amen?

When we see that word 'saint,' sometimes what we think of in our mind is someone who is a **'Super-Christian'.** You know if you are a Super-Christian, you get to be, "Saint-this", and "Saint-that". But it's really important to understand that the **Bible never uses the term saint** that way. It always uses the term consistently as "anyone who has trusted Jesus Christ as Savior." **The word "saints" refers** to all those who have been saved and sanctified, **'set—apart'** in Christ Jesus. It does **not refer** to individuals who have been **canonized** by some ecclesiastical body, as some of us have been taught in the past. **That beautiful word 'saint'** designates all those who God has set-apart from sin to Himself (into salvation), and made holy through their faith in Jesus Christ.

W. A. Criswell preached this: All right, look at the second verse; "Unto the church of God, to them that **are sanctified** in Christ Jesus, called to be saints." **Now, you have it in italics again,** "Called **to be** sainted." **The "to be" is not** in the original Greek, **"Called saints," separated people of God.** All right, look down there in the 9th verse. "God is faithful, by whom ye were called unto the fellowship of His Son, Christ Jesus our Lord." (I Corinthians 1). I wonder what all of that means? **He is a called apostle.** The **church of God are called saints.** And in the 9th verse, "Ye are called unto the fellowship of His Son Christ Jesus." **It means simply this,** now, you listen to me, it means simply this, that the church of God in Corinth is called to separation, **called to holiness,** called to **godliness,** called to **purity,** called to **separation."**

To keep it simple, **sanctification means** "to be **set apart**" for the purpose of "being made holy." Being **"sanctified"** or the word **"sanctified"** is a strange word for most. **The reason** for this is that most **Pastor/Teachers do not spend much time** on this wonderful teaching. **Sanctification is one of the great truths of God's Word,** and we should spend some time here to see what the Word of God says about the subject. **Sanctification prepares us** for the service of God. **It places our feet on a spiritual ground** where there is no retreat. **Sanctification** inspires the inner man to go forward in spiritual harmony with Christ.

When our family lived in the mountains of Colorado, we had several dogs at our mountain home. One was a great **outside dog,** a Norwegian Elkhound, a really large outside dog. One was a little white two pound poodle who **stayed in the house** for the most part. I got to thinking about the **millions of dogs** that are born throughout the world which are **abandoned or destroyed.** We **took them home** and the **children began** to love, feed, and play with them. By the choice of another, those dogs were given honor and fulfillment. **Something like that takes place** when **God names people.** God does not have to explain or justify His reasons. But for **those of us who have been called,** that call is irreversible. **We are the called-out ones** because **God chose us** and **set us apart.** It is because **God took** the initiative that we are who we are.

Sometimes we are just too caught up in the past. For some, the past is the "good old days". **We can talk** for hours about how God **used** to work in our lives. For others, the past is filled with terror. We are so hurt by what has happened to us that we can't move on in life. It's not bad that we remember our past, but if we're not careful, **we'll get swallowed up** in the past and **never take the time to live** in the present, and looking forward to the future.

You may know this story that when **Cortez** landed at Vera Cruz in **1519** to begin his conquest of Mexico with **small force of 700 men,** he purposely **set fire** to his **fleet of 11 ships.** His **men on the shore watched** their only means of retreat sinking to the bottom of the Gulf of Mexico. **With no means of retreat,** there was only one direction to move, forward into the interior to meet whatever might come their way. **Christian, in paying the price** for being Christ's disciple, you too must **purposefully destroy all avenues** of retreat. Resolve that **whatever the price** for being His follower, you will have to pay it.

Before we continue, perhaps we should have some simple 'Biblical definitions'.

Regeneration is the implanting of new spiritual life in a person who was "dead in trespasses and sins." **This new life comes from God,** and is the beginning or inception of the Christian life. It is so dynamic that when a person receives this new life he is said to be "born again" or "born from above." **Regeneration is the work** of the Holy Spirit (John 3:3, 5, 6, 8) and **by this act the believer is indwelt** by the Holy Spirit. **The apostle Paul describes** such a person as "spiritual" rather than "natural" (1 Corinthians 1:12-14).

Sanctification is the work of the **Holy Spirit in us.** Sanctification is specifically the work of the indwelling and directing Holy Spirit in the life of the regenerated person. **Sanctification is the visible result** of that in the behavior of individuals. It is all that change **working out in terms of practice** so that you see that **someone is different.** We for several years have been **hearing** much about **Chuck Colson, Eldridge Cleaver,** and even **Larry Flynt,** and **the claim is made that these men** have received salvation—that is, born again—and, therefore, their **behavior is changing;** they are being sanctified. That is **what Paul refers** to here with the Corinthians **because their behavior** was what was in question.

Justification is the deliverance from sin's penalty, **whereas sanctification** is the deliverance from the power of sin. **Justification is the legal/judicial act of God** at the beginning of the Christian life, whereby we are at once acquitted and forgiven of all our guilt, and **accounted legally righteous** on the basis of the substitutionary atoning death of Jesus. **It is a once-for-all declaration by God** as the **Judge** acquitting the believing sinner.

Justification is the description of the change that God makes within an individual when he comes to Christ. **It is what we also call the "born again"** experience that we are hearing much of today. It means an **inward change of nature,** a deep and fundamental difference in outlook and attitude because of a deep change within.

When Paul walked in and started preaching, no one slept in the church in Corinth! They had sins, which they had committed, real sins, dangerous sins, terrible sins, and these sins had to be rooted out or else. Their lives had been so profoundly changed. There was so much to be excited and enthusiastic about. **We'll never escape sin,** not in this world, not in this life. **And we must deal with sin!**

Justification further, is a declaration by God concerning our relationship with Him. However, **justification and sanctification belong together,** and one cannot be justified without being in principle sanctified because our positional sanctification takes place at the same time. **Progressive sanctification** deals with how the justified person should live the Christian life (II Corinthians 13:4; Galatians 5:13). It involves the daily Christian life.

Regardless of the terminology, a **"sanctified"** person is one who has been "made holy," "set apart," for God's service. **Sanctification begins** with the experience of the new birth. **Being sanctified begins** at the moment we believe. **Paul told the Corinthians,** "you were washed, and you were sanctified, and justified in the name of the Lord Jesus and by the Spirit of our God. (I Corinthians 6:11). At salvation, God **places us in the position**—that we are His. **He never wants us** to make ourselves show a false, sanctimonious, holier-than-thou attitude.

Dr. David Peterson states: "The Corinthian Christians were a holy and distinct people in that corrupt and godless city. **This was so because of God's initiative,** drawing them into an exclusive relationship with Himself. Here the perfect passive participle **'sanctified' should be understood** as another way of speaking about their conversion and incorporation into Christ. **It can hardly refer to their holiness** of character or conduct, **since Paul spends** much time in this letter **challenging their values** and their behavior, calling them to holiness in an ethical sense. He does this on the basis that they are **already sanctified** in a **relational sense,** but now need to **express that sanctification in lifestyle"**

Sanctification continues throughout the Christian's life with a **process of growth** and development. **The apostle Peter challenges God's children to** "grow in the grace and knowledge of our Lord and

Savior Jesus Christ. To Him be the glory both now and forever. Amen." II Peter 3:18. **Sanctification continues** in us, and it is what He is doing in us now. We are to be "set apart" each day for Christ. This is the **growth process** of Bible study, meditation, prayer, yielding, cleansing, seeking to become more like Christ. **This growth continues** throughout our life.

Dr. Bob Utley states, "The New Testament asserts that when sinners turn to Jesus in repentance and faith, **they are instantaneously justified and sanctified.** This is **their new position "in Christ." His righteousness** has been **imputed** to them (Romans 4). They are **declared right and holy.** This is a forensic act of God. But the New Testament **also urges believers** on to holiness or sanctification. It is both a theological position in the finished work of Jesus Christ and a **call to be Christlike in attitude and actions** in daily life. **As salvation is a free gift** and a cost-everything lifestyle, **so too,** is sanctification."

Paul is not commanding the Corinthians to become more sanctified, he is rather declaring the fact that **they have already become sanctified.** This is where you see Paul looking at the Corinthians through the eyes of the cross. **How could anyone look** at the Corinthians and identify them as those who have been sanctified? **Paul could,** because **he viewed them through the eyes of Christ, he identifies them as 'those who are sanctified "in Christ."**

Paul wrote that the church is made up of those who are "together with all those everywhere who call on the name of our Lord Jesus Christ, their Lord and ours". (verse 2). As we have already pointed out: **anyone who has called** on the name of the Lord Jesus Christ for salvation and new life **is a member of the invisible church of God.** He is part of the **true community of faith.** However, **understand the other side** of this statement. If someone has truly put his trust in the saving work of Christ, **he is a genuine believer.** Even though **he has a different** political outlook than we have, he belongs to a different denomination, he reads a different version of the Bible, he worships in a different way, he views communion and baptism differently, or he approaches a particular doctrine differently than we do.

The Gospel is not complicated! John 3:16—"God loved, God gave." "We believe, we receive." **For the intellectuals** who were the Greek philosophers of Paul's day, **this message was foolish** and **too simple** to be **true**. For those with a **religious background,** the Jews, this **message was foolish** and too simple to be of **value.** (1st Corinthians 1:18-25).

Doesn't this sound familiar? So many of my neighbors, friends and acquaintances through the years have **looked down their long intellectual noses** as I've shared the **simple Gospel** with them, and **many religious people,** those who have been christened or confirmed or catechized, or baptized, seem to **have no need for the truth** I am sharing. Yet, if they would accept this simple Gospel, a door to wisdom would open for them that **is so deep** that **only the Spirit of God** can reveal its truths.

Paul wanted to remind the Corinthians (and us) that what makes a person a true believer is not the label that they wear, the church they belong to, or the acts they have performed. **What makes a person a child of God** is that they have turned to Jesus as the one who can alone rescue them from their addiction to sin. **Do we disagree** on some important issues? **Yes.** These issues **should be discussed** and even debated because we seek a true knowledge and understanding of God.

Remember: God isn't finished with you yet! Sometimes we may wonder if the work God is doing in us will ever be finished. **He is constantly working on us!**

One woman tells the story, "My engineer husband is **meticulous** but mild-mannered. While **our new house was being built,** he would **leave notes** for the workmen, politely calling their attention to mistakes or oversights. **Two weeks before we were to move in,** the **floors** still were not finished; the **bathrooms** not tiled, **nor** were **necessary fixtures** installed. I was sure that the work **would never be completed** in time. However, **on moving day,** we found that the house was ready to receive us. **Curious as to how** this miracle had been accomplished, I went and **checked** where my husband always **left his notes** for the workmen. **Posted prominently** on the living room wall was my husband's last note: "**after September 15, all work will be supervised by our 5 children."**

God doesn't need any motivation. He's planning on finishing the work He's begun in you. **God knows** what He has in mind for you. He has plans for you. **And sanctification is consummated** in a glorious transformation of soul and body into the image of the Son of God. (I John 3:2; Romans 8:29). **Finally, one day** we will be made **completely perfect in Him.** The scripture teaches that when we meet the Lord, then, we will be like Him, sinless. **Paul speaks of the church** (those called-out ones, saved ones) **when he says,** "That He might present it to Himself a glorious church, not having spot, or wrinkle, or any such thing; but that it should be holy and without blemish." Ephesians 5:27.

Someone once came to Michelangelo who was chipping away with his chisel at a huge **shapeless piece of rock.** He asked the sculptor **what he was doing.** "I am **releasing the angel** imprisoned in this marble," he answered.

The things that Jesus is doing in our lives aren't something already hidden inside of us, **He's doing His own work,** a new work in our lives. But He sees where we are going. **He has things in mind** for what we are to be. **God's plans for us** include good things that He wants to do in us. **Paul stated in** Ephesians 2:10, "For we are his workmanship, created in Christ Jesus unto good works, which God hath before ordained that we should walk in them."

Sanctification has to do, not only with our soul and spirit, but also our bodies. **Sanctification will not be complete** until our bodies are perfectly redeemed and glorified. Our old nature cannot be eradicated by an experience which renders a person sinless in this life, but one day this also will happen, when we meet Jesus.

A word of caution here: Just as **salvation is not** of man... **sanctification is not** of man! **Sanctification is "of God."** (Jude 1). Sanctification is "of Christ." (Hebrews 10;10; 10:14). **Sanctification is** "of the Holy Spirit."(II Thessalonians 2:13, Romans 15:16). **Sanctification is** by the "Word of God." (John 17:17, Eph. 5:26).

Let me sum up this part by saying: Sanctification is that **inward spiritual work** that the Lord **Jesus Christ works** in a man **by** the **Holy Spirit** when He calls him to be a true believer. He **washes him** from his sins in His own precious blood. He **separates him** from his natural love of sin and the world. He **puts a new principle** in his heart, and makes him godly in life. This is **work which the Spirit effects** in us through the Word of God, though sometimes He uses afflictions and providential visitations "without the word." (I Peter 3:1).

> "Search me O God, and know my heart today;
> Try me O Savior, know my thoughts, I pray.
> See if there be some wicked way in me;
> Cleanse me from every sin and set me free.
> I praise Thee Lord for cleansing me from sin,
> Fulfill Thy Word and make me pure within.
> Fill me with fire where once I burned with shame;
> Grant my desire to magnify Thy name."
>
> J. Edwin Orr

CHAPTER NINE

"In Christ" Everything You Really 'Need' Will Be Supplied.

Philippians 4:19, "My God will supply every **need** of yours according to his riches in glory **"by Christ Jesus."**

Our sovereign Lord is the great Provider. **One of the Hebrew names of God Almighty is "Jehovah—Jireh,"** meaning, "The Lord Will Provide." (Genesis 22:9—14). **He** is the **God of the Bible,** and the God and Father of our Lord Jesus Christ. **It is through personal faith in Christ** that we gain that experiential knowledge of God. **Jesus said,** "I am the way, the truth, and the life: no man cometh unto the Father, but by me" (John 14:6). **Can you say** with the apostle Paul that Jehovah-Jireh is "my God?"

When Israel **needed a leader,** He raised up Moses. When they **needed water** in the desert, He supplied it from a rock. When they **needed food** for their wilderness wandering, He gave it in the form of manna. **Man needed a Savior** from his sins, **so God sent His only begotten Son** to die on Calvary's cross. God is the Great Provider! **The hand of God's provision** is also open to us **in our time of affliction.** This verse states that God has **provided for the need** of His saints.

A story is told by Dr. Richard Newton of an old and **poverty-stricken Indian,** who many years ago made his way into a Western **settlement** in **search of food** to keep him from starving. **A bright-colored ribbon** was seen around his neck, from which there hung a small, **dirty pouch.** On being **asked what it was,** he said it was a charm given him in his younger days. He **opened it,** and took out a worn and **crumpled paper,** which he handed to the person making the inspection. It proved, **on examination,** to be a **regular discharge** from the **federal army, signed by George Washington himself,** and entitling him to a **pension for life.** Here was a man with a promise and provision duly signed. When presented in the right place would have **secured him ample provision,** yet he was **wandering** about hungry, helpless, and forlorn, and **begging bread** to keep him from starving.

Unfortunately, that is a picture of many Christians who are in need of everything when they **might be rich and full!** Perhaps their own life had not been generous, certainly **their faith** has never put in its claim to **God's great bank of promise.** Many have lived a long life, never having been blessed with, "the riches in glory by Christ Jesus." **Many Christians grow old** and go to their grave, never having experienced the full blessings of God that are promised in His Word.

To help us place our trust more confidently in this promise of God, **someone** has put Philippians 4:19 **in terms we can all understand:** "My God (the bank) shall supply (the check) all your need (the amount) according to His riches in glory (the capital) by Christ Jesus (the signature)." **As with any valid check** that we have received, **we need only endorse God's check** through our "signature of faith" and it will be paid in full. **As long as we're willing to be content** with much or little, as Paul was (v.12), we can dare to be generous people. **Only then** will we discover for ourselves that we can **never out give** our rich and generous God.

Growing old is an unavoidable fact, but you know **growing up** is not. **Maturity** is a matter of **choice.** It is a battle we can win. And **God wants us to mature** . . . or grow up spiritually. He mentions this repeatedly in this letter to the Philippians. **For the Christian, maturity is a process we never complete on this side of eternity. Maturity is the ability** to **do a job** whether you are supervised or not; **finish a job** once it's started; **carry money** without spending it. And last, but not least, **the ability to bear** an **injustice** without wanting to get even.

Even if you are young, or wanting to feel young, all of us are constantly **fighting** and losing a **battle-with aging.** Have you noticed that **with age,** our **"needs"** are constantly changing? **Do you remember** the opening words to a **popular soap opera say,** . . . "as sand through the hour glass . . . so are the **days of our lives." We can't stop the physical effects of the ever ticking clock. We try to protect ourselves** against age. We exercise. We take our vitamins. We try to eat right, but those **are just stop-gaps. Eventually we succumb to our overwhelming enemy. Our hair** falls out. **Wrinkles** form around our eyes. Our **energy** fades. Aging is **inevitable.** There is nothing we can to do keep this from happening. **Jesus affirmed this fact.** Remember what **He said** in Matthew 6:25-31? "Who of you **by worrying** can add one inch to your height . . . or subtract one day from your age?"

Charles Swindoll tells of one aging woman who wrote a friend a humorous description of her own aging and said, **Remember, old folks**

are worth a fortune-**SILVER** in their hair, **GOLD** in their teeth, **STONES** in their kidneys, **LEAD** in their feet, and **GAS** in their stomachs. **I have become a little older since I saw you** last, and **a few changes** have come into my life since then. Frankly, I have become quite a **frivolous old gal.** I am seeing **five gentlemen** every day. As soon as I wake up, **Will Power** helps me get out of bed. Then I go to see **John.** Then **Charlie Horse** comes along, and when he is here he takes a lot of my time and attention. When he leaves **Arthur Ritus** shows up and stays the rest of the day. He doesn't like to stay in one place very long, **so he takes me from joint to joint.** After such a busy day I'm really tired and **glad to go to bed with Ben Gay.** What a life!

P. S. The preacher came to call the other day. He said at my age I should be **thinking about the hereafter.** I told him, Oh, I do that all the time. **No matter where I am**, in the parlor, upstairs, in the kitchen, in the yard, or down in the basement, **I ask myself, "what am I here after?"**

F. B. Meyer cautions that we must distinguish between our **needs** and our **desires.** It is possible **to want** a good many things which we do not **need**, and **often want** things which it **would injure** us greatly to have. **Paul wanted to be delivered** from his **thorn,** but his real **need** was for more grace. We want a great many things which it is not possible for our Heavenly Father to give us, except to the great detriment of our best life. **There is no promise that God** shall supply all our desires or wishes, but it is certain that He will fulfill all our **need.**

One of the first things we hear . . . . and unfortunately, one of the **first things** we **forget** as Christians is that God does **provide for our 'needs.' God has promised to supply** all the **'needs'** of His dear people. This one of the **great promises** of all the Scripture. **God doesn't say** that He will supply all our **'wants.' He doesn't promise luxury items** (non-essentials)—**but our needs**. He does sometimes supply luxury items, but this is not the promise. When God does this, it is a surplus that is out of His loving-kindness. **When our 'needs' are supplied, we need to be sure that God gets all the glory.** Almighty God will not share His glory with others.

Have you ever heard the false and unscriptural statement, "God helps those who help themselves." The **real truth** is brought out in this verse: "God helps those who cannot help themselves!" It is easy **to take this verse out of context** and use it as a soft pillow for **Christians who are squandering** their money on themselves with seldom a thought for the work of God! "That's all right. God will supply all your need." **While it is true, in a general sense,** that God does supply the needs of His people, this is a **specific promise** that those **who are faithful** and **devoted** in their **giving to Christ and His cause** will never suffer lack.

When God leads He provides. **Hudson Taylor** observed, "God's work, done in **God's way, will receive God's supply. Our God hasn't changed. When the child of God is in the will of God,** serving **for the glory of God,** then he will have every need met." **Amen!**

How vast is the wealth of God? How rich is the Provider? **I doubt** that we will **ever fully know in this lifetime** the extent of God's riches. He said to His people Israel, "And I will give you the treasures of darkness, and hidden riches of secret places, that you may know that I, the Lord, which call you by your name, am the God of Israel" (Isaiah 45:3). Yes, **God has hidden riches** in secret places about which we know nothing. **The apostle Paul mentioned** "the riches of his goodness" (Romans 2:4), ""the riches of his glory" (Romans 9:23; Ephesians 3:16), **and** "the riches of his grace" (Ephesians 1:7; 2:7). **What an amazing provision from an amazing Provider! Jehovah—Jireh, our Provider!**

Our God has promised to supply our need according to **His** riches. This tells us that **we cannot have a need too great** for God to supply. **Our Heavenly Father knows** what our need is, and **all His riches** are made available to His own. "He that spared not his own Son, but delivered him up for us all, how shall he not with him also freely give us all things?" (Romans 8:32).

As we study the Scriptures, we have seen that **God promises** to graciously supply all you need, so that you can abound in good works. **But this promise in v. 19 is conditional.** His supply is abundant. **He is more than able** to help you do all that He expects of you. Look in the mirror and you will see the problem. You see, there **are several things** we must do if we are to fully experience the abundant grace of God. And if you are to experience a complete and overflowing sufficiency in your life, **some conditions** must be met. **You must be "In Christ."** To whom is this promise given? **Is this an unconditional promise to all people? No!** It is made to **believers only.** II Corinthians is written to believers. **Notice** in Philippians 4:19, that **our needs** are met "in Christ Jesus". This promise is to those who are in vital union with Christ by faith. So, **if you have not placed your faith** in Jesus Christ as Savior and Lord, that is the starting place for you. **Why neglect** the **Source** of a never-ending supply—Jesus? Turn to Christ. Trust in Him today. Receive Him into your heart and life. Make Him Lord and Savior now.

A family had put their Grandma on her **first plane flight**, but she was **not very confident** about the experience of **leaving the ground** on this **modern 'contraption'**. When they **met her at the airport** on her return, one of the family members kidded her by asking, **"Well, did the plane hold you up okay?"** She grudgingly replied, "Well, yes," and **then quickly added,** "But I never did put my full weight down on it!"

Many Christians are like that Grandma. The **truth is,** they are being sustained completely by God, but **they're afraid to put the full weight of their lives down on Him.** As a result, they're **plagued by anxiety** and aren't able to **enjoy the flight.**

Do you see why Paul begins our text with a **reference** to **"my God?"** That God is the center of Paul's life, and that God is so very faithful, He uses Paul in His kingdom, and Paul considers that such a privilege. Nothing else is important as long as he can serve. And see: **Christ supplies his needs so that he can serve!** No matter what your need is, the **need is not greater than God.** But, please **note the pronoun "my."** It **is "my God."** "My God," **"in Christ Jesus."**

Here again we see Paul's intimate, personal relationship with his Savior. Giving to the Lord's work is not for anyone who does not know Him through the cross. **If you know Him as "my God,"** if you know that by faith you are **"in Christ Jesus,"** then the privilege of giving and the **promise of God's faithfulness** applies to you. If you do not know Christ, you **can't give to Him** until you **receive from Him** His gift to you . . . **Jesus!**

The question immediately arises, "Do you really belong to God. **Has Jesus** become your Lord and Savior? **The Apostle John wrote,** "to as many as received Him, (Jesus), to them He gave power (the right) to become the children of God . . ." (John 1:14). **The question remains,** Are you His child . . . to qualify you to call on Him?" **God will provide** the need of His children. Does God know you personally, enough to "supply your needs?" **God is God,** and He is **able to supply** whatever provision His dear child needs. **We must learn to remember:** No matter what the trial or need, **God will supply!**

The Apostle Paul wrote, "And God is able to make all grace abound toward you; that you, always having all sufficiency in all things, may abound to every good work." (II Corinthians 9:8).

When Paul expresses in our text, **his confidence that the Lord will supply** the needs of the Philippians, **he is not thinking first of all of material abundance, or** of relief from persecution **or** even grace to overcome their selfishness. **Paul knows:** on this side of the fall into sin life remains a wilderness, characterized by sweat and tears. Persecution, hatred, oppression are the lot of Christians in this fallen world.

Dr. John MacArthur states, "God is glorified when we trust Him. Unbelief doubts God and implies that He is not to be trusted. That detracts from His glory." **And he goes on to say,** "Sometimes I think that the greatest problem in letting the world know about God's glory is that the message has to go through us! We like to quote the verse, "My God shall supply all your needs according to His riches in glory in Christ Jesus". **But then some crisis comes** into our lives, and we collapse. Sometimes everyone at the job and at home knows it. **Then people say,** "Some kind of God you have! You don't even trust Him yourself." **God is glorified** when we believe in Him, **when we rest in His full assurance.** That gives Him glory."

One of my favorite Bible stories is Daniel and his three friends at judgment time at the blazing furnace. What a **great example** of God's believers who trusted God in the face of a severe trial. **When threatened** with the fiery furnace, **they didn't say,** "We have a practical problem, what verse applies here?" **They just shouted out the announcement,** "Our God, whom we serve is able to deliver us from the furnace of blazing fire; and He will deliver us out of your hand, O King!" (Daniel 3:3:17). **Then they said,** "But even if He does not, let it be known to you, O King, that we are not going to serve your gods or worship the golden image that you have set up." (v. 18). **Listen,** if they had fallen on the ground, and groveled in the dirt before the golden image, that would not have glorified God. **But, they trusted God with their lives, and He was glorified before the entire nation.**

The real question is . . . Do you believe God, and that He keeps His Word? Of course He does, whether we trust Him or not. **Do you live** as if He keeps His word? **Christian, the world watches us,** who say we believe Him. And when they see us waver, they are not to sure what kind of God we have. **We need to glorify God** . . . by trusting Him. **Not to trust Him** is the same as calling Him a liar. (I John 5:10).

Someone once said, "If you can't be happy with what you already have, why should God trust you with anything else?" **Good question!** Far too many people go through life **chronically unhappy** with their circumstances. Yet, in every situation, we have whatever we need to be content (if not happy). **When we focus on material** things, we will **often feel frustrated,** but when we **focus on the Lord,** we **can rejoice knowing** what we have can never be taken from us.

Unfortunately, selfishness will continue to plague even those renewed through the Spirit of Jesus Christ until the Day of Glory. But in the midst of all that brokenness, **the Lord will give peace** in one's heart, and contentment in the privilege of being allowed to serve. **Paul has experienced it himself,** and he's sure that **the God who supplies all his needs, gives grace** to be content. Paul knows how to be abased and how to abound. The God who supplies all his needs will supply the needs of the struggling saints of Philippi also. **And to struggling saints** all over the world!

Truly, friend, **what a great promise that is! And what an encouragement! But a question remains**: is it really true that God will supply the Philippians in the way He has supplied the apostle? More: on what grounds can we today be sure that the Lord will supply all our needs?

Years ago, in the late 1950's, **Dee and I traveled**, with our three little children, **to Northern California,** about 200 miles north of San Francisco. **A little church** of about 6 to 8 members called us to **come pastor their church.** It was a real struggle financially. **This was the days** when Southern Baptists called this kind of work, **'Pioneer Missions.'** I was "pulling green chain" in a local sawmill. I had no church, denominational or other types of financial support. **One cold, wet and rainy evening I was teaching a Bible study** in our home (which was where we had services). **A new man arrived,** and **I took his coat to hang it up.** I happened to make **some remark** to the effect that it was a **very nice coat** and looked like it would be **warm** in the winter and **dry** in the rainy season. When this **man left,** he walked away without putting on his coat. I **grabbed the coat** and ran outside after him. **"Wait,"** I screamed, "you forgot your coat," **He replied,** "That's not my coat; its yours,", and he walked into the night. **I never saw him again.** Do you think God met a need of mine ... before I asked?

Let's look at the guarantee of Paul's statement. The **guarantee of God supplying our needs,** brothers and sisters, lies in the **concluding words** of our text: "according to His riches in glory by Christ Jesus." "His riches in glory." **God is God.** This is He, Paul knows his Bible, who created all things and therefore possesses all things (Ps 24:1). **All the riches of all creation,** from gold and silver on the one hand, to power and peace on the other, belong to this God. **This God who owns all** dwells in eternal glory in heaven, with multitudes of angels who sing His praise and do His bidding. "Riches in glory," **the phrase describes the wealth** of resources that God has at His disposal, resources so infinitely greater than Paul has at his disposal in the confines of his prison cell.

Too often, the **believer forgets** that **God is the great provider!** No matter what our need is ... the need is not greater than God. **To reaffirm, the first word** (the pronoun) in this verse, **"My."** He is **"my God!"** For this verse to have effect, one must truly know God personally, through His Son Jesus. My God is able! **God is the center** of Paul's life, and God is so very faithful, **He uses Paul** in His kingdom, and Paul considers that **such a privilege.** Yes, nothing else is important as long as he can serve. **Notice: Christ supplies His needs so that we can serve, certainly not just to have 'stuff!'** As Christ supplies the apostle's need, even **in the valley** of the shadow of death, so, says Paul, **this God will supply** every need the **Philippians** might have (and ours also). Of that Paul has no doubt.

Sometimes we fail to ask for certain provisions because something may seem too **trivial** or small to trouble God about. **But if it's big enough** to make me anxious, it's certainly big enough to ask God about. **A woman once asked** the Bible teacher, **G. Campbell Morgan,** "Do you think we should pray about the little things in our lives, or just the big things?" **He retorted, "Madam, can you think of anything** in your life that is too big for God?" So whenever you're **anxious, come to God** in reverent, humble, specific, thankful prayer.

Understand, God is not only the **great provider,** but **He has great provision!** Let me take the liberty of changing a question to a statement. "There is nothing too hard for God." (Genesis 18:14) Giving Abraham, age 99, and Sarah, age 89, a child in their old age proves, nothing is to hard for **Jehovah-Jireh** (the God who provides).

This verse 19 is a wonderful source of assurance and contentment: "And my God will supply all that you need according to the riches of his glory in Christ Jesus." **Some read this verse** as a kind of **blank check.** They suppose that it tells them that God is infinitely rich, and that **He will give them whatever they ask.** This is **not exactly** the message that Paul is seeking to convey. Let's step back from this verse and look more carefully at what it says.

Remember the context of the verse. The context of the verse is Paul's response to the gift that the Philippians had sent by Epaphroditus. Paul has been playing down his needs and emphasizing his contentment, even though he is in somewhat dire circumstances. **Paul is the one in need,** and yet he is assuring the Philippians that God will supply their needs.

F. B. Meyer comments that **"Christ is God's Answer to Our Need." In Him** are all the treasures of wisdom and knowledge hidden. It pleased the Father that **in Him** should all the fullness dwell. **In Him** dwells all the fullness of the Godhead bodily. The Divine-Human nature of Christ is replete with every possible supply for His people. He fills all in all. (Colossians 2).

Have you ever come up short at the **Bank** and had a **check returned,** "insufficient funds?" Let **us take note of the infinite resources of God.** There is **no question** as to **God's ability** to provide for our needs. God is infinitely rich. **No request is ever denied** on the basis of **"insufficient funds." Remember:** God supplies **"according to the riches of his glory."** In verse 20, we read, **"May glory be given to God our Father forever and ever. Amen."** I take it, then, that **God's glory is the source** and **the goal** of His gracious provision for the saints. I am reminded of Paul's words in Romans 11:36: "For from him and through him and to him are all things. To him be glory forever! Amen."

There is a modern heresy in many of our churches today **that teaches** that it is God's will for all of His children **to be always healthy and wealthy** in this life. **The eloquent false prophets** of this cult teaching live in huge mansions, drive expensive cars, and indulge themselves in every flagrant luxury that they can, **luring their gullible followers** with promises of the same. It is **completely un-scriptural, and anti-Christian!** While **God promises** to meet our basic physical needs, He knows that our **deepest need is spiritual,** to be rightly related to Him. So **He blesses us** with every **spiritual blessing** in the heavenly places in Christ.

God's ability to supply our needs is limitless. Remember however, God said, "all your **needs,**" not "all your **greeds**" One **T.V. Evangelist—Preacher** said that **when he started** the T.V. work, he had **one home they** were about to lose. He said he were willing to just give it to God, and **now he has 12 beautiful homes** around the world, **filled w/ gold** and **fine furnishings** (giving us the impression that those who can afford it **the least,** that God will do the same for them **if they just support him!)** Ouch! God **hasn't promised** to meet our greeds ... but our **needs!**

Far too many place the emphasis of this verse **on physical "things."** Although it does include food, clothing and shelter, **this verse really refers** to spiritual, mental, emotional, social and needs. It refers to any need that arises, engulfs, or confronts the believer. **No real need is overlooked** ... nothing is too big or too little for God to take care of His dear child. No matter what the trial or need is, God will supply. **Remember: this is His promise ... claim it in faith.**

Having said this, I would also suggest that **we should not assume** that every perceived "need" is a wrong that needs to be made right by sharing that need with others, and expecting them to provide what we think we need. **This mindset** has **become a "given"** in Christian circles. **It is true of those who are in ministry.** I see very few men coming out of seminary who are willing to "roll up their sleeves" and **work in a secular job** because they assume that others should support them in their ministry. **And yet some of the most effective servants** of Christ are those who are "tent makers," those who **support themselves** in ministry by working secularly, teaching school, or . . . . I am trying to say that while each of us has an obligation to share all good things with those who teach us, (Galatians 6:6), those of us who do teach and preach should not demand that we be supported financially.

This is not just a problem with those who have prepared themselves for **full-time ministry.** There are a considerable number of **Christians who refuse to accept** the fact that they **should have unmet needs. I want to caution you here!** They **demand that God deliver** them from **any** "need" or "adversity." **They expect and demand healing** when they are sick. **Some even demand** that God delay death, until they are ready for it. (Most have to admit that God wants them to die, someday, but just not this year). **What I am saying is,** that every Christian **ought to be willing** to cheerfully **accept some unmet need,** as God's will for them. It may be the unmet need of marriage, **or** a full-time ministry, **or** a "fulfilling" **and** good-paying job.

God is not only the great provider with great provision, but **notice the great resource,** "according to His riches in glory." All the riches, wealth, glory and the majesty of heaven are available **to meet the needs of God's dear people.**

Pastor Harold Springstead was driving along, on his way to preach at a little country church, when he felt a sudden vibration. A **tire had gone flat.** As the **78 year-old** pastor maneuvered his car to a stop, **a trucker** pulled up behind him. A **young man** jumped out, assessed the situation, and **cheerfully changed the tire.** Pastor Springstead **got to the service in plenty of time,** and it was **not until later** that he realized his **car didn't even have a jack!**

It was a minor problem. He was a **retired faithful servant of God.** It was a tiny congregation. We might think **God would be too busy** with larger and more important needs than to be concerned about a **flat tire.** But **His promise** to provide for **the needs** of His people covers little things as well as big ones.

Please know that God is infinitely able to meet our needs, and He has **promised** to provide all our **needs.** If we pray for God to provide something that we think we need, **and He chooses not** to provide it, must we **not conclude** that it was not really a need after all? How often **we confuse our "wants" and our "needs."** How easy it is to expect God to indulge **our fleshly desires** (James 4:1-3). Many are those who would question God's promise, His goodness, His ability to provide, or their own faith, when their requests have not been met. What should really be questioned is the accuracy of our perception of need.

We Christians are not to be ruled and **controlled** by our wants, desires and passions. Whether it is lustful passions, anger, bitterness, or jealousy, **God has promised us that,** ". . . sin shall not have dominion over you . . ." (Romans 6: 14). **The only way a Christian's** desires will begin to **rule their life** is if they allow them to reign over them. **Again, Paul said,** "Let not sin therefore reign in your mortal body, that ye should obey it in the lusts thereof" (Rom.6: 12). **Rather than being ruled** by our **wicked desires and passions,** we are to submit ourselves to the **Holy Spirit's control,** for we are **commanded to,** ". . . be filled with the Spirit" (Ephesians 5: 18). **Getting all our desires and wants** isn't all it's cracked up to be, as **this little story** suggests:

One day a boy's mother decided she would **make hot buttered biscuits** as long as her son could eat them. **He loved biscuits** and always complained that he never got enough. **He ate and ate and ate.** She kept pulling them out of the stove. **Finally she** looked around and saw him sitting there looking sort of green. "What's wrong, son, **don't you want some more biscuits?**" He answered sickishly, "No ma'am, I don't even want the ones I ate." **You may get what you want,** but you may **not want what you've got** after you've gotten it! **Make sure your desires** are not **mere selfish wants,** but desires that fall in line with God's will.

The Holy Spirit leads Paul to **describe** to the Philippians a work that **daily takes place** within him. What is that work? **Christ strengthens him.** That is to say: Jesus **Christ gives Paul grace day by day** not to get **despondent** in the face of adversity, not to get **cynical** in the face of injustice, not to get **bitter** in the face of wrong. **The ascended Savior gives** His servant grace to believe that the gates of hell cannot prevail, and so all the opposition and disappointment and unfairness and injustice this life throws at him will ultimately come to nothing. The ascended **Christ gives His servant** grace to believe that He is using all this opposition and disappointment and unfairness and injustice to make His kingdom come.

Paul wrote in chapter 1, how his **imprisonment provided opportunity** for the gospel to come to ears of persons who otherwise would not hear the gospel, all those prison guards and so even Caesar's household (1:12)! For Paul **"to live is Christ,"** he lays himself at Christ's disposal, **willing to be of service** however Christ chooses.

God gives us what we need. This is His promise, time and time again. **God gives** us the **strength** we need to keep going when we want to quit. **He gives** us the **love** we need to keep ministering to those around us. **He gives** us the **ability** to curb our own desires and obey Him.

Philippians 4:19 **says,** "God shall supply all your **need."** We see, then, that there must **be a need** before God will supply. We must **not presume** on this promise and run ahead of God with plans of our own. Neither should **we presume** on God for all our wants or be careless in spending God's money. God does not promise to supply all of our wants, only our needs. **Be aware:** The slothful, the spendthrift or the selfish person **cannot claim** the promise of Philippians 4:19. There must be a legitimate need. **Those who** are slothful and unwilling to work or who are overly ambitious to gain things need not expect to have this verse fulfilled in their lives. **It should also be understood** that God meets our need for a purpose, not to relieve us of our responsibility, but because He has given us responsibility. **When God gives us a responsibility to fulfill,** we can count on His supplying all of the resources that are necessary to accomplish it.

Donald Grey Barnhouse, the great Presbyterian **preacher tells the story** of an uneducated miner in Scotland who began to preach among his fellow workmen with great power. **Soon his witness** took him far **beyond** the confines of the mining **towns. Someone asked him** how he had received his **call to preach.** He replied, "Oh, I had such a burden on my soul for those who did not know the gospel, **I argued with the Lord** that I had no education and no gift. But **He said to me,** "Jamie, you know **what the sickness is,** don't you?" I answered, **"Yes, Lord, the sickness is sin."** "And **you know** what the **remedy is, don't you,** Jamie?" I answered, **"Yes, Lord,** the **remedy is the Lord Jesus Christ."** And He said to me, **"Jamie, just take the remedy** to those who are sick." That is my call to preach. **This is God's call to every believer.**

Let us remember those to whom Paul is speaking. Most of us would like the promise of verse 19 **to be universal,** but **we need to remember** to whom this assurance was given. **Paul is writing to the Philippians,** the most generous church in the New Testament world. These are saints who have given to meet Paul's needs as well as the needs of others, and at great personal sacrifice. **Through Paul, God assured these saints** that He would provide for all their needs. **Paul is assuring those who sacrificially give** that God will continue to provide for them so that they might continue to give. **In other words, God promises** to provide the things we need in order to be generous toward others. **This is not a "blank check"** for those who would indulge themselves; it is a promise to those **who wish to minister** to others. This is what Paul told the Corinthians.

The guarantee to supply our **'needs,'** is cemented in the concluding words of our text: **"according to His riches in glory by Christ Jesus." "His riches** in glory." **God is God.** This is **He who created all things** and therefore **possesses** all things (Psalm 24:1). All the riches of all creation, from **gold and silver** on the one hand to **power and peace** on the other, belong to this God. This **God who owns all** dwells in eternal glory in heaven, with multitudes of angels who sing His praises and do His bidding. **"Riches in glory:" the phrase describes** the wealth of resources that God has at His disposal, **resources so infinitely greater** than Paul has at his disposal in the confines of his prison cell.

D. L. Moody, the great evangelist, **preached on verse 19 on one occasion. His outline was this,** he **called his sermon: 'God's Cheque'.** He said: **'My God'**, that is the name of the firm on the cheque, 'My God.' **'Shall supply'**, that is the promise to pay. **'All your need'**, that is the amount to be paid. **'His riches'**, that is the deposit in the account against which the cheque is drawn. **'In glory'**, that is the address of the bank. **'By Christ Jesus'**, that is the signature that appears on the cheque. **This cheque needs but one thing** to make it a practical and valuable thing, and **that is the endorsement** of your faith on the reverse side—and then, **whatever your need,** God will abundantly supply it.

Paul said in these verses: "I have received full payment"—verse 18: "I have all, and abound: I am full, having received of Epaphroditus." **We don't know** how much Epaphroditus sent from the church at Philippi, but **he is able to cry: "I am amply supplied." Have you ever seen such a paradox** and seeming contradiction as this: **this little man,** bow-legged they say, and with a big nose and bald, sitting in this prison, absolutely poor, impoverished, not a penny to his name, chained to a Roman soldier at the order and will of a Roman tyrant, almost perhaps persuaded at the beginning that he was going to his death, inevitably he would be sentenced to death under Nero—**yet he said: "I am amply supplied".**

Bob Wieland has learned to be content in every situation of life, and that's where the Lord wants to take us. Right now you may **feel like you're on mile marker one** of that **spiritual marathon,** and you are fading fast with 25 miles to go, but Jesus Christ can give you all the **strength you need. Bob completed** the **New York marathon in 1986,** finishing **19,413th,** that's **last.** It took him **4 days, 2 hours, 48 minutes and 17 seconds.** Where did Bob Wieland get the strength to do all of that? It came from above. **As Bob once said,** "Through faith in God, dedication, and determination, there is nothing within the will of God a person can't achieve."

Bob Wieland is a believer. Bob completed the **Los Angeles** and **New York City marathons twice** and the **Marine Corps Marathon** once. Those races are **26 miles** long! Bob also **rode a bicycle** from Los Angeles to Washington, covering **2,700 miles in 35 days.** He broke the **world record** for the **bench press four times,** once lifting 507 pounds. He also **completed the Iron Man Triathlon in Hawaii.**

All of that is phenomenal, but the thing that **makes it amazing** is that **Bob Wieland** is a '**double amputee.**' His legs were blown away by a **land mine** in **Vietnam in 1969.**

Now take note of the intent of God's provision. God supplies "**according to the riches of His glory.**" In verse 20, we read, "**May glory be given to God our Father forever and ever. Amen.**" God's glory is the source and the goal of His gracious provision for the saints. **Read Paul's words** in Romans 11:36: "For from Him and through Him and to Him are all things. To Him be glory forever! Amen."

Imagine, if you will, **your child coming to you and asking for a bicycle.** The child pleads and **pleads.** Finally, you decide to **reward the child** with what he asks. **He wakes up** one morning to find a **bright and shiny bike,** a beautiful **red one,** all ready to be ridden. The **child looks at you** and, with a whining voice, **says "But I wanted a blue one."** How would you feel?

Do you know the reason that people are **unhappy, unsatisfied, and unfulfilled** is because **Jesus Christ is not the center** of their lives. **As the old country song says,** "they are **looking for love** and fulfillment **in all the wrong places.**" They have not learned to trust in God. **Remember:** You were made for a purpose and that is to **have a relationship with God** through Jesus Christ. **You were made** with a God shaped vacuum in your life that **only God can fill.** When you try to find satisfaction in life through people, popularity, possessions, or prestige, **you will never be content, you**

will never be satisfied. **Jesus said,** "I have come that they may have life, and that they may have it more abundantly." (John 10:10) **Abundant life comes from** having a **relationship** with God and **learning to trust Him.**

Sometimes we, as humans, do this same thing to our Creator every day. We receive His bounty. **The Bible tells us that God continually** does good toward us, giving us rain from Heaven, and fruitful seasons, filling our hearts with food and gladness (Acts 14:17). **God has been so good** to all of us, whether we have believed in Him or not. Although God does not have pleasure in wickedness (Psalm 5:4), He has done good to all. **He is, as He told His servant Moses in** Exodus 34:6-7, "The LORD, The LORD God, merciful and gracious, longsuffering, and abundant in goodness and truth, keeping mercy for thousands, forgiving iniquity and transgression and sin . . ."

Have you ever felt like everything was going wrong for you? I've lost my job. **I've gotten** a bad report from the doctor. **My mate** has let me down. **My child** is in trouble. **My finances** are not meeting needs. **I have miserably failed.** I am **going through a rough time** in life, **and I need someone** to strengthen me. Let me tell you, "**Jesus Christ can give you** all the strength you will ever need."

Remember: God does not give us what we **deserve, but what we need.** Time and time again the children of Adam came to Christ for healing, and He turned none away. **The leper** was cleansed, the **blind** given sight, the **dead** were raised, and the **lame** were given strength to walk. **Jesus healed**, forgave, and made whole all who came to Him in faith. How was He treated? Many times Jesus healed, then sent those He healed away with the admonition "go and tell no one".

Did you hear about the young man got engaged to a young woman and went to **meet her parents** over dinner. After dinner the **father takes the young man** into the drawing room to **find out his plans** for life with his daughter. "So, what are your plans?" The father asks the fiancée. "I am a Biblical Scholar," he replies. "A Biblical Scholar. Admirable, but **what will you do to provide a nice home** for my daughter to live in, as she deserves," the father asks? "I will study," the young man replies. **God will provide for us.**" "And how will you buy her a beautiful **engagement ring,** such as she deserves," the father asks? "I will concentrate on my studies, **God will provide for us,**" the young man replies. "And children" the father asks, "**how will you support your children?**" "Don't worry sir" the young man replies "**God will provide.**" The conversation continues to proceed like this. **Each time** the father asks a question, the **young man insists that God** will provide.

Later, the wife asks about the discussion, "So, how did it go?" The man replies "He has **no job**, and **no plans**, but the good news is, he thinks I'm God." **Trusting God doesn't mean** that we don't work, **it means** that instead of sitting around and worrying, we should pray. And if we aren't working, we ought to get a job.

Jesus did what He did because God is love, and needed no reward to do good. But there were other times when Jesus healed, and, like humans will do, those healed quickly went away to live their lives without God. **Jesus healed ten lepers** but only **one** returned **to thank Him** for His wondrous gift. **Jesus said** in Luke 17:17-19, "Were there not ten cleansed? But where are the nine? There are none found that returned to give glory to God, save this Samaritan." And he said unto him, "Arise, go your way: your faith hath made thee whole (well)."

There's a lesson in this. God has given us great things. **If we have received** of His bounty, and there's no one who hasn't, then we need to stop and thank Him for what He has done. God is good! **The Children of Israel suffered** great desolation because they developed the all too human habit of complaining instead of praising.

If you're drawing air into your lungs today you ought to be praising God. **If your belly** is filled, you ought to be praising God. **If your soul** is saved because you called upon the Name of Jesus for salvation, **you ought to be so thankful you'd be praising God. If you are a citizen** of America you ought to **be praising God.**

As a pastor I have seen many call upon the Name of Jesus while they were in adversity. **These same people,** once blessed by His gracious love, **walk away** from the hospital, the courtroom, the prison, the valley of the shadow of death to **go back to a life without Him.** I ask that we all stop our busy-ness, our running to and fro, and thank God for what He has done for us all.

It's amazing how soon we forget just how big God is, and that God wants to provide for you. Now that we've seen the Scripture, **don't miss the promise—God wants to provide for your needs.**

The following story was told by **Dr. Helen Roseveare, former missionary** to Zaire. **A young mother at our mission station died** after **giving birth** to a premature baby. We **tried to improvise an incubator** to keep the infant alive, but the only **hot water bottle** we had was beyond repair. **So during devotions** that morning we asked the **children to pray** for the baby and for her little sister who was now an orphan. **One of the girls responded,** "Dear God, please **send a hot water bottle today.**

Tomorrow will be too late because by then the **baby will be dead.** And dear Lord, **send a doll** for the sister so she won't feel so lonely."

That afternoon a large parcel arrived from England. Eagerly the children watched as we opened it. **Much to their surprise,** under some clothing **was a hot water bottle!** Immediately the **girl who had prayed** so earnestly started to delve deeper, exclaiming, **"If God sent that, I'm sure He also sent a doll."** And **she was right!**

Listen, the Heavenly Father knew in advance of the child's sincere requests, and **5 months before,** He had **led a ladies group** to include both of those specific articles. **Paul reminds us in Romans 8:32,** "He that spared not his own Son, but delivered him up for us all, how shall he not with him also freely give us all things?"

I don't know if you were **growing up in the seventies,** but do you remember at **youth group or in church singing** a praise song by Merla Watson, **"Jehovah Jireh,** my provider, **His grace** is sufficient for me? **My God will supply** all my needs according to His riches in glory. He gives His angels charge over me. **Jehovah Jireh** cares for me . . . for me . . . for me. **Jehovah Jireh:** the God who sees, the God who cares, the God who undertakes, the God of providence—**Jehovah Jireh cares for me."** This is the theme from Genesis 22:7-14; Philippians 4:19.

Well, my friends, that's the theme song of contentment! The song of contentment is, "My God, **I believe** that Your supply of my needs is more real than the air that I'm breathing right now. **I believe** that Your supply of all my needs is more real than the food that I eat. **I believe** that Your supply of my needs is more real than the skin that I'm in. **I believe** that Your supply of my needs is more real, more lasting, than any circumstance that I'm in right now. **That's my theme song."**

And **until the truth of God's** providence has **worked** deep down **into our hearts** so that is the reflex reaction the minute that we're in any difficult circumstances of life, **we haven't yet apprehended** the **secret of contentment** in the way that we need to. **"Your need:"** may be very big: **but it is so little to Him,** Yes, vast and varied may be our need. **"My God:"** in all **His majestic mightiness,** He will supply. Paul depends on Him as **"my" God:** and you and I are allowed the same **privilege;** up alongside of Him, **our need does not seem** so insuperably big, after all.

Anna Warner, author of the hymn **"Jesus Loves Me,"** constantly faced financial pressure. Her father had been a **wealthy powerbroker** in New York City, but the **stock market crash of 1837** wiped out his finances. As a result, **Anna faced over-whelming debt** all her life. But **she**

learned to trust God with her needs. **A friend wrote** this about her: "**One day when sitting** with Miss Anna in the old living room she took from one of the (book) cases a (sea) shell so delicate that it looked like lace work and holding it in her hand, with eyes dimmed with tears, she said, 'There was a time when **I was very perplexed, bills** were unpaid, **necessities** must be had, and someone sent me this exquisite thing. As I held it, **I realized that if God** could make this beautiful home for a little creature, He would take care of me.'"

Oh, how hard it is for us to comprehend that with all the resources at God's disposal, He can provide for our every need. Not only does He have access to everything, He knows everything! A **crucial note here, we must not forget, that God does nothing** apart from Jesus Christ. **The key to having your needs met** is that **before you can approach God,** you must be in a right relationship with Jesus Christ. The **question is:** have you surrendered your life to Jesus as your Lord? **I have never seen one verse of scripture** that promised blessing or supply **for anyone who is openly rebelling against God and His will.** Think about that.

This verse ends, "**by Christ Jesus.**" All these 'needs' are met through Christ Jesus. **Remember:** God has only one son, the Lord Jesus Christ. God the Father and God the Son have such a close, unified relationship that the Father will do nothing for a person, unless that person knows and honors His Son.

The American pastor Wilbur Chapman had a family tragedy occur that made it necessary for him to travel to the West Coast. **A Christian banker** who attended his church **visited with him** just before he left. As they talked, the **banker took a piece** of **paper** out of his pocket and slipped it into his pastor's hand. Chapman looked at it and saw that it was a **blank check** made out to him, **signed by the banker. Stunned,** he asked, "Do you mean you are giving me a signed check **to be filled out as I please?**" "Yes, exactly," said the banker. "**I don't know how much you might need**, and I want you to draw any amount that will meet your need."

Chapman gratefully took the check, but he **didn't need to use it** on his trip. Later he commented, "**It gave me a comfortable, happy feeling** to know that I had a **vast sum at my disposal.**" Friend, our **supply** is as sufficient as the **Bank of Heaven,** a **blank check** for all our needs. **But how do we know** the check is good? **It is good, because Almighty God promised it!** The check is signed by: "**My God shall supply . . . .**"

Blank checks are no good if the person who signs them is destitute or a crook. But if the check is **signed by "my God," the God** I know personally, **the God** who is also my Father (4:20), **the God** who has never in human history failed His children, **the God** who demonstrated His great love for us **by giving His only Son** on the cross, **then the check is good!** "He who did not spare His own Son, but delivered Him up for us all, how will He not also with Him freely give us all things," wrote Paul. (Romans 8:32). **If we meet the condition** of being in His will, **the promise is certain** our God and **Father will meet** all our **needs. You can count on it!**

Here is a lesson many soon forget: All of nature depends on **hidden resources. The great trees** send their roots down into the earth to draw up water and minerals. **Rivers have their sources** in the snow-capped mountains. The **most important** part of a tree is the part you **cannot see,** the root system, and the **most important part** of the **Christian's life** is the part that only God sees. **Unless we draw** upon the deep resources of God **by faith,** we fail against the pressures of life. **Paul depended** on the power of Christ at work in his life.

But the key to it all is in Christ Jesus. He **mediates to us** all the benefits and blessings of God. More than that, He is Himself the sum of all the blessings, for the preposition is **not 'through' but 'in.'** He is not a channel along which they flow, but a place in which they are deposited. It is finally **because of Christ** that Paul is contented, and it is Christ whom he offers to us as the means and guarantee of our contentment. For Paul, **"the person who possesses Christ possesses all."**

Years ago, a man gave his testimony, "I was born just a few miles from here. **My mother was not married** at the time.... and **the reproach** that **fell on her,** fell on me as well. **They had a name for me** when I started to **school.** The **taunts of my peers** cut so deep. What was **even worse** was to go to town with my mother on Saturday and feel all those **eyes literally piercing thru me,** and realize they were asking, **"Whose child is he?"** "I wonder who his father is?" When I was about 12, **a new preacher came** to the little **church in our community** and people began to talk about his power and his eloquence. **I began to go myself** and was intrigued by him, although **I always slipped in late** and tried to **get out early** because I was afraid that people would say, **"What's a boy like you doing in a place like this?"**

Well one Sunday, the benediction got said quicker than I realized, and I found myself **caught with a lot of people** crowding around. Before I knew it, there stood the **preacher,** looking at me with those **burning eyes** of his. **He said:** "Who are you, son? Whose boy are you?" **And I thought to**

myself, "Oh, no .... here we go again!" **But then a smile of recognition** broke across the preacher's face and he said, "Wait a minute .... **I know who you are!** I see the resemblance! **You are a son of God!**" And with that he **patted me** across the back and said, **"Boy, you've got quite an inheritance!** Go and claim it!" The **words of that one statement,** said the old man, **literally changed my life.**

Questions to answer .... Do we ever lack? We have our **moments** that we certainly feel we do. Health or finance, good work or moral support or love: time and again **we feel that we lack, that we don't have what we need** (or perhaps deserve). **Cynicism and discontent** lie then so close at hand, But Paul sets us straight. **Do we lack?** That depends on **who** is central to our lives. Self? Own comfort? Own reputation? Yes, then we lack so much, lack so often ... **Or Christ? Then, says Paul, we never lack.** Whether our struggle be with material shortage or devilish persecution or strife in the communion of saints, whether we be abased or abound, we can be content—for our God through Jesus Christ is bringing praise to Himself. **To achieve that goal** He'll ensure that we always have all we need.

God is for you like an ever-flowing artesian well, constantly **re-supplying** you with strength, courage, wisdom, and financial resources. **By His grace He will** enable you to succeed in the Christian life, and do many good works for His glory. But you must meet the conditions. **You must make sure that Jesus** is the head of your life. He must be your Lord and Savior. **You must** be diligent in your Christian growth in a local church. **You must** give a generous portion of the time, talent, and treasure that God has given you, and invest it in the lives of others and in kingdom work. **You must** trust God to multiply the seed you have sown into a great harvest. **If you have not been living** out of the riches of God's grace, **begin today!**

The reason why Paul was so sure is because he was **aware of the source.** When you get a grasp of the source, you can know the assurance of it because you know that **this God is the one who supplies** your need and **He cannot fail** to do so, because of who He is. **When others fail** to come to your rescue, **remember: my God is able!** When the **well** runs dry, when the **barrel** is empty, when the **path** runs out, when the **light** is dim, when your **energy** runs low, when **you cannot,** my **God is able!** When **there seems to be no way** of reaching your needs at all, **humanly speaking,** what a blessing to know even when you can't see it, **but by faith my God shall supply!**

The prophet Isaiah stated, "Do not be afraid for I am with you, do not be dismayed (do not hesitate); for I am your God: I will strengthen you, yes, I will help you, yes, I will uphold you with the right hand (the victorious right hand) of my righteousness." (Isaiah 41:10).

> "He gives more grace when the burdens grow greater,
> He sends more strength when the labors increase.
> To added affliction He adds His mercy,
> To multiplied trials, His multiplied peace."
>
> Annie Johnson Flint

CHAPTER TEN

"In Christ" the 'Peace of God' Will 'Guard' Your Heart and Mind.

Philippians 4:6 & 7, the Apostle Paul states, "Be anxious for nothing (do not worry about anything), but in everything by prayer and supplication (earnest pleading), with thanksgiving let your requests be made know unto God, And the peace of God, which surpasses (transcends) all understanding, will guard (shall keep) your hearts and your minds '**in Christ Jesus.'**"

The Bible gives us secrets for experiencing **a joy** that cannot be stolen, **a peace** that baffles our comprehension, **and a contentment** that transcends circumstances. We can learn how to dance even when it hurts. **In this passage,** I want you to **study** about the attitudes of **one mature Christian** who learned the **secrets of joy** and **passed them on to us,** even while he was practicing these very secrets. This is what makes Paul's message all the more profound.

Paul alerts us to the fact that there are **thieves that steal our joy. Worry is one** of the thieves. **There are other thieves** that come in through our thought life. **What music** do you live by? **What thoughts** run through your mind? **What noise** distracts you from the dance? **Can you shut out the thieves** of the mind? Some distractions are self imposed. **Has worry** become the center of your gyro putting you off balance? **Worry can become** the center of your focus. **It's wonderful** what happens when **Christ displaces worry** at the center of your life. **Anxiety can** set you off balance. Christ is the answer. **You can't dance** when you are off balance. **There's no joy** when worry sets you off balance.

Why do we, as Christians, continue to worry? We live in a world shot through with worry and anxiety, gloomy in the deepest and most pervasive sense. **We worry** about yesterday. **We worry** about today. **We worry** about tomorrow. People in this world are just anxious worrying people. **We just worry. WHY?**

Someone has said, "Worry is stewing without doing." **Worry is wrong** because it assumes that God can't take care of you. **He promised**

to care for you, but **when you worry, you are saying,** "Lord, I don't believe you can take care of me so I'm going to take matters into my own hands."

The verses that precede verses 6 and 7 above contain the best **prescription for worry** ever given to mankind. For most of us, it almost comes as a mocking, because of our lack of trust in the truths of God. The **first exhortation** that we examined was in **Philippians 4:4,** "Rejoice in the Lord always, again I will say rejoice." The **second exhortation** that we examined was in **Philippians 4:5** "Let your moderation be known to all men, the Lord is near." The **third exhortation** is at the very beginning of **Philippians 4:6 "Be anxious for nothing."**

We seem to forget so soon that once we have **"made peace with God,"** then the **"peace of God"** floods our lives. **Why is it** that we can't seem to maintain that peace? **How do we keep** the "peace of God" ruling and reigning within our souls and in our lives? **Remember,** the peace that God is offering is not based on the belief that I will get what I ask for but rather that I will get what I truly **need** based on God's purpose for my life. **Peace is a wonderful thing.** Peace is something that the **whole world desires** and to some degree at various times enjoys but a peace that the world might enjoy **apart from God's peace** is a very **poor substitute** for the peace that **can be ours through prayer.**

Do we have any 'worry warts' who are reading this? Of course we do! For **all those of you** who are prone to worry, did you ever stop to think how dangerous worrying is? **Did you know that over 100 diseases** have been directly attributed to worry! **Worry** will not only **take away your physical energy,** it will also **rob the soul** of its stamina as well. Why? Worry is the **ultimate act of rebellion** against the rule of God in a believer's life. **How? Worry says** that **God is dead;** and if He is alive, then He is incapable of doing anything about my situation!

The great theologian Ann Landers (?!?), received around **10,000 letters a month** from people requesting advice on various topics. When asked **what her most common question is,** she answered that people seem to be **afraid or worried about something.** They're **afraid** of losing their **health,** they worry about their **job,** and they're filled with concerns about their **family.** People are **wacked out** about their **neighbors** or frustrated with their friends. A great many of her letters describe relational ruptures and family friction. **In short, people are looking for peace** but **never can seem to find it.**

Dr. Charles Mayo, M.D., of the renown **Mayo Clinic said,** "Worry affects the circulation, the heart, the glands, the whole nervous system. I have never known a man who died from overwork, but many who have died from doubt (worry)." **And,** the **Mayo Clinic** actually estimates that **more than 80%** of their total caseload is directly related to worry on the parts of their patients. **Along with that,** the Clinic stated, "52 percent of the people in the hospital could get up and leave if they could rid themselves of fear, worry and frustration." **Someone has said, "About 80%** of what we worry and fret about **never happens** and the **other 20%** turns out **better** than we probably imagined it would.

As a matter of fact, **worry could be called** the most **popular pastime** of the human race. **One elderly lady said,** "I always feel bad when I feel good, for I know that I'll feel bad after awhile!" **What a tragic outlook,** yet many people live right there. Friend, **the bottom line** is this, **When we worry** we have **ceased to trust the Lord,** and **that worry is a sin!**

Let's face it, as long as we are in this flesh, we are all going to be tempted at times to become anxious. But **for the Christian** there is absolutely **no reason** for us to succumb to their **anxious thoughts.** There is help available. **The help** that I am talking about is not the help that is being extended by the world. I am talking about the **help** that is being **extended to us in Christ.** He is the source of help that is perfect and deserves not only our attention but our accolades. I am extremely disappointed when **the help** that is **available** to us **in Christ takes a back seat** to the help being offered by the world and subsequently the praise that should be going to Christ is deflected and diminished. **This worry leads to stress!**

Did you know that "forty-eight percent of Americans say they're **more stressed now** than they were **five years ago,** and the same percent report regularly **lying awake** at night because of **stress,** according to a new study by the American Psychological Association. Stress **continues to escalate,** and it's **affecting every area** of people's lives," said Russ Newman, a psychologist and executive director of the APA." **Psychosomatic diseases,** in layman's terms, are physical disorders of the body originating in or aggravated by the psychic or emotional processes of the individual. **These disorders can** lead to major physical and major mental disorders. It's no wonder that Dr. Mayo said what he did.

Newsweek magazine stated that **23 million Americans,** or in other words, **12.6%** of our population, will **suffer an attack** of acute **anxiety** this year. You might ask, "What is acute anxiety?" **Acute anxiety** is often referred to as a "panic attack." Those **suffering** from a **panic attack** will take a rather benign and harmless incident and turn it into a **three-alarm fire mostly brought about by worry.**

In addition to the great number of people suffering from **acute anxiety** or **panic attacks** you can add all those **suffering from chronic anxiety.** Chronic anxiety is characterized by less intense reactions but of **much longer duration.** Those with chronic anxiety are trapped, in a sense, on Ole' MacDonald's farm. Rather than "here a pig, there a pig, everywhere a pig, pig" for them it is "here a fear, there a fear, everywhere a fear, fear." **Those suffering** from chronic anxiety **can suffer it indefinitely.**

Years ago, I spoke to **a lady** who **visited our church** in Long Beach, California. She had no job, no place to stay, no money, and no food. **She did have a husband.** He **was in prison** for many years to come. In addition to all of that, she had a **stomach disease** that was slowly taking her life away from her.

As I talked to her, I asked her **how she was coping.** She smiled and said she was **doing okay. She said God was keeping her safe.** Here this woman was, in living conditions that were sub-human, and she smiled and **said she wasn't worried.**

Isn't it amazing how **some people** who **suffer** a lot **worry very little,** while others, who **suffer a little** seem to **worry a lot? Could that** have something to do with the **depth of our faith?** Does your mind ever seem to just run away with thoughts of what "could happen"? Dear God, "When will we ever learn to trust in You?"

We all know that stress is keeping people **from sleeping** at night. According to **one study,** the anxiousness from stress also **leads to things** like **fighting** with family members and loved ones, to **drinking** alcohol, to **giving up** on working out and exercising. **Long term consequences** range from fatigue, to obesity, and even heart disease. **Fifty-four percent** of people studied nationwide, said their stress and anxiety has led to fighting with people they love. **Eight percent** said it has led to divorce. **More than three-quarters** of the respondents said that stress and anxiety is making them sick. **Forty-four percent** report getting headaches because of the anxiousness produced from stress. **Thirty-four percent** report getting upset stomachs. **Seventeen percent** say that it makes them grind their teeth. Forty-three **percent** said that to deal with it, they eat unhealthy junk foods, or they eat too much food. **One third** say they lose their appetite and start skipping meals. **25 million Americans** have high blood pressure due to stress/anxiety; **1 million** more develop high blood pressure **each year.**

Being "In Christ" | 175

8 million have stomach ulcers, and every week **112 million** people take medication for stress related symptoms.

John Edmund Haggai, in his book, "How to Win Over Worry," **tells of a woman** who **worried for 40 years** that she was getting **stomach cancer.** Every cramp had to be cancer she thought. **When she was 73,** she **died of pneumonia.** She **wasted 40 years** worrying about the **wrong disease! Even though we may know these things,** it doesn't change the fact that people worry. As a matter of fact, **worry could be called** the most popular **pastime** of the human race.

My friends, **worry is like a rocking chair,** it keeps you busy, but it doesn't get you anywhere! **If worry is eating** you alive and is **destroying** your physical and spiritual life, I want to help you defeat its power. **In these verses, the Bible** sheds some light on how we are to handle our cares. **Worry distorts our thinking.** When we worry we **tend to look at situations** through a magnifying glass which makes things bigger than they really are. When we worry **molehills become mountains.**

Worry is not constructive; it is destructive! It does not contribute to the solution, but **becomes a part of the problem.** I am sitting in front of my computer as I write this. There are times when **I give my computer another task.** For example, sometimes I begin **printing one sermon manuscript** while I am writing another. The printing process takes up enough of my computer's resources that **I have to wait** to continue writing. In this case, both the printing and the writing are productive, at least hopefully they are. **But worry saps energy and focus** that could be employed for productive tasks. **Worry is not only unproductive; it is counter-productive.**

In our desire to be **conformed** to Christ perfectly, the peace that comes from God **through prayer** will be viewed as far superior to the peace derived from any other source. **I don't want to know the peace** that might come to my life through **drugs. I don't want** to know the peace that might come to my life through various **psychological techniques. I don't want** to know the peace that might come to me through the **various written declarations** signed by the leaders of the most powerful countries in the world. **These are but fleeting things which will not last.**

In the original Greek, this word 'worry,' means: "to be pulled in different directions." **Our hopes** pull us in one direction and **our fears** in another, and we are pulled apart **by fears and worries. Sometimes we excuse ourselves** by saying, "I just can't help it . . . it's a panic attack. . . . I'm defeated before I even had a chance to put up a struggle." **Careful!**

We must look at how **important prayer** is as the safeguard to **protect us** before the temptation of fear or anxiety strikes. **Jesus said,** "Who by worry can add a single hour to his life?" **Worry is wasted energy.** There is **nothing productive** about worry. It leads to nowhere! **Worry hinders** us rather than helps us. **Worry paralyzes** rather than energizes us.

Worry and Anxiety are different from concern and excitement. **You can be excited** about something and be thrilled with anticipation. That is **not the same as worry.** You can be concerned about something (like preparing for retirement, saving for college, etc.) **and make plans** to address these concerns and that is not the same as anxiety. **It is when our concerns** become all-consuming and debilitating that we have become anxious.

Chuck Swindoll calls **worry** the **"universal addiction." Paul understood** the **natural tendency** to become anxious. **He knew that anxiety** is one of the greatest thieves of joy. **Worry robs us of our strength** for today doesn't it? **Question:** Have you ever **been so worried** about something, that **you felt paralyzed by fear?** Have you ever **been so worried** or fretful that you found it **difficult to concentrate** or accomplish anything worthwhile or be productive? Have you ever **been so worried** that you **failed to follow through** on something good God had called you to do?

How many of you have apprehensions about flying. My great grandpa once said, "If God wanted man to fly, he'da put wings on us." **Do you like to fly?** My first plane flight was in a Stearman Bi-Plane, the old two wing military trainer of WWII. We took off out of a field behind my uncles house in Ennis, Texas. It was great!

Did you hear about the family that had to put their Grandma on her **first plane flight,** but she **hadn't been very confident** about the experience of leaving the ground on this **contraption.** When **they met her at the airport** on her return, **one of the family members kidded her by asking,** "Well, did the plane hold you up okay?" **She grudgingly replied,** "Well, yes," and then **quickly added,** "But I **never did put my full weight down** on it!"

Many Christians are like that Grandma. **The truth is,** they're already being sustained completely by God, but **they're afraid** to put their full weight down on Him. As a result, **they're plagued** by **anxiety** and aren't able to enjoy the flight.

Worry does that to us—it **robs us** of precious opportunities to do what is right, to do what is good, to do what is helpful. **We get so gripped**

by worry that it hinders us from being effective for the Lord. **Instead of standing fast in the Lord** and being spiritually stable, we are filled with worry, we are wavering, ineffective and unstable. **These words about worry** aren't just for the Philippians. These words are from God's Word and **apply to each of us today** as believers. We are **commanded** not to worry.

I once read about a paratrooper in the **US Army** who had made more than **50** successful **parachute jumps** without a single serious injury. But the first day back home after being discharged, he **stumbled over a rug,** fell against a table, and broke four of his ribs! **He had worried a great deal** about his parachute jumps, but then something happened he had never worried about: **He tripped over a rug.**

Did you realize that worry is a sin? God has clearly **commanded** us in His Word not to worry and when we do worry we are sinning. Often we make light of worry but we shouldn't! **Worry is sin.** Worry is not something that should characterize the life of a child of God. This is **not the only place** we are told not to worry. **Listen to the words of Jesus** in Matthew 6:34. "Therefore do not worry about tomorrow, for tomorrow will worry about its own things. Sufficient for the day is its own trouble."

This will be hard for some reading this, but God orders us through direction and inspiration of the Holy Spirit: **stop worrying!** That worry is sin! Can you accept that? **John Wesley, the great Methodist evangelist** said: "I would no more worry than I would curse or swear." **It's equally as much a sin** as any other sin, and just as any other sin in the life of a believer **robs you of your peace** between you and God, and the peace in your own heart, **so worry does exactly the same.**

I wonder, when you **find yourself worrying,** biting your nails, or your insides being wrenched like a wet rag being wrung out, do you stop in your tracks? Do you get on your knees? Do you lift your head high to heaven **and do you confess it as sin?** That's what it is! **It is just as much a sin** as adultery or murder or idolatry, **yet** how often do **we as believers** treat anxiety and worry as some kind of light thing before God? **You hear people say:** "Well, that's just me, that's my make-up, that's the way I am, I'm just a worrier." **God says** that when you worry you need to realize that you have fallen into sin.

Some people just love to worry. They have made it a pastime. **Did you hear about the guy who** came home from the **doctor** looking very worried. His wife said, **"What's the problem?"** He said, **"The doctor told me** I have to take a pill every day for the **rest of my life."** She said, **"So**

what? Lots of people have to take a pill every day their whole lives." **He said,** "I know, but he **only gave me four pills!"**

We need to learn the most important steps in possessing this peace that only God can give. **Today's verse** shows us **how to have** this peace and maintain peace. These steps will show us how to receive the peace of God, and allot it to rule and reign in our hearts and lives. **When learned,** we will never lose God's peace and God's power.

Prayer is the replacement for worry. If you don't want to worry then you need to pray. Pray about a few things and worry about others? **No,** it says **in everything,** by prayer and supplication, with thanksgiving, let your requests be made known to God. **Pray about everything!** Pray about the big things and the little things that concern you. Don't worry about anything but pray about everything! **Instead of worrying,** the child of God is counseled to pray. When Paul talks about praying, he uses three words in this verse. He writes about prayer, supplication and requests.

William Ward said, "Worry distorts our thinking, it disrupts our work, it disquiets our soul, it disturbs our body, it disfigures our face, it destroys our friends, defeats our faith, demoralizes our life, debilitates our energy, it unfits us to meet our difficulties, it prevents us from thinking clearly, it causes our hands to tremble so much that we cannot perform any delicate operation at all. **Worry is what causes** the crease on your brow, it's what ties your stomach in knots and makes you irritable and hard to get along with." **There are even those who,** when they find themselves not worrying, that they start to worry about not worrying. **I know some** of you are that person. **An unknown poet put it like this:**

> "I've joined the new Don't Worry Club, And now I hold my breath,
> I'm so afraid I'll worry, That I'm worried half to death."

Worry and prayer are opposites . . . like water and fire. **You can worry, or** you can **pray** but you **can't do both** at the same time. **God wants us to know** that there are some **precious promises** that can be ours, if we can come to the place **where we refuse** to allow worry to be our master; and we learn to **bring our needs to Him.**

The real, lasting, Godly peace comes through **"real" prayer. Notice the charge of God,** that "everything (is) by prayer and supplication." **Caution:** Now I am **not talking** about some simple, simplistic "now I lay me down to sleep" prayer.

Question: How peaceful is God? His peace is **absolute.** God enjoys **perfect** peace. He is **free** from all anxiety. **Why is that?** He is **sovereign.** He is subject to none, influenced by none, absolutely independent. **God does** as He pleases, only as He pleases, always as He pleases. **None can thwart** Him, none can hinder Him.

The Bible and history shows that the **Christians at Philippi were suffering** persecution, and humanly speaking, they had every reason to worry and be anxious. **There was persecution** from the **outside** of the church (1:18-19), and disturbances **inside** the church with disunity and quarreling (1:27,42). They had **carnal members** (given to the things of the flesh), while some were prideful, super-spiritual and self-centered (2:3,4; 12). They faced false teachers who were in the congregation (3:2,3; 18-19). **On top of this** they were having a struggle with not having the necessities of food, clothing and shelter. (4:19).

And you think your church has problems? What else could go wrong with these believers? They were facing every trial and temptation imaginable, **these were the kinds of trouble that arouses anxiety and worry. Listen:** They needed to receive an injection of supernatural power. **So . . . they prayed, and prayed, and prayed!**

Brethren: If anybody had an excuse for worrying, it was the Apostle Paul. His beloved Christian friends at Philippi were disagreeing with one another, and he was not there to help them . . . Added to these burdens was the possibility of his own death! . . . What is worry? Being pulled in different directions! **Our hopes** pull us in one direction; **our fears** pull us the opposite direction; and we are pulled apart!

Why are we always in such a hurry? The way that you know when your care is **too excessive** is when you **hurry into hasty and ill-advised situations.** When you **get into a frenzy,** so as to make decisions quickly and unadvisedly and in the heat of the moment, **that is a sign** that you are **over careful** and that **you're too anxious** and **that you worry too much.** In Isaiah 28:16, **the prophet wrote,** "He that believes shall not make haste." Many times, **hurry is part of worry,** but to be a careful person that **waits on God,** you don't need to hurry because **God is in no hurry;** and God is an eternal being. **It's hard for us to remember, God Almighty is** outside of time, and **time is not a factor** or an **issue with God**—therefore we need not hurry or make haste in our decisions. **Someone said,** "Our society is one of **"Worry—Hurry—Bury!"** And, we suffer for this!

From the spiritual point of view, worry is **wrong thinking** (the mind), and **wrong feeling** (the heart), about circumstances, people, and things. **Worry** is the **greatest thief of joy.** It is not enough for us; however, to tell ourselves to 'quit worrying,' because that will never capture the thief. **Worry is an 'inside job,'** and it takes more than good intentions to get the victory. The **antidote to worry** is the secure mind. We must meet the conditions that God has laid down for a Godly faith **Have you ever wondered why we all have a problem with unnecessary worries?** We, as Christians, know better. The **ineffective thing in worry is** it doesn't do a single thing except **depress you** and **discourage** those around you. **It doesn't give you more control** over the situation that you're out of control of. All it does is **depress** you and **discourage** those around you. And **the Apostle Paul says** here's **the solution: instead** of worrying, **pray** to the one who **is in control** of **everything** in your situation, **because He loves you** and **He'll take care** of you.

Years ago, I heard a story of the pioneer days of aviation, a pilot was making a **flight around the world.** After he had been gone for some **two hours** from his last landing field, he **heard a noise** in his plane, which he recognized as the **gnawing of a rat.** He realized that while his plane had been on the ground a **rat had gotten in.** For all he knew the rat **could be gnawing through a vital cable or control** of the plane. It was a very **serious situation.** He was both concerned and anxious. At first **he did not know what to do.** It was two hours back to the landing field from which he had taken off and more than two hours to the next field ahead.

Then he remembered that the rat is a **rodent.** It is not **made for the heights;** it is made to live on the ground and under the ground. Therefore the **pilot began to climb.** He went up a thousand feet, and then another thousand and another until he was more than **twenty thousand feet up.** The **gnawing ceased.** The **rat was dead.** He could not survive in the atmosphere of those heights. More than two hours later the pilot brought the plane safely **to the next landing field** and **found the dead rat.**

Friend, worry is like a rat in your heart and in your mind. **If left alone,** it will **gnaw at you** until it destroys your life and until it steals away all your joy, power and energy. But, the **rodent of worry** cannot live in the secret place of the Most High. **It cannot breathe** in an atmosphere that is steeped in prayer and influenced by the Word of God. **Worry dies when we ascend** to the Lord through prayer and His Word. What do you need to carry up to the throne of grace this evening?

Faith must lead to constructive action. Negative anxiety must be replaced by positive habits. (Ephesians 4:25, 28-29). **After praying,** a believer must get involved in **right thinking and doing.** The two imperatives ("'think" and "do") give these two apostolic directives....a **popular axiom:**

> "Sow a thought, reap an action.
> Sow an action, reap a habit.
> Sow a habit, reap a character.
> Sow a character, reap a destiny."

You and I must always remember that there is **power,** then there is **supernatural power** which only God Almighty can bring. **Oh God help us to learn** that the God of our salvation will **infuse us** with this power to overcome the trials in our life, no matter how terrible, troubling and pressuring they may be. **God can, and will infuse the believer** with this peace—the peace of God Himself—the very peace so great and so wonderful that it carries the believer right through the trial.

Of course, this does not mean that the believer is not concerned about the situations and problems he is experiencing. **But, with God's peace** we can walk through the tribulations confronting us. **But dear Christian, there is a difference between concern and anxiety or worry.** I personally know people who suffer greatly because of anxiety and worry . . . **they simply lack the peace of God!**

In His book, "Experiencing God Day by Day," **Dr. Henry Blackaby writes,** "As you no doubt have discovered, becoming a Christian does not make your problems go away. But it does give you an advocate to whom you can take every concern." **Remember:** "Casting our cares is a choice. **It means consciously handing** over our anxiety to Christ and allowing Him to carry the weight of our problems. At times this is the most difficult part of trusting God. **Sometimes we don't like** turning over the responsibility for our problems. God asks us to turn over all of our problems—big ones as well as little ones." **Dr. Blackaby continues,** "God sees you as His frail child, burdened with a load that surpasses your strength. He stands prepared to take your load and to carry it for you." **Will you let Him?**

Why are some people so negative about life? **I'm sure you have heard about the lady** who went to the **doctor** for more tests. After the tests, he came into the room and said to her, "There is **nothing else** we can do for you . . . perhaps **you should go home and go to God in prayer.**" "Oh, no," she lamented, **"has it really come to that?"** Christian, **why is it** that we make prayer our **last resort?**

You've met some of these folks, haven't you? They face disease, death and all kinds of **difficult circumstances,** not with a sense of resignation but **with confidence.** There is a difference. **One says,** "There's nothing I can do about it so I guess **I'll just have to live with it."** These people **become negative,** withdrawn, depressed. The **other group says,** "There is nothing I can do, but **God will do what's best** and I will trust Him." **This person lives without fear.** They may even joke in a crisis. They **even face death** joyfully and faithfully. And they do all this **because their focus** is **on the Lord** and **not** themselves or their circumstances.

Have you ever gone to a Bible class and heard someone say: "Why do you have to let God know about things that He already knows about? **Doesn't it say** in the Bible that He knows what we're going to ask before we even ask Him?" **Of course it says that!** The way some people pray, sometimes you'd think God didn't know some of the things. **You hear some people say in the prayer meeting:** "Lord, I don't know whether You saw the news tonight, but . . ."—**as if the Lord didn't see it! Of course, He saw it** . . . in fact, **He saw it before it happened,** and while it was **happening, before the T.V. News got it.** We **don't need to tell God** things He knows, and let me say **we don't need to preach to God** in the prayer meeting either. **When we bring** our cares and requests to God, **we are communicating to God** our needs. **We are transferring our cares** from ourselves unto Him!

Notice: This verse teaches us **to pray "about everything."** We should be in tune with God so much that **we are to pray about everything** no matter how small or insignificant it may seem. **He wants us to acknowledge Him** in "in all our ways," because He wants to care and look after our every step. Did you notice "how we are to pray?" **The scriptures teaches,** that "Do not be anxious (Don't worry), but in everything by prayer and supplication, with thanksgiving, let your requests be made know unto God." (Philippians 4:6)

When your eyes are on the Lord, you can **face the future with thanksgiving! Thanksgiving is the key to lasting peace.** When you **look up** you will find **abundant reasons** for **thankfulness.** When you **look around,** even more reasons for thanksgiving present themselves to the saint of God. When you **look ahead,** you can do so with thanksgiving **when you know Who holds your tomorrows. Faith is thankful** when it faces the future because real **faith does not concern itself** with tomorrow. **Faith contents itself** to look into the face of God, knowing that while

tomorrow might be filled with its share of pain and disappointment, **faith knows** that **He holds all the tomorrows** of life in His hand.

For example: In 1621, a band of 46 Puritans and 91 Native Americans held a **special day of thanksgiving to praise the Lord** for a bountiful harvest. A bad winter had reduced their number from 102 to 46. A hard winter, disease and illness, a lack of food had dwindled their number. **We may wonder** what they had to be thankful for: **they were thankful for God's grace,** His **provision** and His **mercy! The Pilgrims looked up!** God's blessings came down, and they were thankful.

The **"peace of God"** does **pass all** our understanding. It is beyond anything we could ask or think. **God's peace** in our lives, while there is turbulence and trouble all around us, surpasses all our imaginings. **Perhaps you have gone through, or are going through** a terrible situation in your life. **Remember:** God is far greater than anything you can ever think about or experience. **Peace cannot be explained.** We **can experience** peace, but we **cannot explain** it. It is a **divine gift** that comes from God so our circumstances cannot change this peace.

Know this: the **peace** that the **world offers** is very fragile. It is **not found in a pill** or a **bottle.** It is not found, even in the very **best of religions. The peace** that is offered in and by the world is **here today and gone tomorrow.** Why? Because the very factors that were at work to produce the initial peace can change at any moment. The world and everything in the world is very fluid. **If you had a choice, what would you rather have?** The peace that the **world** offers, which is fragile and transitory, **or God's** peace, which is perfect and forever? **Is there really even a choice?**

We must understand that there is **no peace** with God except through Christ! **Peace** is God's extraordinary **gift** to His children. **Peace** is the legacy, which He alone, has the power and resources to leave to His family. **All other peace which the carnal mind** thinks about, besides this, is a mockery and a delusion. **When hunger** can be relieved without food, and **when thirst** can be quenched without drink, and **when weariness** can be removed without rest, then, and **not till then** will men find peace without Christ, and believe me, it can't be done.

The Bible is full of God's peaceful promises. The reason you don't know about them is **you don't study the Bible!** Didn't Isaiah say: "Thou wilt keep him in perfect peace whose mind is stayed on Thee?" **How can you do that?** Well, **it's so simple it's profound.** It's what **Peter** said in 1 Peter 5 verse 7: "Cast all your care upon Me, for I care for you." **If God can't handle it, you sure can't! Amen?**

A lady said to her husband: "Why can't you sleep? You've been walking up and down, pacing the bedroom floor since 3 a.m. this morning." He says: "Honey, **I've borrowed a thousand dollars** from the next-door neighbor, and I haven't got it to give it back to him. I can't pay him and I've to pay him back tomorrow." **The wife** jumps out of bed, flings open the windows, sticks her head out and **shouts:** "Sam! Sam!" **After a few minutes** the groggy **neighbor opens** his window, and stuck his head out: "What is it?" he mumbles. "You know that thousand dollars that my husband owes you?" "Yes!" "Well, he hasn't got it!" **She closes the window,** goes back to bed, **turns to her husband and says:** "Now you go to sleep and let him pace the floor and worry about it!" **In other words, learn to give** your **worries** to God and let Him handle them.

There are some people who don't understand **how God can help them. One person may say,** "My problem is **so big that you could not understand it."** That may be true, but God can understand your problem. There is no **problem** you can have that is **so big that God cannot understand. Someone else may say,** but my problem **causing me anxiety** is so small that I would not want to trouble God with it. **Let me tell you** that there is **no trouble** that is **too small.** That is **what the Bible tells us** to do, to take anything that is causing us anxiety to God in prayer. **Do you remember the Joseph Scriven's poem,** "Oh, what peace we often forfeit, oh, what needless pain we bear, all because we do not carry, everything to God in prayer."

Now, let me ask you, do you have this kind of peace that Paul is writing about? **Bought by Christ** with His own blood, **offered by Christ** freely to all who are willing to receive it—**is this peace your own? My friend,** you should not rest or sleep until you have given this question a satisfactory answer. In fact, one reason some of you **cannot sleep** at night, and need a sleeping pill is, you lie there '**worrying**' about things you can do nothing about.

The **fountain** from which **true peace** is drawn is the **justification of God.** The peace I'm trying to describe is not some dreamy feeling, without any reason or foundation. The reason a child of God has lasting true peace is that **he knows his sins are forgiven. The Bible says that our sins** are blotted out of the book of God's remembrance. They are cleaned away, pardoned, wiped out. **God says** He casts them to the depths of the sea . . . and, casts them behind His back.

The greatest area of sin in the believer's life is not the area of **actions** but the area of **thought.** There is a whole classification of sins that we would have to call sins of the mind. What was the **first sin of Lucifer?** It was **pride.** What is that? A **sin of the mind.** What is **lust?** A sin of the mind. What is **covetousness?** A sin of the mind. **Greed?** A sin of the mind. **Suspicion?** A sin of the mind. **Jealousy?** A sin of the mind. **Discouragement?** A sin of the mind. We could go on and on.

Those sins are more real to the child of God than such sins as adultery and murder and theft. **That is a testimony** to the fact there is **a warfare going on. Satan** always **attacks the mind.** Therefore this word of the Apostle Paul concerning the use we make of our minds is so relevant to us today: "meditate, ruminate, dwell on these things."

To Paul, God is the God of peace. This, in fact, is **his favorite title** for God. "And the God of peace will crush Satan under your feet shortly. The grace of our Lord Jesus Christ be with you. Amen." (Romans 16:20) **To a Jew,** peace was never merely a negative thing; it was **never merely the absence of trouble;** peace was everything which makes for a man's highest good. **Only in the friendship of God** can a man find life as life was meant to be. **To the Christian,** this peace issued especially in right relationships. It is **only by the grace of God** that we can enter into a right relationship with God and with our fellow men. **The God of peace** is the **God who is able** to make life what it was meant to be, **by enabling us** to enter into fellowship with Himself and fellowship with our fellow men.

Now notice what this peace does, (verse 7). "The **peace of God** which surpasses all comprehension shall guard your hearts and your minds in Christ Jesus." **Guard you from what?** From anxiety, from doubt, from heartache, from fear, from distress. **What great truth! That term "shall guard" is a military term,** it literally means shall keep guard over, shall **protect.** The Philippians **lived in a garrison town** where Roman soldiers were stationed to watch out for the Roman interests in that part of their world. They knew what a sentry was, what a guard was, what a garrison was... a **protector.**

I can tell you right now, beyond the shadow of a doubt, the **world will not** be able to understand this peace, **when we are in it.** They will look at us when everything around us might seem to dictate to them that we should we anxious and all that they see in us is an absolute and perfect peace. **This is a supernatural peace** that is ours **'in Christ'** which **they will not** be able to fully **understand.**

We have learned the solution to anxiety **from these scriptures.** For many **people in** the **medical world** the **solution** to the **problems** of anxiety and worry and stress is **medicinal.** Usually **various** benzodiazepins such as Valium, Xanax, Activan or Klonopin are prescribed as the first level of treatment. **A pill for this ... and that!**

At other times this help is found in **various therapies** offered by most mental health professionals such as "cognitive restructuring", "relaxation training" or "distraction." **Without being too critical,** should we, as the disciples of Christ start lining up at the doors of these **well-meaning counselors** and pay the **$75 to $200 per hour** for their help in overcoming anxiety? **I believe** that **the answer** to this question is, **NO!** And why is this? **We already know** the **answer** to this question as we continue our study of **Philippians 4:4-9.** (Read it slowly again).

Friend, if we fail to pray about our cares and concerns then of course we can be anxious even if we are a true Christian and truly desire to live for Him. **If you are a Christian reading this, let me ask you a question. How can** a true born again Christian who is **seeking to live** for the Lord **continue to be anxious** if they have truly turned all their anxiety over to the Lord and are trusting Him for the perfect outcome? **The answer is it can't be done.** What is **God's solution** to **anxiety** or even the threat of it? **Prayer!** Do not discount the power of prayer!

I am a firm believer that there are many people who **come to Christ** because they **are anxious** and they want the peace He offers. **But if they do not** confront the fact that they are living to **please themselves rather** than God, they will simply settle into a **self-centered life** where they "use God" for their own peace and comfort. **Jesus said,** "Whoever wishes to save his life shall lose it; but whoever loses his life for My sake and the gospel's shall save it" (Mark 8:35). **The peace Christ** offers is the by-product of **enthroning Christ as Lord** and **living for** His kingdom.

And look what Paul says, if you know your God, and you know your God is near, and you **confidently trust** your God in the midst of any trial, knowing that it is effecting His purpose, then being thankful in the midst of that for the purpose of God even in the difficulty, **grants you the peace of God.** That peace will guard you and protect you from anxiety, difficulty, distress, dissatisfaction, discontent, and doubt.

Here's a silly little story, with a point! A man used to worry about everything, and his **friends knew him as a chronic worrier.** One day his friends saw him with a **smile** on his face, **whistling,** and they said: **"That can't be our friend!** It can't be ... but it is!" **They stopped him** and they said: "What has happened?" **He said: "I'm paying a man** to do **all my worrying** for me." "You mean you aren't worrying any more?" **"No!** And whenever I'm inclined to worry, I just let him do it for me." **"How much**

do you pay him?" He said: "I pay him $250. a week." **They said:** "Well, how can you afford that?" **He said:** "Well, that's not my worry!"

Friends, **here's the J. B. Phillips translation of 1 Peter 5:7?** "You can throw the whole weight of your anxieties upon Him, for you are His personal concern." **Worry** about nothing, **pray** about everything, **be thankful** for anything, and the peace of God will defend your heart through Jesus Christ our Lord. **Wow! God give me the spiritual knowledge and ability to teach and do that. Amen!**

Think about this: Isn't it interesting how **God never tells** you to do something that isn't **ultimately for your good?** So each of the exhortations in this passage, including the exhortation to be reconciled, is **designed to do what?** So that **in your hour of need** when all the lights go out, you are ready by your heeding of these exhortations **to experience the peace** that passes understanding. **Remember:** this can **only be obtained "in Christ Jesus."**

What is our response to this **unlimited generosity from the Lord? Too often our response is, "I don't have time right** now. I pray before meals. I take care of my family, and before I go to bed, I pray again. **Isn't that enough?"** We join with the people in Jesus' parables who said, "I have bought a field . . . please have me excused." "I have bought oxen . . . please have me excused." And "I just got married . . . Therefore I cannot come." **We often see prayer** as a chore. **We don't see the privilege** or grace in God's invitation to pray. We often see it as one more verse that commands us to do something.

I'm reminded of a cartoon that I saw a few years ago. **The scene portrayed** the **waiting room** of an **executive office** from late nineteenth century Washington D.C. **A man sat** there next to the **prototype of a new weapon** set up on the floor of the room. **An officer in the Union army** bent over and talked with him. **The caption at the bottom read,** "I'm sorry Mr. Gatling, but General Grant is **too busy** fighting the war to see you right now." **Are we too busy for God?** Do we find ourselves telling the **One who created time** and gave it to us that **we don't have time for Him?**

Dear friend, there is a day fast approaching when all who are **not justified** shall be in utter despair. **Paul and John both** tell us that one day, the voice of the archangel and the trump of God will scatter to the winds the false peace which now holds up many a man. **At the day of Judgment** it will be to late. There will be **no peace** which shall stand in that awful day, **but the hope** of the **justified soul.**

Read out loud, and listen to the words of Christ to His disciples as He is getting ready to leave them. What did He say? **"Peace I leave with you; My peace I give to you; not as the world gives, do I give to you. Let not your heart be troubled, nor let it be fearful."** God's everlasting eternal peace is in our possession in the person of Christ (John 14:27). **Please know this:** The peace of God which will be enjoyed by you and I who are Christians, will protect our mind and hearts from further worry. **Thank you Lord!**

To receive this peace that God gives, **we must give Him our lives,** committing to serve Him as Lord. **As you travel along I-10** in Louisiana, there is a **large billboard** which catches your eye. **It stands high above** the city just as you start up the **Mississippi river bridge.** On it is a **picture of Jesus Christ on the cross** of Calvary. He has **His head bowed.** The **caption underneath** says **in bold letters, "It's your move."** And it is. **Anyone who wants** to become a Christian **must personally make a move.** They **must respond** to all **Jesus has done** for us. **As John 1:12 says,** "To all who **received** Him, to those who **believed** in His name, He **gave the right to become children of God."**

> What a friend we have in Jesus; all our sins and grief's to bear,
> What a privilege to carry everything to God in prayer.
> Oh, what peace we often forfeit. Oh, what needless pain we bear,
> All because we do not carry everything to God in prayer.
> Have we trials and temptations? Is there trouble anywhere?
> We should never be discouraged. Take it to the Lord in Prayer.
>
> —Joseph M. Scriven

CHAPTER ELEVEN

"In Christ" You Have 'Eternal Life'

The Word of God states in Romans 6:23 "For the wages of sin is death, but the free gift of God is **eternal life "in Christ Jesus" our Lord."**

The majority of us would recoil at the very thought of **owning a slave,** or especially, at the thought of **being** a slave. **To our modern minds,** especially here in the United States, **slavery is a concept** that is very much out of place. The idea **that one human** can have the power to force another human to serve him is very offensive to our modern minds. **But I want you to know that slavery** is alive and well, not only in our society, but in the whole world. **As you read this book,** would I shock you if I told you that **you are a slave.** In fact, **we are all slaves!** The difference of this slavery and what you may be thinking of, **is that we have the choice** of which master we serve.

Paul wrote, "But God be thanked that though you **were slaves** of sin, now you have obeyed from the heart, that the form of doctrine to which you were delivered." (Romans 6:17). He refers to the fact, in this verse, that **they had been slaves of sin. While many may live** like this and think that they are free, **Paul makes it clear** that they are slaves!

The literal **meaning** of the **word slave** is the word **servant!** The **rebellious life** would be any life that is lived outside the will of God. It is a life **yielded to the master of sin.** They made a choice to change masters. **Friend,** choices and decisions concerning how we live our lives come knocking every day! **When Christ knocks** at our heart's door, do we open that door? We can either be a slave to sin or we can be a slave to Jesus. It is a choice that you must make!

Let us never forget that the dividing line between the old life of bondage (slavery) and death, and the new life of liberty and life is our faith in the Gospel of Christ. **It is His salvation** that makes all the difference! **Never forget,** when we trust Jesus, we are reshaped by the power of God. **He re-makes** our character into His image. **He changed us** when we believed, (II Corinthians 5:17).

Let me say, I recognize that **slavery, sin and death** are **unpopular subjects to hear and discuss.** It is just not part of our daily routine to get into discussions on sin. **However, slavery, sin and death are universal,** and perhaps this is one reason why the term is so frequently ignored, **and the results of sin are terrifying. Many are sinning so frequently** that it is a **way of life!** It has **become the norm** and now has become **acceptable** because everybody is doing it! **How could this be true?** Because we are slaves. **Did you know that the Bible** says that we are **slaves** (servants) **of sin** (Romans 6:6, 19). Although many would deny that, it's true.

Ray Stedman who was pastor in California, **tells the story** of a man walking down the street one day. He **sees him wearing a sandwich sign.** On the **front** are the **words, "I am a slave for Christ."** After the **man passes by**, and on his **back** the **sign reads, "Whose slave are you?"** Good question: **Whose slave are you?**

The word "redeemed" used by Paul many times, comes from a **word that means** "to loose after the payment of a ransom price." It **carries the idea of a slave** who is **purchased** in the market and **then is set free!** As we put all this together, it becomes **clear that in Jesus,** we enjoy a redemption that bought us, secured us and freed us to serve the Lord. **What a wonderful purchase that is, making salvation ours!** When did all this happen? At the **very instant we trusted Jesus** as our Lord and Savior! "And they sang a new song saying: You are worthy to take the scroll, and to open its seals; For You were slain, and have redeemed (bought us back) us to God by Your blood, out of every tribe and tongue and people and nation, and have made us Kings and Priests to our God, And we shall reign on the earth." (Revelation 5:9, 10). **Hallelujah!**

Mankind's greatest fears revolve around **terminal illness,** dying, and death itself. **We try to sanitize** and **rationalize** it because of its dread. With over 55 years in the ministry, I have observed **many people take their last breath on earth. Death** is the **ultimate humiliation** of mankind. **It comes to all** in the same way, rich and poor, young and old. When they take their last breath, **they all look alike.** That is the **end result of sin in our world,** but praise God, **it is not the end for the child of God.**

Paul brought his thoughts to a summary conclusion in verse 23. **The principle** stated here is **applicable to all people,** believers and unbelievers. **It contrasts the masters of our life,** sin and God with their outcomes, death and eternal life. **Paul also distinguished** the means whereby death and life come to people. **Death is the wage** a person **earns** by his or her working, **but eternal life** is a **free gift** to those who rely on the work of Another—Jesus.

Sin is a curse of being lost. A person whose **lifestyle** is characterized as **one of sin** must be a lost person. They are **spiritually lost.** Sin is their **way of life.** It may be the **sin of pride** as they think they can handle any situation and don't need God. In fact, **their pride makes them god.** It may be adultery, lying or drunkenness, or stealing. **Whatever the sin,** they are powerless to break its strong hold.

"Sin" is a little word and it is often a misunderstood one. It is **a word that does not** communicate well **in our society** today because people tend to think of sin as one specific kind of obvious immorality and if they don't happen to be guilty of that kind of immorality, they don't see themselves as sinners. **They think, since I don't** rob banks or do drugs I'm not a sinner. I've **never killed** any one, so I'm not a sinner. **Listen: Sin is not just bad things that we do**-whether they be big sins or little ones. No! ... **Sin is a state of total imperfection** ... a **'state of depravity'** into which we **are all born.**

According to Webster the word **'depraved' means** marked by corruption or evil, perverted, crooked. **When we hear that** we think, That **doesn't apply to me.** I'm not evil or perverted. **We think depraved** is a word describes **others but not us** ... and that in our estimation we are pretty good. **According to the Bible** sin and depravity have nothing to do with our estimation of ourselves but rather of God's estimation. **Dwight Pentecost writes,** "The Scriptures do not measure men by man; they measure men by God Who has created them. The creature is measured by the Creator and is found to be wanting."

"The wages of sin is death." **The result of Adam's sin** was physical death. Physical death means the separation of body and soul. Remember the curse pronounced by God upon Adam? **Every single death** is a reminder of God's curse. From God's point-of-view every death is necessary and no death is surprising or arbitrary. **Open your paper each day and go** through the **obituary column.** Behind each name you can write, "The wages of sin is death."

Have you ever been lost? There was **a time** in my life when **I was lost.** I'm **not** talking about being lost in the woods or on a highway traveling. I am talking about being **lost 'spiritually.'** I had broken God's laws. I was living in sin . . . oh, and I was just a boy . . . **but, thankfully I realized I was a sinner** who needed to get rid of my sin. I needed salvation and forgiveness. **And Jesus made all that possible!**

As Pastor in Long Beach, California, on one occasion **I went to visit a person** who had **visited the church.** As I **started up the stairs** a man came out. **I asked him if Mrs. Blank** lived there and he said, "Yes, but you don't want to talk to her; **she is a crazy woman;** follow me." I went out by this **man's car** and he took **out a bottle** and said, **"Let's have a drink."** When I related that I was a Christian and **didn't drink,** he began to tell me many things, but finally said, **"I'd like to quit** drinking, and many times I have taken my bottle and **tried to throw it** in the sewer but it **won't come out of my hand."**

Face it, whatever it is, as sinners **we love our sin** more than anything else. **This man had the curse of sin** upon him. **I tried to witness** but he wouldn't listen. I learned quickly as a **young preacher** that when someone is **under the 'spirits' of alcohol,** they cannot understand the 'Spirit' of God. If you have not accepted Christ as your Savior, **the curse of sin** has the power to enslave you. You need to turn from sin and to the Savior. **The life of God is imparted through grace,** but how graceful would God be **if he allowed us to continue practicing lifestyles** which bring death and destruction? **It wouldn't be any different** than sending your children to play a soccer game on the **I-95 Freeway during rush hour.** It might sound exciting, but it will surely lead to destruction.

Paul writes, "I am the chief (the worst) of sinners." (I Timothy 1:15), "All have sinned and fall short of the glory of God." (Romans 3:23). That's what **you need to say to yourself** and about yourself. **Acknowledge** who you are. That is the first step in cleansing, and getting rid of your sin.

Except for Jesus, of all the people who live, of all the people who have ever lived, of all the people who will ever live, **none are righteous.** No one seems to understand this. **No one seeks God.** All have turned away. All have become worthless. No one does good. **A one hundred percent failure rate** ... that is **what Paul is talking about. Imagine a teacher** who has to fail every student. Imagine a **baseball team** that loses every single game. **Imagine every marriage** ending up in divorce. **What a condemnation:** no one, not even one, all! **The third Chapter of Romans is an indictment on my life (and yours), before Christ!**

Here's honesty, although I'm not sure the same thing would happen today. **Years ago,** in preparation for a meeting in a large city, **famed evangelist Billy Sunday** wrote a **letter to the mayor** in which he **asked** for the name of **individuals** he knew who had a spiritual problem and needed help and prayer. **Sunday was certainly surprised when he received** from the mayor **a phone book** of the **entire city. This mayor** must have known and **understood the words** of our text: "All have sinned."

How else have we sinned? Paul says, in Romans 3:11, "There is no one who understands." They don't understand what the **righteousness of God requires** of us, and they don't understand God's righteousness. **God is righteous.** That is the message of the Bible. **This means God alone is holy.** This **means** there is no moral blemish, no defect, no stain of wickedness within God. **He is** morally excellent and ethically perfect in His being and His actions. As the Holy One, God hates all sin and evil.

God's Word says, "all have turned away" (Romans 3:12). Turned away **from Him,** Who is the way, the truth, and the life (John 14:6). Turned away from the **perfections and loveliness of God. Turned away** from Him Who is our all-in-all. **Turned away** from the knowledge of God. **Turned away** from the paths of righteousness. We are all so **blinded** by sin, so **deafened** by evil, so **maimed** by wickedness, that we **turn away** from whatever is noble, right, pure, lovely, admirable, excellent, and praiseworthy (Philippians 4:8).

Paul states, "they have together become worthless" (Romans 3:12). **How useful** is a **wagonload** of sweet corn that you can't get to market? How worthwhile is a **house** at the coast or in the mountains **if you never get there?** What is the value of a **tree** full of **peaches** if you never pick the fruit? **Because of sin,** we all are useless, we all are worthless, in the sight of God. We don't live up to our created purpose. We are like a **peach** that is **not eaten.**

Bruce Thielemann writes about a collection of letters that children wrote to **Santa Claus.** Some of them were pretty good. **My favorite** went like this: **"Dear Santa,** there are three little boys who live at our house. There is **Jeffrey;** he is 2. There is **David;** he is 4. And there is **Norman;** he is 7. Jeffrey is good some of the time. David is good some of the time. **But Norman** is good all of the time. **I am Norman."** Poor, misguided, little Norman. **He needs to hear the truth** about himself: "there is no one who is good, not even one" (Romans 3:12).

"All have sinned." **What an indictment** on the morality of mankind. **We all stand condemned** before God. **We all are worthy of judgment** and death because the wages of sin is death (Romans 6:23). I am sure you get the point. **In the same way as an employee** has a right to his or her **wages,** so **the sinner** has a right to his or her wages. **In the same way as justice** demands that an **employee be paid,** so justice demands that a **sinner be paid.** In the same way as it **would be unjust,** and therefore wrong, to **defraud the laborer** of his wages, so it **would be unjust,** and therefore **wrong,** to allow the sinner to go unpaid.

Do you realize that there are those who feel that they are 'not-so-bad,' and that the word **sinner** is abusive to their character. **Don't ever be fooled** by the veneer of **cultural "goodness."** Just because you haven't killed or raped or stolen or committed adultery or used drugs, **don't think you are better than those who have. Do not make the mistake** of thinking you are more righteous than all those sinners out there. You need to be willing to say with Paul, "I am the worst of sinners" (1 Timothy 1:16). You need to be willing to say the words of our text: "all have sinned and fall short of the glory of God." (Romans 3:23).

Some people say, "Oh pastor, you know that isn't such a bad sin," **or,** "it's such a little sin, and after all no one will be hurt," **or,** "no one will ever know." **That's like the kid who had a pet raccoon.** It was such a small animal, so cute and as a baby was a wonderful pet. **What the little girl, who was feeding and loving it . . . didn't know,** was that **Raccoons** go through a **glandular change** at about two years. After that they often **attack their** owners.

Since **a 30-pound raccoon** can be **equal** to a **100-pound dog** in a scrap, the pastor felt **compelled to mention** the change coming to a pet raccoon **owned by** this young friend of mine, **Susie.** She listened **politely** as I explained the coming danger. **I'll never forget her answer.** "It will be different for me" And she smiled as **she added, "Bandit wouldn't hurt me.** He just wouldn't." **Three months later** Susie underwent **plastic surgery** for **facial lacerations** sustained when her **adult raccoon attacked** her for no apparent reason. Bandit was released into the wild.

Listen: I know that some **sin is beautiful, enticing and alluring. Did you know** the Bible even says, that people "enjoy the passing pleasures of sin." (Hebrews 11:25). **Sin often comes dressed** in an adorable guise, and as we play with it, how easy it is to say, "It will be different for me." **We have all indulged in sin, every one of us!** Believe me, the results are predictable.

In his book, "Whatever Became of Sin?" **Dr. Carl Mennenger,** M.D., **tells the story** of a stern-faced, **plainly dressed man** who was **standing on the corner** of a busy **intersection in Chicago.** As people hurried by, **he would solemnly lift his right arm, point to the person nearest him, and speak loudly the single word, GUILTY!** Then without any change of expression, he would resume his still stance for a **few moments,** and then he would **again raise his arm, point** to someone else passing by, and **pronounce** the one word: **GUILTY!** When he did this, **one man turned to another** and exclaimed, **How did he know?** This street corner prophet had odd methods but **his sermon** was **absolutely accurate.** I could repeat it this morning and **point** at everyone in the congregation **including myself** and accurately say the same thing: **GUILTY!** because as Paul says in **this verse from Romans, everyone is GUILTY of this thing called sin.**

"The wages of sin is death." **Sometimes this phrase** is used to explain what happens to notorious sinners. **When Jeffrey Dahmer,** the serial killer from Milwaukee who ate parts of his victims, was beat to death with a pipe more than one person said, 'The wages of sin is death.' **Almost two decades ago Magic Johnson** admitted he **had AIDS** because of a promiscuous, irresponsible lifestyle. 'The wages of sin is death.' **When a serial killer** is put to death by lethal injection we want to say, 'The wages of sin is death.' **When it comes right down to it, every single death** is the result of sin. **Every single death** is a reminder of God's curse. **From God's point-of-view every death** is necessary and no death is surprising or arbitrary.

The result of Adam's sin was also spiritual death. **Spiritual death means** the separation of man from God. **Do you remember** what Adam and Eve did when they fell into sin? **They** "hid from the Lord God among the trees of the garden" (Genesis 3:8). **Suddenly man was afraid of God.** Suddenly man could not stand to be in the holy presence of God. Suddenly man **was ashamed** and could not measure up and was unworthy. Man was separated from God. Remember also how **God chased** Adam and Eve **out of the Garden?** He drove them out from His presence. Man was separated from God. **Without being "in Christ,"** we are still separated.

To be away from God means to be away from life. To be away from God **means** to be in the **presence of death.** And, to be eternally away from God means to be in the **presence of eternal death.** In fact, that is **what hell is like.** Separation from Himself is God's eternal punishment upon those who are unrepentant sinners: "Depart from me, you who are cursed," **He says,** "into the eternal fire prepared for the devil and his angels" (Matthew 25:41). One the meanings of Hell is: **to be eternally separated** from the presence of God. "The wages of sin is death." **Many people object** to this teaching. They think it is unfair and unjust of God that people end up in hell.

A man said to a minister one day, "I did not like your sermon today." "Why," asked the minister? "Well," said the man, "I do not like your Savior." "Why would you say that," asked the minister? **The man said,** "Because He sends men to hell."

The pastor replied, "I have never heard of Him sending anyone there. Men send themselves there, because they refuse love."

That is true! Men **send themselves** to hell. **It is what they earn.** It is what they deserve. **Jesus is never at fault** because a soul goes to hell. Never! Never! No soul confronting Jesus in that great and awful Judgment day can ever say, "I am lost through your fault." **None can ever say** that to Him. For don't forget, "The wages of sin is death."

Here is a riddle: What do ministers, teachers, hermits, presidents, and guilty prisoners have in common? **The answer is sin.** But many people don't see this.

And many people don't believe this. "All have sinned..." (Romans 3:23).

Sin is 'not' like a disease that some contract and others escape. **Some may self-righteously think** they are **better than others** because of outward appearance—living by sight—**but we have all been soiled and ruined by it.** "There is none righteous, no, not one." (Romans 3:10). **Perfection is gone,** and because of sin, we have all come short of the glory of God.

I have had people tell me, "If I want to sin . . . it's my business." **and,** "It won't hurt anybody but me." **If you think that sin is just a private thing** that we just do by ourselves, or with consenting adults, look around. **There is someone who is reading this,** that will **tell you** from experience **that sin never happens in isolation.** It always has an effect way beyond what we'd like to believe. And if you don't believe this, look around at your friends, family and neighbors (be honest), and **see the brokenness of unfulfilled lives.**

I read this poem in a sermon by Ray Stedman.

> *"I said a very naughty word only the other day.*
> *It was a truly naughty word I had not meant to say.*
> *But then, it was not really lost, when from my lips it flew;*
> *My little brother picked it up, and now he says it, too."*

Sin never happens in isolation.

There are Gospel tracts that I have given out that have this on the front: "What you have to do to go to Hell . . ." **Then, on the inside,** the tract is **blank.** Suggesting that **the sinner must do nothing** to go to Hell. I know what they are saying, and if the **sinner does nothing,** spiritually speaking, he will go to Hell. However, I would like to **submit to you** that in fact, **the sinner must work hard** to get to Hell! To go there, **he must**

get over several obstacles God has placed in his way. **Question:** What obstacles are in the way? **Answer:** The Bible, Jesus, the church, the blood, the Holy Spirit, the prayers of God's people, and many more. **The fact is,** God does not want you, or anyone for that matter, to go to Hell. **2 Pet. 3:9 states,** "... not willing that any should perish, but that all should come to repentance." **But you will** if you don't come to Jesus! **What a waste of life** it is to live without God!)

According to Paul's words in our text, **sin is an addiction.** Modern psychology may be right in drawing our attention to our addictions, **but it fails in many ways to deal** with sin as it should. **First, psychology tends to avoid** the fact that addiction is sin. **Often,** the **label of addiction** serves as an excuse for sin and not as an identification of sin. **Psychology is also wrong** in the way it seeks to deal with addiction. **Its "cure" for addiction** is really a curse. **Jesus Christ is the only cure** for our addiction to sin, any sin. **The many "Twelve Step" programs** which seek to deal with addiction refer to a **"higher power,"** but they **do not point to Jesus Christ, Who is that Higher Power, and the cross** of **Calvary alone** as the means of deliverance. Man's help comes from a "higher power," a "god" of our own definition. Man will find no deliverance in a higher power, other than Jesus!

Especially in our public schools, there is a contemporary slogan that expresses the best "deliverance" the world can offer from addiction: **"Just say no."** This is no different than the **legalism of the Judaizers.** As Paul will make clear, **we are not able to say no. Adding rules does not remedy sin;** it even promotes sin. **The only remedy to the addiction of sin is "Just say yes." What? Just say yes to the offer** of salvation in Jesus Christ. **Have you received God's deliverance** from sin's penalty and power? If not, I pray that you will.

Charles Haddon Spurgeon told this story about the 'results' of sin: "**A cruel king** called one of his subjects into his presence and asked him his occupation. The man responded, **I'm a blacksmith. The ruler then ordered him** to go and make a **chain of a certain length.** The man obeyed, returning after several months to show it to the monarch. **Instead of receiving praise** for what he had done, however, he was instructed to make the chain **twice as long.** When that assignment was completed, the blacksmith presented his work to the king, **but again** was told to Go back and **double its length!** This procedure was **repeated** several times. **At last** the wicked tyrant directed the man to be **bound in the chains of his own making** and **cast into a fiery furnace.**" Like that cruel king, **sin exacts** from its servants a dreadful price: "The wages of sin is death".

But **the good news** is the last part of that verse: "**but the gift of God is eternal life** through Christ Jesus our Lord."

We must, according to the scriptures, know that deliverance from the addiction of sin comes **only from our Lord Jesus Christ,** and His death, burial, and resurrection. **Whatever your bondage** or addiction might be, **it is rooted in sin,** and its **only resolution** is the cross of **Jesus Christ.** Jesus Christ died for sin, bearing the penalty of God's wrath for sin. **He also died to sin,** delivering men from the power of sin. **Have you trusted** in the work of Jesus Christ? Here is the only deliverance from the addiction of sin God has provided for men. **Jesus Christ is not a way;** He is **the way,** the only way: **Jesus said to him,** "I am the way, and the truth, and the life; no one comes to the Father, but through Me." (John 14:6).

"**I'm not so bad**" **or,** "I don't feel like a sinner" **or,** "compared to my neighbors, I'm a pretty good sinner," (whatever that means . . . I've heard it all). **If you** were to do a **survey** in your community, you **would run across many people** who think they are **"good."** And **if they would admit** to sin, they would **call themselves "good sinners."** Many people here generally think of themselves that way. They would tell you that they **haven't** committed murder or anything. That **they don't hurt anyone.**

Oscar Wilde, great writer, brilliant mind, very esteemed man, **secretly was involved in homosexual relationships** and other deviant behavior. **When he was discovered. he wrote,** "I forgot that what a man is in secret, he will some day shout aloud from the housetop." **Sin begets sin.** It's discovered. There's no way to stop it.

Guess what sin leads to. Sin and more sin. Sin begets sin. **Folks, it is cancer,** it reproduces itself. It is a **cruel master.**

Know this: Deliverance from sin does not come by our **mastering sin,** but by a **change in our master.** In our sin and unbelief, sin, and ultimately **Satan, is our** master. We cannot master sin, but **we can submit to Jesus Christ** as our Master. When we do so, we not only die to sin in Christ, but God's power and victory over sin becomes ours.

My daddy used to tell me, "Glen, you become like those you associate with. Be extra careful who you run with." He was right! ". . . **Be sure, your sins will find you out!"** (Numbers 32:23). I sometimes think about **Sinclair Lewis** who was the **toast of the literary world.** He wanted to **mock Christianity** so he **wrote "Elmer Gantry."** Elmer Gantry was a **blast at Christian preachers** and **evangelism,** making the featured character a Bible—pounding, Jesus-preaching, alcoholic, thief, fornicator, and everything bad. **The literary world toasted** Sinclair Lewis, **but few**

people know that **he died an alcoholic in a third-rate clinic** somewhere outside the city of Rome, **totally devastated.**

Listen: You don't get away with sin, it just **begets itself.** And **that's what Paul is saying.** You used to be under sin and as your position was under the bondage of sin. Your practice was there as well. And sin begot sin, and as we'll see in a moment, there's an ultimate end to all of that. But he says this, **"Now you are redeemed by a new master."** As you were 100 percent **yielded to sin** before Christ, so you should now be 100 percent yielded to righteousness, **now that you are "in Christ."**

If you know eating a certain food is going to **make you sick,** you will **avoid** that food. If you know a certain **customer never pays his bills,** you will stop doing business with him. If you know **your girlfriend doesn't like** to be called "lamb chop", you won't call her that . . . **if you know what is good for you.**

Dr. Tony Evans writes, "How do you **grow the new you** while shutting down the old you? You do it by **feeding your spirit** while you **starve your flesh**—those **old, corrupt impulses** and desires and habits. **You cannot feed the flesh,** neglect the inner you, and expect to have victory over the flesh. **But too many Christians** are like people **in a cafeteria line.** They get a steak smothered with brown gravy, mashed potatoes, bread with plenty of butter, and a big dessert covered with whipped cream. **Then they come to the end** of the line and **get a diet drink, hoping somehow** that it will **cancel out the effects** of the other stuff."

Another common mistake that people make is **comparing themselves** with other people (II Corinthians 10:12). **Nearly everyone has heard,** "If the hypocrites down there at church make it, then I'll make it." **The only thing wrong** with that thinking is that the hypocrites down there at church **aren't God's "measuring stick."** Everyone is going to be **compared to Jesus**, the glory of God, and therefore everyone will come up short. **We all need a Savior.** His name is **Jesus!**

Question: How long is eternal life? You say, "Forever!" Right! Now, **how long** is forever? You say, "It has no end!" Right! **Please keep that in mind,** as you think about eternity . . . . **eternal death** and/or **eternal life. Eternal life is indeed** a free gift as this verse states.

You may be wondering, "How can this be?" **The reason** that eternal life cannot be purchased, worked for, earned, or secured is because it has already been paid for by Christ, who paid our ransom with His own precious blood. (Hebrews 10).

There is an interesting paradox which becomes difficult for some. **Salvation is both** free and costly. **God paid** a terrible price to procure salvation for sinners (you and me). **It cost Him** his only begotten Son, Jesus. **Jesus paid** the **full price** in order that it might be **free to us.** (Romans 6:6; II Corinthians 5:14; Romans 6:11). **A holy, righteous God** cannot simply wink at or overlook sin, and act as if it never happened. There **must be atonement for sin.** Law demands a penalty for sin, and it is a penalty that must be paid: "The wages of sin is death." (Romans 6:23).

As already stated above, everyone knows what "wages" are. That's why we work . . . for wages. Paul told his fellow preacher, "If anyone does not provide for his own, he is worse than an infidel." (I Timothy 5:8). This is why we work for wages . . . to get paid . . . to provide. **God says that the "wages" of sin**—that is, **what you "earn"** for transgressing God's law—**is death.** He does **not say** that the **unrepentant sinner** will live eternally in some sort of torment but that **he will die. Sin gives a complete paycheck,** you are **paid completely** what you are owed.

When you work **the job of "sin,"** you **get a paycheck** at the end of the day, **written** out for **the full amount,** no deductions, and the **amount is "death".** Mankind's greatest fears revolve around physical death** and dying. We try to **sanitize and rationalize** it because of its dread. That is the **end result** of sin in our world, **but praise God,** it is **not the end** for the **child of God.**

Almighty God is life! **Almighty God** is holy! **To be away from God** means to be away from life. To be away from God means to be in the presence of death. **And, to be eternally away** from God means to be in the presence of **eternal death.** In fact, that is **what Hell is like.** God's eternal punishment **is man's separation** from God Himself. God's eternal punishment upon those who are unrepentant sinners: **Jesus said, "Depart from me, you who are cursed,"** He says, "into the eternal fire prepared for the devil and his angels" (Matthew 25:41). **Hell means** to be eternally separated from the presence of God. **God, being holy,** cannot allow sin or sinners into His holy presence . . . into Heaven.

Look at verse 24, "and are justified freely by his grace through the redemption that came by Christ Jesus" (Rom 3:24). **The Bible condemns all of us in our sin.** But the **Bible also tells us** about **salvation in Christ.** In other words, sin does not have the last word **if** you are in Christ. Rather, in Christ, your throat, tongue, lips, mouth, feet, and eyes are used for the glory of God. This, of course, is the **real focus** of the **Lord's Supper** (communion) that **sinners are set free** by the blood of Christ!

In this life . . . when we sin, unfortunately, the **Devil is the paymaster,** and he sees to it that you get paid. **This reminds us of the eternal truth that,** "whatever a man sows, that shall he also reap." (Galatians 6:7) Let me illustrate: **As my daddy used to say,** "Glen, if we **sow bean** seeds in this garden, we will **NOT grow peas."** You harvest what you sow!

Dr. R. G. Lee told a story about a **young man** who called himself the **"Kangaroo Kid."** Dr Lee **preached daily over the radio** and this person would **call or write** to express all kinds of **criticism and insults.** They always said or were **signed, "The Kangaroo Kid."** One night Dr. Lee received a **call from the Baptist Hospital.** The nurse said, "There is a **youth here** in the isolation ward who is **asking for you.** He may not live through the night." Dr. Lee said, **"Who is he?"** and **the nurse said,** "he told me to **tell you he's the Kangaroo Kid."** Dr. Lee went and this young man raised up in bed and **told Dr. Lee,** "Tell all the youth you can that the **devil pays in counterfeit money."**

The gift of God is eternal life **"in Christ." The salvation from sin that we all need** must be God-given, God-driven, God-empowered, and God-originated. **This gift is not** from man to God. It is **from God** to man. As I John 4:10 says, "It is not our love for God; it is God's love for us in sending His Son to be the way to take away our sins." **Those who have accepted this gift** understand this principle.

Did you hear the story of the man whose name **was listed** in the **obituary column** of a daily paper by mistake. Greatly upset, he went to the newspaper **office** and exclaimed, "This is terrible! Your error will cause me no end of embarrassment and may even mean a loss of business. How could you do such a thing?" **The editor expressed regrets,** but the man remained angry and unreasonable. **Finally the editor** said in disgust, "Cheer up, fellow, I'll put your name in the **birth column tomorrow** and give you a **fresh start!" We may smile** at this suggestion, **but in the spiritual realm** that's **exactly** what happens when we find **new life "in Christ."**

People who have followed God describe man's efforts at earning salvation in repulsive terms. **Isaiah said our good works are,** ... like filthy pieces of cloth. referring to menstrual rags. (Is. 64:6) **Paul equated our efforts** at righteousness as the pile of stink you avoid in the cow pasture. (Philippians 3:8) **These men and others have learned** that God's love is activated not by our goodness but by our need, not by our spiritual depth but by our spiritual depravity.

As Romans 5:8 tells us, God's action in history to redeem sinful man was not initiated by our loveliness but by His love. **God did not see Christ dying** for His own crimes. **He had committed none!** No ... **Jesus died for your** crimes and for mine. **He paid my penalty and yours. Hebrews 9:15 says,** Christ died as a ransom to set us free from our sins.

As prophesied through the Prophet Isaiah, our Redeemer was, pierced for **our** transgressions. He was crushed for **our** iniquities.

In this world we sow the **seeds of sin** and destruction. **QUESTION:** Do you know what a **tornado** is? It is an ever increasing **whirlwind**. I have seen the **destruction** it brings in property and lives... and you have too. I was born in North West Texas and have **seen first hand** the destruction that a tornado can bring. We had a **storm cellar,** behind our house, where mother and daddy would take us when a storm was on the horizon. **It was a safe place,** filled with food, (vegetables, meat and water). It was **dug out of the ground** and was a cool, secure place where a person or family could stay for days. **The Bible says,** "They sow the wind, and reap the whirlwind..." (Hosea 8:7a). When the whirlwinds came, we always had a place to go for safety.

Christian, once we are saved, what benefit is there in sowing to the flesh and reaping its reward? **Most of us have sown** a **few 'wild oats',** how many of us have spent a **lifetime reaping** what we have sown. How much fun is it to **live in regret? Some Christians continue** to sow their 'wild oats,' while at the same time, they are praying for **a 'crop failure.'** How gracious would God be if his grace encouraged us to continue such lifestyles? Christian, I'm reminded of the Scripture which says, "Be sure, your sins will find you out." (Numbers 32:23).

Did you hear about the **radio station** that decided to do a poll. They **asked listeners** to call in who have **committed adultery. Not one person called in.** Then they asked any listeners who have **had an affair to call in.** The phone lines were **swamped. I find that very interesting! No one broke** the seventh commandment; but **all sorts of people** had **extra-marital affairs.** No one was a sinner; but all sorts of people had a fling. **No one wants to believe** that the little bit of wrong they have done **is going to reap death.** But you listen to me here, sin is real. And its punishment, its wage, is also real. **None of us,** are **"good sinners."** All of us, deserve the wages of sin. **And whether** you agree with this or not, **you will someday receive your wages** ... eternal death .... eternal separation from God.

Did you know that here are people who don't know Christ who **think** they're **good people. The truth is** they're **slaves to sin** and they're totally void from righteousness. **Righteousness has no cause** to which they must respond. What a statement! **The world is full of people** who think they're good people. They think **they do right things** and **good things** and **honorable things.** And **on a human level,** they do. **But when God starts talking** about the standards that **are His** standards, they are **totally void from righteousness.** They're not bound to obey righteousness, they're not bound to keep the righteous law, there's no need for that because **they have no capacity for that.**

In fact, and this may surprise some of you 'super-spiritual,' self-righteous church members, **Paul has a good word** for the arrogant, prideful, self—righteousness, of man doing his best apart from God. **Do you know what he called it? Dung!** (It is translated in other versions: refuse, rubbish, but I think Paul called it by name, and the translators won't write it. Interesting, isn't it?) **If you wonder where that is,** it's Philippians 3:7, 8. **Individuals without Jesus Christ** have no obligation to righteousness at all because they couldn't fulfill it. When I say you're either a slave of sin or a slave of righteousness, that is exactly what Paul is saying here. And nobody's in the middle.

The wages of living in continued sin is death and destruction . . . now and for eternity. We are challenged, as Hosea did to Israel, to "sow for yourselves righteousness, and reap in mercy." (Hosea 10:12). **You may ask,** "Brother Glen, how do I do this, and what must I do to reap (inherit) eternal life?"

You must realize that Jesus, the Son of God, "emptied Himself, taking the form of a bond-servant, and being made in the likeness of men. And being found in appearance as a man, He humbled Himself by becoming obedient to the point of death, even the death of the cross." (Philippians 2:7,8).

Jesus, the sovereign Lord of all, surrendered everything, even to the point of being willing to die the most painful, humiliating, excruciating death known to mankind. **He did this on your behalf!** "He Himself (Jesus) bore our sins in His body on the cross, that we might die to sin and live to righteousness." (I Peter 2:24). **Our sovereign God,** came to this earth **for you! Jesus was God's gift to you.**

This verse also states, "The gift of God is eternal life in Christ Jesus our Lord." **Eternal life is God's gift "'in Christ'** Jesus our Lord." Do you know what this means? It is a reference, **a pointer, to the cross.** You see, **Jesus faced** death, eternal death, so we wouldn't have to. **Jesus suffered** the anguish and torments of hell so we wouldn't have to. **Jesus suffered separation** from God—remember those three awful hours of darkness, remember that cry of, "My God, My God, why have you forsaken me?"— Jesus suffered this separation **so we wouldn't have to.**

Christ's death was the ultimate sacrifice for sin. The penalty for **our sin** was paid in full! His sacrificial death paved the way for every believer to have **lasting peace with God. Paul wrote,** "While we were yet sinners,

Christ died for us ... having now been justified by His blood, we shall be saved from the wrath of God through Him." (Romans 5:8).

Paul states in Romans 8:1, "There is therefore now no condemnation to those who are in Christ Jesus, who do not walk according to the flesh, but according to the Spirit." **You are not condemned** when you are "**in Christ.**"

This reminds me of the 'rescue capsule' on the **oil rigs** in the Gulf of Mexico. These **rescue devices** are there in case of fire, hurricanes or storms. The workers can get into the **tube-like module** when there is a sign of danger. When everyone is in, the door is shut. It then releases down a chute to the water below. **The capsule** then **bobs on the water** until there is a rescue. **The rig may topple** in the hurricane, but those in the rescue module are safe in the storm. **The welfare** of the workers depends on whether they are 'in' the rescue device. **For those** who are '**in Christ,**' there is **now** no condemnation and destruction. **We are safe when we are in Jesus!**

Let me share a note about the last two words in this verse, "our Lord." Even in death, this horrible death, **Jesus was Lord!** He proved this (that He is Lord) with His resurrection from the dead. "Therefore also God highly exalted him, and bestowed on Him the name which is above every name, that **at the name of Jesus** every knee should bow, of those who are in heaven, and on earth, and under the earth, and that **every tongue should confess that Jesus Christ is Lord,** to the glory of the Father." (Philippians 2:9-11).

Jesus is Lord! Salvation belongs to those who receive Christ, "... as many as received Him, to them He gave the right to become the children of God, to those who believe in His name." (John 1:12). **When they receive Him,** they receive Him for all He is—"the blessed and only Sovereign, the King of Kings and Lord of Lords." (I Timothy 6:15). **Please understand,** Jesus is **not** just some "fire insurance" policy to keep you out of Hell. ". . . . He is Lord over all." (Acts 10:36).

Wayne Barber states, "When you refer to Jesus as Lord Jesus Christ, **you're not** just referring to **the position** He holds, but you're referring to **the compassion** He feels for the people whom He oversees . . . . Whatever He does in the authoritative position that God has put Him in is for our good." The **word "Lord"** is used over **745 times** in the New Testament, **92 times** in the book of **Acts** alone, while calling Him Savior only twice. **The heart of the Christian message** in the early church's preaching/teaching was **the centrality of Jesus' Lordship.**

Being "In Christ" | 205

Those who present Jesus as Savior **without presenting Him as Lord** are doing an injustice to these biblical invitations in their teaching. **Dr. Luke records that Peter, in his Pentecost message in Acts 2:21,** for instance, "Everyone who calls on the name of the Lord shall be saved." And in **Acts 2:36,** he continues, "Let all the house of Israel know for certain that God has made Him both Lord and Christ—this Jesus whom you crucified." (Ref: Romans 10:9, 13).

John Calvin said, "As soon as **the godly** begin to be enlightened by the Spirit of Christ and the preaching of the gospel, **they freely acknowledge** that their whole past life which they lived without Christ is worthy of condemnation. So far from trying to excuse themselves, **they are in fact ashamed** of themselves. Indeed, they go farther and continually **bear their disgrace** in mind so that the shame of it may make them more truly and willingly humble before God."

One thing is certain, the **Bible presents Jesus Christ as Lord and Savior** and demands that those of us who receive Him, **take Him for Who He is.** When we offer Christ to a lost and dying world, we offer Him in all His offices. Those willing to receive Him **must agree to submit to Him.**

Martyn Lloyd Jones, who so often captures thoughts in such a **graphic way,** says this, "**As you go on living the righteous life** and practicing it with all your might and energy and all your time and everything else, you will find that the process that went on before in which you went from bad to worse and became viler and viler is **entirely reversed.** You will become cleaner and cleaner and purer and purer and holier and holier and **more** and **more conformed** to the **image of the Son of God."**

To receive Jesus as Savior **without** accepting Him as **Lord** is not a biblical teaching. Those who receive Him must surrender to who He is. No individual can accept Him as Lord without knowing Him as Savior. **Those who refuse** to receive Jesus as Savior cannot know Him as Lord. I'll admit that when I turned over my life to Jesus, I did so as Savior. I was a young man, and didn't fully understand the Lordship of Jesus. **But, I want you to know,** that as soon as I understood the meaning of Lord, it was easy to embrace Jesus as my Lord . . . (my Boss and Master).

"Death", in this verse, **refers to a spiritual condition.** The persons without Christ **don't hear spiritually.** They **can't communicate** spiritually; they **can't produce** anything spiritually. **Death is the consequence** and **punishment** of sin. It speaks of a process and an ultimate end. **Sin causes spiritual death** that rules life and robs it of ifs best qualities. **One could explain** this concept with the words **'decaying'** and **'decayed'.** This process of day by day **death climaxes** when someone **dies without Christ** and is eternally separated from Him. **Death is ultimately final** in its separation.

Many years ago, I was just 19 years old, attending Baylor University and pastoring my **first church** in Texas. Several youth in a nearby town, **who were friends** with some of the youth in our church, **were killed in a car wreck. To my knowledge none** of them were Christians. My youth questioned what happened to them now, what was their fate? **God's Word teaches that,** if they **were lost,** they were **dead in trespasses** and sins before that fatal car wreck. They **entered eternity separated** from Christ Jesus and all His blessings.

"Life," in this verse refers to a **spiritual condition also.** The person who has **accepted Christ's salvation** has received life. They can hear, see and communicate **spiritual truth.** They are alive in Christ. **Jesus said,** "I came that they might have life, and might have it abundantly." (John 10:10). **What a contrast between Life and Death. Amen!**

Jesus is not looking for people who want to **add Him to their sins.** He's not looking for people who want to **add Him to their life style. He is calling men who want to die and rise again.** He's calling men and women who **want to say no** to the **present master** and **yes to a new master.** Grace covers sin. That's right. But it **never condones it.** And further, **it transforms the sinner.**

Because of Jesus, we who are **spiritually dead, are now made spiritually alive. Because of Jesus,** we are **no longer cut off** from the presence of God. **Because of Jesus,** we, like Adam, can **talk** with God and enjoy His presence. **Because of Jesus,** we can **look forward** to a time when the dwelling of God is with men, when He will live with them (Revelation 21:3). **Because of Jesus we have spiritual life.**

Do you remember the 33 miners trapped a half mile below the ground **in Chile,** who were rescued after **two months** of being **trapped underground.** Their obedience to the **rescue workers' instructions** meant their freedom, not their bondage. **In the same way, our freedom from sin** is not bondage **to some divine dictator** who is going to take the fun out of life. **Our freedom from sin** allows us **to serve** each other in love, **to live** our lives with a thankful heart, **to avoid** the earthly consequences that often accompany our old sinful ways, **and to be the revived soul** that God has made us to be.

But that is not all. Because of Jesus, **those who physically die "in Christ,"** will one day be **made physically alive.** Our **bodies will be raised** and will never again die. **Our bodies** will be raised and God will wipe every tear from our eyes. **Our bodies** will be raised and there will be no more mourning or crying or pain (Revelation 20:11 and 21:4). **We shall be made like Him!** The Apostle John wrote, "Beloved, now we are children of God; and it has not yet been revealed what we shall be, but we know that when He is revealed, we shall be like Him, for we shall see Him as He is." (I John 3:2).

This is the all-important phrase: "in Christ Jesus our Lord." We should, of course, ask: **How can sinners like you and me** hope to receive eternal life? Why should we get the gift of life and not the wages of sin? And the **answer is** that we are **"in Christ Jesus our Lord." In Him** we are righteous. **In Him** we are forgiven. **In Him** we are loved.

The question is ever before us, how did we get **into Him?** And how do **you know** you are in Him? In the only way that accords with a free gift, and not a wage. **That is, by faith. Faith sees the offer** of a free gift of grace held out to the world by Jesus. **And faith receives** the gift as a treasure. If you will receive Jesus Christ as your treasure, **then you will be "in Christ Jesus"** and have eternal life. And **Romans 6:23** says that "the free gift of God is eternal life **in Christ Jesus** our Lord."

It is your choice whether you are dead or alive spiritually. Today you need to **make your choice.** You can be a **living example of God's grace** or an **example of Satan's curse. You can be like a cut flower "appearing"** to be alive, but dead. because all your life's flow has been separated from the source. **Or you can be** a **living plant rooted** and **grounded in Christ.** The **choice is yours!**

Paul and Silas presented the claims of Christ to the Philippian Jailer saying, "Believe on the Lord Jesus, and you shall be saved." (Acts 16:31). **And one scripture I have shared** as much as any other when attempting to lead someone to the Lord, "If you confess with your mouth Jesus as Lord, and believe in your heart that God raised Him from the dead, you shall be saved." (Romans 10:9-10).

That Jesus is God is the **fundamental component** of the gospel message. **Those who deny** that Jesus is divine (deity) cannot be saved. "... Every spirit that confesses that Jesus Christ has come in the flesh is God, and every spirit that does not confess that Jesus Christ has come in the flesh is not of God. And this is the spirit of the Antichrist, which you have heard was coming, and is now already in the world." (I John 4:2,3).

The idea of deity is the one of authority, dominion and the right to command. If you are **unwilling** to be obedient to Christ, or live in rebellion against the teachings and commands of Christ, **you have not accepted Him** as Lord. **Paul wrote Timothy,** "They profess to know

God, but in works they deny Him, being abominable, disobedient, and disqualified for every good work." (1:16)

One of the greatest challenges for **affluent Christians** living in an affluent society is **to value the things of God** more than the **things of this world.** Precisely because we have much of this world, it is possible **to be distracted by the things** of this world, to **become preoccupied** with them, to use them sort of like a **spiritual pacifier** as the answer to any particular calamity; **to find a greater delight** in them than in the riches of God.

Do you know the difference between temporal blessings and spiritual blessings. Sometimes they come together. Some of **the godliest people** of the Scriptures were people who **had both** like Abraham and David. Sometimes of course they don't come together. Some of **the godliest people** in the Scriptures were people who **had absolutely nothing.**

There are many 'supposedly' Christian preachers, who are doing their best to confuse you about that fact. In fact, if you **turn on what is so-called 'Christian television,'** most of the teaching that you will be hearing will be specifically designed to confuse you about these things, and to **lump together** spiritual blessings and earthly blessings. **So, if you send** in a **five-dollar check,** you'll get a **fifty-dollar blessing.** And if you send in a fifty-dollar check, you'll get a five hundred-dollar blessing. **Oh, and remember, God promises you health and wealth** if only you will just believe. There are **'supposedly' Christian** teachers who are **doing their best** to confuse you about the difference. And the first thing you need to know is **not** to value the **blessings of this world** over the **greater spiritual blessings** of God, **there is a difference.**

When confronted by such scriptures that cannot be broken, our only possible conclusion is that **the sin-debt that each person** owes to God absolutely cannot be worked off. **It is so huge and serious** that an already sin-defiled person cannot pay it off. **Once a person sins,** his debt is absolutely **irredeemable** by anyone or any action **except through death.** Either each individual pays for himself, or Christ pays in his place. These are the only acceptable payments.

This is important! Scripture teaches that Jesus came to pay the sin issue. **He paid a debt** He did not owe, because **you and I owed a debt** you could not pay. He died for you. **He paid our debt!** You are saved by faith in Christ. You will then live by faith.

There was a little first grade boy who was **quoting** John 3:16 in Sunday school. And **as little boys often do,** he **misquoted** a crucial word. "For God so loved the world that he gave his only '**forgotten**' son." The **problem with so many of us** is that **we have 'forgotten'** God's only son. **We're so proud** of what we've done.

We're so proud of our good works, **we're so proud** of our religiosity, that **we have forgotten** what Jesus, God's son, did for us. **Do you want to go to heaven?** You can. **The free gift of God** is wrapped up **in the person** of God's son, **Jesus Christ.** In your heart and life, if you want to **repent** of **your sin, say yes to Jesus,** and **invite Him** into your life forever.

If you are not a Christian, would you pray: "Dear Lord Jesus, I know that I'm a sinner. I know I deserve your punishment. I know I've broken your law. I cannot be good enough to save myself. **Thank you, Lord Jesus,** for dying on the cross for me. **Thank you for paying the price** for my sin. **Thank you for taking my sins** away. Come into my heart and life, Lord Jesus, and be my Savior. Amen."

Who is your master? Is it **sin?** If so, the wages of your service to him are death and Hell. **I am glad that I can tell you** that you have the opportunity to change masters today . . . now! **Is your master Jesus?** If yes, **then rejoice!** For in Him, you have found **life and liberty.** You have found peace and purpose. You have found all you need. The difference is plain to see! **And, it all lies** in those **last few words** of Romans 6:23, "through Jesus Christ our Lord." **He is the only way** into eternal life. **He is the only way** out of bondage into freedom. **Are you a slave? Yes you are!** But, **who is your master** . . . sin or the Savior?

Pastor David Dykes, pastor of the Green Acres Baptist Church in Tyler, Texas reminds us that **Abraham Lincoln** issued the **Emancipation Proclamation on September 22, 1862.** Although this document declared **all slaves on American soil were free,** it wasn't **until December 18, 1865** that **Congress ratified the Thirteenth Amendment prohibiting slavery.** Many slaves **walked off** the plantations as **free people singing,** "Free at last, Thank God Almighty, I'm Free at Last!" **Sadly, thousands of slaves never left** their masters and **died in slavery** because **they refused to accept the free gift of liberty** that they had been given.

Friend, It is just as sad, when Christians who have been **set free, still chose** to live in bondage and defeat. **Chained** to their past, **imprisoned**

in their impurity, and **held captive** by their fears, **they live as though the cross never happened.**

> "Jesus is Savior and Lord of my life, My hope, my glory, my all.
> Wonderful Master in joy and in strife, On Him you too may call.
> Will you surrender your all to Him now? Follow His will and obey,
> Crown Him as Sovereign, before His throne bow;
> Give Him your heart today."

LeRoy McClard

CHAPTER TWELVE

"In Christ" You Will be 'Raised From the Dead' at the Coming of the Lord.

As I Corinthians 15: 20-23 shows us, "But now Christ is risen from the dead, and has become the first fruits of those who have fallen asleep (died). For since by man came death, by man came also the resurrection of the dead. For as in Adam all die, so also '**in Christ**' shall all be made alive. But each one in his own order: Christ the first fruits, afterward those who are Christ's at His coming."

For the people in the Corinth church, there was no doubt, Jesus had been raised from the dead. Paul didn't have to convince them of that. **It was the resurrection** of the dead that he was speaking to. "So all will be made alive **in Christ**," he says. And he meant it. All will be made alive.

For over 55 years, I have preached many sermons on the **resurrection of the dead.** When I was younger, **I just took it for granted** that people understood death and resurrection. The older I get, and the nearer I get to my own mortality, **I realize** that many actually **do not understand** what happens at death, and after death. Although I am retired from the active pastorate, **I fill the pulpit almost every Sunday** some-where. As I open the Word of God and share the vital message of life and death, I am **surprised** at the **immaturity** shown by some Christians about this subject.

I have noticed that the thought of death often gets people upset, while others began asking questions? **Both, as a pastor and a father** (who has lost two of my children), **death** seems to stimulate questions from others for me. When **my children** were young, more than once they would come to me with **questions such as:** "What if you and mom died?" "What happens to dead people?" "Why do people die?" "What if you aren't ready?" Then the final question was from Steve, our oldest son..., directly, exactly to his mom, "Mom, where is your tombstone?"

Throughout history, people (mostly atheists, intellectuals, and the unbelieving), have come up with some **interesting explanations** to promote the idea that death was truly **the end for Jesus.** People have come up with almost **every possible explanation** for the **empty tomb.** For the last 2000 years there have been people who have questioned, "What if death was really the end for Jesus?"

In 1929, a man by the name of **D.H. Lawrence** wrote a short story about the empty tomb. **His conclusion** was that Jesus had survived His crucifixion, and then he had **fled to Egypt** where He fell in love with an **Egyptian priestess** and lived happily ever after. Can you believe that fairy tale?

In 1965, a British author by the name of **Hugh Schonfield** published a **book** that gained much attention. In "The Passover Plot," he contends that Jesus intentionally planned out and faked his own crucifixion and resurrection to deceive the world.

In 1972, Donavan Joyce published the **book**, "The Jesus Scroll," where he describes his ideas about what happened. He believes that a **Doctor was planted inside the tomb** by Jesus' disciples and once Jesus was laid to rest and after everyone had left Him, the **good doctor revived Jesus** and he went on to live into His 80's. He goes on to say that **during this time,** Jesus married Mary Magdalene, led revolutionary quests for the Jews against Rome and finally retired to a small community where **he died as a Monk.**

In 1995, it got worse. The **empty tomb theories** took an even greater step toward the ridiculous. **A man by the name of Robert Gregg Calvin** argued that **Mary** actually had identical twins: **Jesus and Hurome.** The twin grew up and as he watched Jesus die, he **developed a masterful plan** to **steal the body** of Jesus and **live out the rest of his own life as Jesus** and fool the entire world.

Question: Why do people work so hard to come up **with crazy concepts** for the empty tomb other than the Bible describes? **Listen:** It takes more **'blind faith'** to come up with, and believe some of these stupid ideas and made up stories. Why have so many people wanted the Christian community to ask, **What if? In other words,** "What if the Bible was wrong? What if death was really the end for Jesus? Why do they work so hard to prove it to be wrong?' **I will tell you why.** It is because you can ignore anything else **other than a resurrected King. Here's what I mean . . .**

You can ignore a man that fakes his own death and slips off to Egypt to become a monk. **You can ignore a man** who plotted a fake resurrection to gain prestige and power. **You can ignore a man** who lost his twin brother but tries to make a tragedy look like a triumph. **BUT YOU CANNOT IGNORE**

A MAN THAT CONQUERS DEATH AND WALKS OUT OF THE GRAVEYARD ALIVE!

When Jesus defeated death on that first resurrection Sunday morning, it was, and still is, the **most incredible moment in all of history.** That **one single event** has **changed everything** in this world and the world to come. **I would suggest that each of you,** once and for all **settle the issue** in your heart and mind about the empty tomb, and **deal with the fact** that Jesus came back to life from the dead.

Almost two thousand years ago, in the city of Jerusalem, **Jesus Christ defied all** the odds and conquered death. From a **human standpoint,** it was a long shot. **No,** from a **human standpoint it was a physical impossibility.** It was, and always will be, the **most incredible moment of history. Don't risk your eternity** on something human with better odds, **or in the end you will lose it all.**

Let's remember that resurrection brings us to a quality and a dimension of life we have never lived before. **It is not simply a return** to existence as we know it now; **it is a lifting to a higher,** more free, more marvelous dimension of existence than we have ever known. **Jesus was the first one,** to be resurrected from the dead. **It was the same Jesus,** He came in the same body, but he came back to **a different level of life.** So Paul says that **Jesus' resurrection is a sample of ours.**

The Lord Jesus Christ was the first man (He became a man, but He is much more than just a man), to leave death behind and be harvested into God's eternal kingdom with a glorified body. **He is "the firstfruits"** of the coming harvest. There is wide-spread agreement that Jesus was raised on the very day, "the sheaf of the first fruits of (the agricultural) harvest" was presented before the Lord. (Leviticus 23:10).

The "first fruits" look forward to and consecrate the harvest to come. Then, as 1st Corinthians 15:23 shows, **at the time of Christ's second coming,** His people, all **true believers,** which includes all the believers from old-covenant days, and all true Christians will be harvested into the glory of God's kingdom. **All believers** who **have died** will be **resurrected, and Christians** still living on the earth when He comes will be transformed. (1 Corinthians 15:50-52; 1 Thessalonians 4:13-17).

Christians are united with Christ in His death, burial, resurrection, ascension. **In Christ we are taken** to a place much higher than what Adam had before the fall (1st Corinthians 15:44-50). **In 1 Corinthians 15:45, Christ is called** "the last Adam. **All true believers** will be caught up into the fullness of eternal life when Christ returns. It's also true that

Christians are "made alive" at conversion, but the fullness of eternal life (including most of the glory) is reserved for the age to come.

In simplicity, all those united to Adam in the first humanity die. **All those united to Christ** in the new humanity rise to live again forever. **This verse tells us that a Christian** is one who is **implanted** in the power of God. (Romans 5:18-21).

As believers, the foundation of our lives is Jesus Christ. **In Him we are saved, restored** to the Father, **forgiven and justified** before God. This is **a standing** that is ours by faith, and remains forever. **It is unalterable! Woe to those** who have as their foundation **their own works** of righteousness, **their own** personal goodness, **their own** efforts to remain sinless! **Self righteousness** is no foundation at all! It is quick sand! **It is as Jesus said,** speaking of the foolish man who built his house on the sand, and when the rain, floods and wind came "and beat on the house, it fell. And great was its fall." (Matthew 7:26, 27).

Let me ask you this question: How many families are there in the world? Well you would say, **thousands, and indeed millions,** which would be true. But **there are only two families in the world, as far as God is concerned,** which are extremely important, **more important** than all the other families upon earth. **And these two families** are those mentioned in our text: "Since by man came death, by man came also the resurrection of the dead. For as in Adam all die, even so in Christ shall all be made alive." (v. 20-22).

The Bible simply explains the **condition** of the **world like this.** There are **two families** upon earth: there is **Adam's family,** and there is **Christ's family.** Each of us, and all others, **are either in the one family** or **the other.** You **cannot be in both** at **the same time,** you are **either in the one family,** or else you're **in the other.** If you are **in Adam's family** you are **lost** and on the way to **hell,** which is very bad news; but if you're **in Christ's family** you are **saved** and on the way to **heaven,** which is very good news. We **are not born** into Christ's family, we are born in Adam's. **To get into Christ's family** we **must be born-again,** what we call the second birth or the new birth. (John 3).

Remember: In Adam you **die. "In Christ"** you are **made alive** for eternity. **Paul tells us that,** "by the disobedience of one (Adam) the many were made sinners." (Romans 5:15). **In human history, mankind** continued a breakdown in every level of life, and disobedience to God. **The marks of death** are upon each of us today, the stains of sin, of hatred, of mockery, of rebellion against Almighty God, **all the decaying fruit** of the self-life. **What happened to us?** We submitted to sin. **Submission to sin** means **slavery** (to sin). **Submission to Christ** means **deliverance** from sin and its results.

You may ask, "How is this done?" There is failure of the first Adam, who was of the earth, a doomed man. **There is victory** of the **Last Adam, Who was a life-giving Spirit and was the Christ**, the Lord from Heaven, **slated for victory** with the Father. Each the head of a creation, but **one in contrast** to the other, in Adam all die, but **in Christ all will be made alive.** All that bear Christ' image will come forth from the grave, victoriously, unto eternal life.

Going back through some old sermons and Bible studies I found this idea that I got from **Ray Steadman. It is a rather sobering thing** to realize that we are all dying. **We begin to die the moment we are born,** and the process keeps going on relentlessly. Though **we can cover up** the outward appearances for a while, the **inward decay** cannot be arrested; we are all headed for death. **There was an epitaph written on a tombstone** once that said:

> "Remember, friend, as you pass by,
> As you are now, so once was I.
> As I am now, soon you will be,
> Prepare for death, and follow me."

Some wag had written underneath it:

> "To follow you, I'm not content,
> Until I know which way you went."

Content or not, that is the way we are going to go. Paul is arguing very strongly here, "**. . . as in Adam all die."** This is certain. You do not have to do anything; you do not have to work at it, although some of you do. **Let time take its course** and **it will happen,** because it is not up to you to die.

To be clear: the **word "resurrection"** comes from the Greek, and **means** a raising up, rising as one would rise from a seat. So, what is to rise up? **I Corinthians 15:11-12 says,** "Therefore whether it were I or they, so we preach, and so you believed. Now if Christ be preached that He rose from the dead, how say some among you that there is no resurrection of the dead?"

The word "resurrection," has to do with dead bodies! **The soul does not need** a resurrection, it goes immediately into eternity to first meet God, and then either to Heaven or Hell. **It is the body** that dies and returns to dust. **It is the body** that is laid in the grave or cast into the sea. So the **resurrection has to do** with a time when dead bodies, corpses, if you will, shall be **quickened back to life,** rising up from the grave! **Those bodies sleeping in the dust** are those bodies that lie dead in the ground awaiting the resurrection. **The righteous will awake** to eternal life, but there **will be those** who awake from the resurrection who will not be given eternal life, but will be consigned to history in shame and **have no future part** in the kingdom of God.

Paul writes, "For we know that if our earthly house of this tabernacle (body) were dissolved, we have a building of God, a house not made with hands (glorified bodies), eternal in the heavens. For in this (body) we groan, earnestly desiring to be clothed upon with our house which is from heaven: If so be that being clothed we shall not be found naked. For we that are in this tabernacle do groan, being burdened: not for that we would be unclothed, but clothed upon, that mortality might be swallowed up of life." **The resurrection provides** that new glorified change of clothes! Who will be resurrected? The answer is obvious, . . . those who have died.! (I Corinthians 15:35-58).

One day soon, maybe sooner than we think, this is going to happen and **the dead will be resurrected.** There is a resurrection of both the **just and the unjust,** we are taught in other Scriptures, **but the** "resurrection to life" (John 5:28-29) involves only those who are **"in Christ."** The apostle makes that very clear. **When will it happen?** Paul answers that **great question** in Verse 23: "But each in his own order: Christ the first fruits, then at his coming those who belong to Christ." (1 Corinthians 15:23).

That's the answer: "at his coming." **This agrees** with other passages in Scripture where the apostle says there will be some who will never die. I just wrote that **death is at work in all of us,** and it is, but nevertheless, for at least one generation there will be some who will never die. **Paul describes this in** I Thessalonians 4:16-17: "For the Lord himself shall descend from heaven with a shout, with the voice of the archangel, and with the trump of God: and the dead in Christ shall rise first: Then we which are alive and remain shall be **caught up** together with them in the clouds, to meet the Lord in the air: and so shall we ever be with the Lord." (1 Thessalonians 4:16-17) This is called by many, the **"rapture,"** being **"caught up"** to meet Jesus in the clouds. These are the living Christians at His return.

So there are some who will never die, even though death is at work in them. **For nineteen hundred years,** every generation has hoped they would be **alive when Christ returned** so they might be part of that **glorious rapture.** That hope blazes high in many hearts now because of the **things that are taking place** in the world today. We see the nations gathering in what looks like may well be the final arrangement before the Lord returns. **No one can say for certain** when this event will take place.

It was **Sigmund Freud,** lauded to be the founder of psychology, **who said,** "And finally there is the painful riddle of death, for which no remedy at all has yet been found, nor probably ever will be." **In once sense, Freud was correct.** There is nothing we can do to avoid the inevitability of death. **Yet in another sense** he was **dead wrong.** A remedy has been provided that will enable us to life forever after death in a better existence than the one we currently enjoy. **Rather than sweep death under the carpet** or numb our minds to its chilling reality, we must accept death and **fix our minds completely on the message of hope** we find in the Scriptures. **For God has decreed** a way where death has lost its sting, and the **remedy that Freud never discovered** comes through the **Savior, our Lord Jesus Christ.**

The Bible plainly teaches that, "It is appointed for men to die once, but after this the judgment." (Hebrews 9:27). **Friend,** you and I are going to die, unless Jesus comes first. **I know that I am going to die!** One day the hearse will back up to my front door and load a lifeless body and take my body away. My heart will beat for the last time, and my lungs will breath my last breath. My eyes will be closed and my arms will be folded over a motionless breast. **I want you to know something. I will not be there! I'll be with Jesus!** Like Paul, I can say, "We are confident, yes, well pleased to be absent from the body and to be present with the Lord." (II Corinthians 5:8). **Talk about victory, "in Christ!" Hallelujah!**

Harry Houdini, was considered to be the **greatest escape artist** of all time. I remember as a **boy** being fascinated by stories of this legendary showman. I would have loved to have been in the audience at one of his performances. **He would free himself** from jails, handcuffs, chains, ropes, and straitjackets. When that got boring, he moved on to being immersed into a water-filled milk can, locked inside, and then escaping. **His most famous feat** was escaping from what was called the Chinese Water Torture Cell. **In that trick,** Houdini's feet would be locked in stocks, he'd be suspended upside-down in midair with his ankles in a restraint brace, lowered into a chamber overflowing with water, and then the restraint would be fastened to the top of the chamber. **And somehow, Houdini would escape** from that.

But I want you to know that his **greatest escape never happened.** Before he died, **he told his wife Bess** that he would **come back from the dead.** He even **gave her a secret code** that **only she would know** so that she could be sure it was him. **He was going to escape death.**

But then he died. And for ten years, on the anniversary of his death, which happened to be Halloween, Bess **took part in séances** and **kept waiting for him** to return. **Of course, he never did. In fact,** Houdini's grandnephew announced that he was going to ask the courts to exhume Houdini's body so that they could confirm the cause of death. (Because there's been a lot of debate and speculation about that over the years.) **But how could they do that?** Because they know where the body is. **I mentioned that his wife** took part in séances for ten years **waiting** for his return. **After that final séance,** she **blew out the candle** that she kept by his picture, and later said, "**ten years is long enough to wait for any man.**"

What a terrible thing he did to her. This great escape artist convinced his own wife that **he'd come back from the dead.** And because of that, she couldn't go on with life. For ten years, **she just kept waiting.** How wasted were those ten years? How pointless? How meaningless?

Let me ask you this . . . **What if Jesus** pulled the same stunt? What if He claimed to have power over life and death . . . **and what if He claimed** He could come back from the dead . . . but what if He never did? **What if the resurrection of Jesus** never happened?

Christianity is based on actual **historic events,** particularly in the life, ministry, death, and resurrection of Jesus Christ. **Disprove any of that,** and you've destroyed Christianity. But, praise God, after almost 2,000 years, after being attacked by every philosophy, every religion, every atheist, **the truths of Christianity still stands!**

Through the years, I've been doing a lot of reading and listening and watching in the area of the **debate between Christianity and atheism.** One of the **atheists** that I've read is **Dr. Brian Edwards,** and this is what he has to say . . . "Deprived of the basic tenets of the Christian faith, **the Protestant churches** in particular have become wishy-washy institutions, peddling confusing, warm-fuzzy messages of non-judging reassurance. **God has been redefined** out of existence. Although one could respect the old-time religion, one can have nothing but contempt for the modern **liberal cleric** who believes in nothing but lacks the intellectual or moral courage to toss his dog collar in the wastebasket and call himself an atheist."

Think with me on this, I agree 100% with what he's saying. You **take away** the **core beliefs** of Christianity, then Christianity is worthless. Particularly in terms of the resurrection. **If the resurrection didn't happen, then our faith is useless.**

Do you know what? Brian Edward was **not the first person** to present this argument. **As early as 20 years** after the crucifixion, the apostle **Paul addressed this same problem** of throwing out the core of the Christian faith. When you read I Corinthians 15:12 to 19, you will see his argument.

Let me just give you a few thoughts about what happened to these people that had been following Jesus, and the **great transformation that took place in their lives.**

What happened to the disciples after the crucifixion? **They were** disheartened, they were depressed, the felt defeated . . . they **basically gave up** and went back to fishing or whatever else they did to earn a living. They **certainly didn't expect Jesus** to be coming back. They thought it was over. **But what happened?** This disheartened group of depressed, frightened, mostly uneducated men went on to change the world. **What made the difference?**

John Stott states, "Perhaps the transformation of the disciples is the greatest evidence of all for the resurrection . . . When Jesus died, they were heartbroken, confused and frightened. But within less than two months they came out of hiding, full of joy, confidence and courage. What can account for this dramatic transformation? Only the resurrection, together with Pentecost which followed soon afterwards."

The British scholar N.T. Wright looked at the change in the disciples and how they went on to change the world, including how on one day they convinced 3000 people to place their faith in a risen Jesus . . . **and he concluded** . . . "That is why, as a historian, I cannot explain the rise of early Christianity **unless Jesus rose again,** leaving an empty tomb behind Him."

The great truth of the resurrection is a **final word** to the **skeptic and unbeliever,** and it will be **the seal of his final condemnation,** if he goes down to the grave in unbelief. It is also the **ultimate comfort to the believer,** whose heart may be heavy with grief for a **loved one** who has been separated by death from him or her, and the precious, persecuted believer who is looking away from the persecution and unto Jesus Christ for the victory in his life; **or the believer** who is amid great trials of affliction, in faith, looking to his ever-present Lord for deliverance and victory.

What will the resurrection body be like? In one of his lighter moments, **Benjamin Franklin penned his own epitaph.** He didn't profess to be a born-again Christian, but it seems he **must have been influenced** by **Paul's teaching** of the resurrection of the body. **Here's what he wrote:** "The Body of Ben Franklin, Printer, Like the Cover of an old Book, Its contents torn out, And script of its Lettering and Gilding, Lies here, Food for Worms, But the Work shall not be wholly lost: For it will, as he believed, Appear once more In a new & more perfect Edition, Corrected and amended by the Author."

The transformation brought about by the resurrection will do more than correct and amend. **Our resurrected bodies** will be **transformed** and will be marvelous! **The difference** between our **present bodies** and our **resurrection bodies** will be with few exceptions, like night and day!

I was speaking on the campus of Long Beach City College in 1966, and after I finished the study, **a student asked me,** "Is there any proof of a resurrection?" I opened this passage in I Corinthians 15:22-23, and read, "For as in Adam all die, even so in Christ shall all be made alive. But every man in his own order: Christ the first fruits; afterward they that are Christ's at His coming." **The empty tomb is proof** that Christ is risen, **therefore guaranteeing** our own future resurrection at His coming.

He then asked me, "Why is a resurrection so important, and is it necessary?" **I told the group that it was important and also necessary for our salvation.** The resurrection is necessary for the purpose of redemption. **We have a "great salvation with a living Savior."** God has made provision for all of us, body, soul, and spirit. **Our salvation encompasses regeneration, sanctification, and glorification.** In Ephesians 1:13-14 **we read,** "In whom you also trusted, after that you heard the word of truth, the gospel of your salvation: in whom also after that you believed, you were sealed with that Holy Spirit of promise, Which is the earnest of our inheritance until the redemption of the purchased possession, unto the praise of His glory." Jesus is the "author and finisher of our faith." (Hebrews 12:2 **Listen: Jesus will reclaim everything lost in the fall!** We have a great Redeemer!

The resurrection is necessary for the purpose **of residence.** I Corinthians 15:47-50 says, "The first man is of the earth, earthy: the second man is the Lord from heaven. As is the earthy, such are they also that are earthy: and as is the heavenly, such are they also that are heavenly. And as we have borne the image of the earthy, we shall also bear the image of the heavenly. Now this I say, brethren, that flesh and blood cannot inherit the kingdom of God; neither does corruption inherit incorruption."

The Resurrection of Jesus Christ is the cornerstone of history. At the time of the Resurrection, not only was **Jesus declared Lord,** not only did God accept the atonement He made for our sins, but the **resurrection of Jesus Christ** also became **the prototype of others** to follow in like manner.

Remember, these verses say that Jesus was the "first fruits" (1 Corinthians 15:20—23), **the beginning of a great harvest yet to come. And that great harvest is the bodily resurrection** of the sons and daughters of God. **The church** as we know it, the beginning and end of the **redemptive mission** of Christ, exists between these two great periods of history, these two great resurrections.

How do astronauts dress when they are strapped into the Space Shuttle and launched into space? **They must wear space suits** especially prepared for a new environment! **Street clothes** will not cut it in outer space! So it is with the resurrection. **Flesh and blood** will not cut it in Heaven! **We need a new body,** especially prepared for a new environment!

We all know that life now is stressful, and it can be hard physically and emotionally. **It can be frustrating.** We **now have bodies** that are not immune to injury, pain, illness or death and it becomes ever more apparent to us, that as we get older, not only to ourselves, but to others around us. **As children,** we are generally in good health and we don't usually see or hear much of death. We **don't know many older people,** other than our grandparents, or others who go through illnesses and have bad health.

Be Aware: All these frustrations and situations will **go away with immortality.** The appeal to us is obvious, especially as we get older. **The promise of renewed strength** is particularly appealing to those who have lost their youth, and those who can no longer run can look forward to running again. It's an idea that I think grows on us over the course of our life time.

Not having to worry about frailties and weaknesses of the body is certainly a wonderful picture, but what about the forever bit? Wouldn't it get a bit boring? What are we going to do for eternity? **In the book of Revelation** we're told that for **the first 1,000 years** or so we'll be kings and priests in God's kingdom, helping to rebuild the earth, but what will happen after that? What is going to happen for the rest of eternity? I can't wait to find out, although, I guess I'll have to.

Christ brings resurrection from the dead. This is what verse 23 tells us: **He gives life** and **also he brings us resurrection of the body.** That's what resurrection means; **it means the body being dead and yet being brought to life again;** that's the meaning of resurrection. **This is of great importance to you and to me** because we're **all going to die,** every one of us, sooner or later, perhaps sooner than we think. **We're going to die.** Are you ready for that event? There are plenty of **countries** in the world **where there is little or no gospel still.** We have the gospel, we have Christ preached to us, and the resurrection from the dead. Therefore value this glorious message. **Make sure that every one** of us is **trusting in Jesus.**

Erich Sauer, once said, "The present age is Easter time. **It begins with the resurrection of the Redeemer. It ends with the resurrection of the redeemed.** Between them lies the spiritual resurrection of those called into life through Christ. So **we live between two Easters,** and in the power of the first Easter we go to meet the last Easter."

In 1971, John Lennon released his **hit song, 'Imagine.'** The first few lines say, "Imagine there's no heaven . . . . It's easy if you try . . . . No hell below us . . . . Above us only sky." **In the remainder of the song,** he described a world of peace and hope that would **result from living a life 'void' of faith** and **ignorance of spiritual rewards** and **consequences** for our actions.

Some people consider 'Imagine' the greatest song of all times, but to be honest with you, **I don't get it.** It would take a mighty **big dose of mind-altering drugs** for me **to believe life** would be better **without faith in God** and an afterlife.

I don't want to ask you to imagine there is no heaven, like Lennon did in 1971. Instead, I want you to **imagine there is a resurrection,** like the Apostle Paul did in 1 Corinthians 15:13-22. **What would life be like** if there was no resurrection?

Paul wrote, "But if there is no resurrection of the dead, not even Christ has been raised; and if Christ has not been raised, then our preaching is vain (has no value), your faith also is vain (useless)." **If Jesus did not raise from the dead,** there is no **reason or no need** to **proclaim** from the **teachings of scripture,** because this is the truth that all other Christian truths are built upon. **The same is true of your faith.** Without the resurrection, **your faith is foolishness.** The **faith that brought** you through your trials, **the faith that sustains** you when you are tempted, **the faith that is the conduit** for God's grace in your life when you need forgiveness, **without the resurrection,** your faith would be **foolish and worthless.**

Friend, I don't know if John Lennon believed in heaven and hell or not. I just know **that he asked us to imagine there was no afterlife,** but I do know **what Paul believed.** Paul believed in the afterlife because he believed in the resurrection. **He wrote:** "But now Christ has been raised from the dead, the first fruits of those who are asleep. For since by a man came death, by a man also came the resurrection of the dead. For as in Adam all die, so also in Christ all shall be made alive." **What an inspiring Scripture 1st Corinthians 15:20-22 is.**

Paul uses the word "mystery." (I Corinthians 15:51). Paul cues us in that he is about to **unfold a previously hidden truth** inconceivable to the human mind, but one that is now revealed to us by God, something into which angels long to look.

Obviously **some Christians will be alive** when our Lord returns. This is affirmed in verse 51 by saying "we will not all sleep (die)." **When our Lord returns,** the Christians who are alive will never experience physical death, for they will receive their resurrected bodies immediately. As the verse says, "we will all be changed." (verse. 52). **How fast will this transformation take place?** The verse adds, "In the twinkling of an eye." Probably faster than a blink. **This will occur** "at the last trumpet." **When that trumpet sounds,** according to verse 52, "The dead will be raised imperishable and we will be changed."

The believer has much on every side to base his hope. He looks up to Jesus Christ, the Author and Finisher of our faith, and away from life's trials. **He looks beneath,** where the everlasting Arms are bearing him up. **He looks around,** where the other Comforter, 'the Father hath sent,' is 'hovering' around him. **He looks inside,** where the indwelling Holy Spirit's presence comforts, guides, corrects and challenges to be "steadfast, unmovable, always abounding in the work of the Lord, forasmuch as we know that our labor is not in vain in the Lord." (15:58)

Having been privileged to **fly all over the USA,** I've boarded gigantic jet planes waiting to take off. **As we look at this monstrosity,** we might well stare and question, "**How does this plane** get off the ground with tons of dead weight, especially with hundreds of people, and all their luggage. Will it ever fly?" Suddenly, the engines began to whirrr and whine, and the airship roars down the runway ... and begins to lift off.

Has the law of gravity ceased to operate? **No! This plane,** now with mighty power speeds down the runway. **Now, a new law,** the law of **aerodynamics .... becomes** the **new authority** that lifts the plane against gravity. **The law of sin and death** has not ceased to operate, but **the new**

law in Christ's death and resurrection has overtaken the power of the old law.

QUESTION: Have you **experienced this change?** Some have exclaimed to me that they are **not sure if they are in the family of God.** Some say that they have **had salvation, but** are not sure they possess it now. Some say that they are afraid that they **have lost** this experience . . . and **lost their salvation.** Others, being totally honest say that they have never had a personal experience with Jesus.

As stated, there are two groups . . . . the saved and the lost, God's children and the children of Satan, the sheep and the goats, those on the broad road to destruction, and those on the narrow road that leads to life. In **which group** are you?

God's word dramatically teaches, "For you did not receive the spirit of bondage again to fear, but you received the Spirit of adoption by whom we cry out 'Abba Father.' **The Spirit Himself bears witness** with our spirit that we are children of God, and if children, then heirs, heirs of God and joint heirs with Christ, if indeed we suffer with Him, that we may also be glorified together." (Romans 8:15-17).

In our sinful condition outside of Christ, we are slaves of sin, following the mandates of the tempter. We are captive to our self-serving desires leading us to eternal destruction. Being **"In Christ"**, not only **are we freed** from this terrible bondage, but we are actually **adopted** into His family. **This is one of the most intimate of relationships beyond our wildest imaginations.** Jesus is our Lord and Savior, and through Him the Heavenly Father becomes our Father too. "Our Father, Who art in Heaven," is now our personal prayer.

Being in God's family, we can call on our Heavenly Father. He listens, provides, forgives, loves, cares, chastens, nurtures, grows character and is always faithful. **He is not like our earthly Father,** because He is perfect and eternal. For us today, these eternal truths are mind-blowing. **And in Romans 8,** we are told that our Heavenly Father's love **can never be taken from us as we are 'in Christ.'**

In our new position "in Christ," we also have the Spirit of God bearing witness with our spirit that we truly are **in** the family of God, having full privileges of that family. Why? Because we are **now heirs** with Christ of all that God has. **Today, we may now suffer with Christ,** but one day soon, we will be **glorified in Christ.**

One of the blessings of God that we have **been promised** is: as a child of God, one of the things we can look forward to, is the day **we will**

Being "In Christ" | 225

be resurrected to live with God forever in Heaven. **God doesn't just forgive us** and make us "okay again." **The** end of our **salvation is total glorification,** that is, we who are **"in Christ"** will be raised from the dead and **perfectly conformed to His image.** (Romans 8:29).

As a minister, I often talk with Christians who are having struggles in their lives, and almost invariably I find their struggles come from an **unwillingness to believe that God can supply** what they need. **They feel** that somehow they have to lean **upon human beings** to get what they need, and that if they are denied what they feel they need, life is hardly worth the living. **But God continually** works in us to show us that is not true. **He is all we need. He knows** we need bread, food, shelter, and the necessities of life.

This is our Lord's argument in the **Sermon on the Mount,** "Your Father knows that you have need of all these things. Do you think he is unable to supply them to you? If he can feed the birds of the air and clothe the lilies of the field do you think he cannot find some way to meet your need as well?" (Matthew 6:26-28). **This is a constant rebuke to our little faith** that we do not trust God and believe that if we obey him and walk with him he will give us all we need. **This is the struggle.** But **the mark** of maturity, **the mark** that indicates that man has come into his own, has fulfilled his purpose, **is the time when** he understands with all his heart, mind and soul that God is everything to every one. **God the Triune God. is everything to every one who is "in Christ." Amen!**

Have you heard the old gospel song? "This world is not my home, I'm just a—passin' thru, my treasures are laid up somewhere beyond the blue; the angels beckon me from heaven's open door, and I can't feel at home in this world anymore." **You may be from New York, or Texas, or Florida** or some other state, and you may love it there, **but Paul said in Philippians 3:20 that** "our citizenship is in Heaven, from which we also eagerly wait for the Savior, the Lord Jesus Christ, who will transform our lowly body that it may be conformed to His glorious body."

One day we are going to be changed. We will be **transported** to our true heavenly inheritance! **Paul teaches us in I Thessalonians 4:16,17 that** the children of God who have died before His return will be the first to join the Lord. **It says,** "the dead **in Christ** will rise first." **Those who are His . . . 'in Christ,'** will be resurrected with Christ when He comes. **then,** "those who are alive and remain shall be caught up together with them in the clouds to meet the Lord in the air. And thus we shall always be with the Lord."

For those 'in Christ,' the power of death, the sting of death and the sting of sin have been defeated by Jesus. Death will no longer haunt us. **Actually, for the Christian** there should be **no fear of death!** Revelation 14:13 says death is a blessing for Christians. For the child of God, death is looked upon as a wonderful thing and a great blessing. **John wrote,** "Then I heard a voice from heaven saying to me, 'Write: Blessed are the dead who die in the Lord from now on.'" "Yes, says the Spirit, 'that they may rest from their labors, and their works follow them.'" (Revelation 14:13).

After the funeral service of my mother, a man came up to me and said, "Glen, I'm sorry you lost your mother." **I knew what he meant, but it was a teaching opportunity,** so I said, "Oh, Bill, I didn't lose my mother. I know exactly where she is." **What a blessing!**

The greatest proof of the resurrection is the **transformed life.** II Corinthians 5:17 **says,** "Therefore if any man be in Christ, he is a new creature (creation): old things are passed away; behold, all things are become new." **Ask yourself:** Is there any proof in your life of the resurrection? **I really believe some people** have a profession, but have no possession. **Are you ready** for the return of Jesus Christ in the air? **Will your resurrection** be unto damnation or unto life?

When was the last time you shared your changed life testimony with someone else, or have you ever done that? **Through Jesus,** God gives each of us **the ability to have purpose** in this world. It doesn't have to be anything extremely grand or earth shaking in the world's eyes; it just has to be meaningful in the eyes of God. **Still some people never try.** Have you ever noticed that? **Some people go through life** just wanting to **keep from rocking the boat;** they just **don't want to cause a scene.** They are afraid that if they try and they do something they **might make a mistake** and everyone would know that they failed. So they don't ever do anything, **they just exist.** That can be seen through the **epitaph of a tombstone:**

> Here lie the bones of Mary Jones.
> For her life held no terrors.
> She lived as an old maid, she died as an old maid.
> No runs, no hits, no errors.

There is simply no way to overemphasize the importance of the Resurrection to the Christian faith. **The resurrection of Jesus is the very foundation** of the Christian faith. **Christianity stands or falls** on the validity and the historical reality, of the Resurrection. **The apostle Paul says in** I Corinthians 15:17 **that** "if Christ be not raised from the dead, your faith is in vain." **The Apostle Peter** makes a similar statement in I Peter 1:3, where he states that **our lively hope is based on** "the resurrection of Jesus Christ from the dead."

Paul included many references to Christ's resurrection and in his letter to the Romans, began by referring to Jesus with this qualification, "he was declared to be the Son of God with power and holiness by his resurrection from the dead." (Romans 1:4). **By Him and his resurrection** we have **received grace,** and may know the power of his resurrection. (Phil. 3:9)

In Romans 4:23-25 the death and resurrection of Christ are declared to be '**essential**' to our justification. **The words,** "it was credited to him" were written not for Christ alone, **but also for us** who believe and are credited the righteousness of God. **Jesus was in fact delivered** over to death for the payment of our sins, and **He was raised to life by God for our justification. Wow!** When I consider the "awe-someness" of that fact, **I am stirred deep** down within my soul! **Do you realize that if Jesus** had died for our sins, **but had not risen** from the dead that there would **still be no basis** for our justification, and therefore **no hope** of our resurrection?

We must come to the realization that this life in the flesh, **is not going to last forever. Psalm 90:9-10 tells us that our lives** here on this earth are but a sigh, and that we are fortunate if we might live 70 or 80 years. **James records life as only** "a vapor that appears for a little while and then vanishes away." (4:14).

Folks, this is not morbid, it is beautiful, graphic language about our future. The writer of Hebrews states, "It is appointed for men to die once, but after this the judgment." You might think that news is bad ... but it definitely gets better. **Being 'in Christ'** means that all those who are at your Memorial or Funeral to mourn your death will know that you have passed on to a much better place. **What a blessing!**

There is a story about an elderly grandfather having a **last talk** with his teenage **grandson.** The grandfather, knowing that he had but a **few days to live,** decided to impart some wisdom to his offspring. He sat the young man down and **asked him about his plans for life.** The lad conveyed to his grandfather that he planned to graduate from High School and **get a job. The grandfather asked, "What then?"** Well, the young man said, "I guess I'll look around and **find a girl to marry."** The grandfather asked again, **"What then?"** The boy responded, "well, I guess we will **have some kids** and raise a family." Again, the grandfather asked, **"What then?"**

The young boy by now was a **little annoyed** with grandfather's repetitious question, but wanting to please he responded that he guess he'd someday retire and see his kids start their families also. **Grandfather smiled** and calmly asked again, **"What then?"** By now the young man **was running out of things** that he imagined that he'd do in life, and just said, **Well, I guess I'll die. Then Grandfather asked** the young man, **"Will you be ready to die ... what then?"**

If you want real peace today and for an eternity to come, **give yourself** to the one Who has risen. **Turn your life over to Jesus Christ. Please:** Make sure you belong to Him. **One of my favorite hymns was written by Bill Gaither.** These words perfectly explain the **peace in the midst of the hardships of life** because of the resurrection.

> "Because He Lives,
> I Can Face Tomorrow
> Because He Lives,
> All Fear Is Gone
> Because I Know He Holds The Future,
> And Life Is Worth The Living,
> Just Because He Lives"

Today, if you are struggling with peace, maybe ... just maybe it is because you have never come to grips with **the truth of the resurrection.** No matter what life throws at you, **you can face the future because of your faith in Him.**

As I watch society, it seems that practically **nobody prepares for death** or even plans on dying, yet it is **the most inevitable thing** in life. **It is a subject** that we just **don't like to think about.** Most people think that it is a little **bit morbid** to even give a thought to dying, but we need to pause to **consider the fact** that **this life is** but a mere **vapor** that appears for awhile, then **vanishes.** That death is a simple doorway into eternity. **We need to realize** that on the other side of death's valley stands our Creator and our Judge.

Christian, if the God of the universe is on your side, who can be against you? **You do not have to live in defeat,** discouragement, or doubt. **If God can raise Jesus** from the dead, is there anything in your life too hard for Him to help you?

Is there any besetting sin so strong that God can not give you the power to live in victory? **By counting yourself dead to sin** and alive to Christ, **by yielding** your bodies to be an offering of righteousness, **by reaping** the benefits of holiness, **by living** in obedience to God's Word, and God's ways, **you can experience** the **abundant life that Jesus promised to us. Jesus said,** "I come to give you life, and that you might have it more abundantly." (John 10:10). **Hallelujah!**

> "When I shall come to the end of my way,
> When I shall rest at the close of the day
> When "Welcome Home" I shall hear Jesus say,
> O that will be sunrise for me.
> When life is over and daylight is passed,
> In heaven's harbor my anchor is cast,
> When I see Jesus my Savior at last,
> O that will be sunrise for me.
> Sunrise tomorrow, sunrise tomorrow,
> Sunrise in glory is waiting for me;
> Sunrise tomorrow, sunrise tomorrow,
> Sunrise with Jesus for eternity.

W. C. Poole

CHAPTER THIRTEEN

"In Christ," We Have Ultimate 'VICTORY!'

God's Word shouts to us in I Corinthians 15:56-57, "The sting of death is sin, and the strength of sin is in the law. Thanks be to God, Who gives us the **victory** through our Lord Jesus Christ, therefore my beloved brethren, be steadfast, immovable, always abounding in the work of the Lord, knowing that your labor is not in vain in the Lord." **I Corinthians 15:22 states,** "For as in Adam all die, even so **in Christ** shall all be made alive."

Whether you are 16 or 66, **in your life,** what has been **your greatest victory? When** did you enjoy **your finest triumph?** Maybe it was playing **on a High School or University** team. Perhaps it was a solo sports performance. Maybe it was that one time you managed to **beat your brother or sister** in competition you felt was very important. Perhaps it was in an argument, or even in a fight. Maybe it was a great **business achievement at work,** and your project was the best. Friend, there is something within each of us, that we all like to **recall times of victory,** no matter how small. **We celebrate victory!** Even at my age **I like to put the pressure** on my sons in a **competitive golf game** . . . and perhaps, from time to time, even win. **I like to be victorious!**

Paul takes all of chapter 15 to tell us that Jesus has given those who believe in Him **absolute victory over death!** By entering death and rising again, Jesus forever took away the power of death. If you know Jesus Christ as your personal Savior and He is the Lord of your life, friend, **He has forever pulled the stinger out of death** for you and me, (1 Corinthians 15:55-56).

A little boy crawled up into his grand-mama's lap one hot summer day and just sitting there, loving mama, and mama loving him. **Then the little fellow became afraid** and pulled closer to his mama she said, "What's the matter, Son?" **And the little boy said,** "Oh, Mama, look at that bumble bee buzzing around me. **I'm afraid of that bumble bee."** She said, "Aw, Son, you don't have to be afraid of that bee." "Well, Mama, that bumble bee will sting me." "No, Son. **That bumble bee won't sting you,** you don't have to be afraid." "**Why don't I,** Mama?" **Mama reached**

out her hand and she **showed** the little boy her hand and in her hand **she pulled out a stinger and she said,** "Son, you don't have to be afraid of that bumble bee; that bumble bee just **stung me** and it can't sting you. I've got the stinger."

All those who have placed their faith in Jesus need not fear death. Jesus has conquered death for us. **He has pulled** out death's stinger! He has **given His children victory** over death! **The victory Christ has won.** For there to be a victory, there must be an enemy, an **opponent,** someone who is defeated . . . that enemy was Satan. **Thank God for His victory!**

Someone once said, "the only two certainties in life are **death and taxes.**" That's really not true. **Our enemy is death.** There's a **sting to death,** and that **sting is sin,** the needlepoint that threatens and does the damage. **Death comes as a result of sin,** and grieves us so. **Sin gets its power** from the law, from God's command. **As we break God's law,** as we disobey and rebel, then that sin stings us, and we fall into the hands of our enemy. Sometimes bee stings can kill, but with the sin sting, death is a certainty. **The Bible clearly states,** "The wages of sin is death." (Romans 6:23). **What can we do,** in the face of such a **powerful adversary?** Our enemy will triumph. We must **find a remedy** for this attack. Christ died for our sins. He died the death we deserve, and has been raised again, He has won the victory over death, because **Jesus didn't stay dead** in the grave, **He arose and lives forevermore!**

The fact that Jesus rose from the dead showed that He was **not just another** one of those **numerous mortal religious leaders** who come and go, cluttering the pages of history, **people whose deaths silenced** their outrageous claims. **No, in spite** of the predictions of many, **the historical record** shows that the **movement Jesus Christ started,** the church, still thrives and grows, **precisely because He still lives.**

Voltaire, the famous French philosopher once said that the Bible and Christianity would pass within a hundred years. Well, **Voltaire died** about 230 years ago and **the church** of Jesus Christ is still here.

In 1882 Friedrich Nietzsche said, "God is dead." He **believed the dawn of science** would be the **doom of the Christian faith.** He was obviously **very wrong.**

The Communist dictionary once defined the Bible as, "A collection of fantastic legends without any scientific support." **Communism is** diminishing. **The church** is thriving.

Max Lucado sums this all up by saying, "Everyone who has tried to bury the Christian faith has discovered the same thing. **It won't stay buried any more than it's Founder.**"

Dr. Warren W. Wiersbe has a **saying** that I have found **helpful** for many years. **It says,** "We **aren't** fighting **for** victory; we're fighting **from** victory." This simply **means** that **while the child of God, "positionally In Christ,"** possesses victory over the world, the flesh, and the devil. **Because of faith** in the Lord Jesus Christ, they do not always possess spiritual victory in the practical sense. **Sad but true** is the fact that **many saints** are living **in spiritual defeat** on a regular basis. They just do not know or realize that Jesus has already won the battle over Satan. And, because of this (at our conversion), we have been placed **"in Christ."** And, as the Apostle Paul points out in our texts, **spiritual victory is** the positional possession of every Christian.

Eternal 'victory' can only come from an **Omnipotent God! French thinker, Auguste Comte,** once **told Thomas Carlyle** that he was going to **start a new** religion to **replace Christianity.** "Very good," **replied Carlyle,** "all you'll have to do is to be crucified, rise again on the third day, and get the world to believe you are still alive." **Then your new religion will have a chance.** The idea fizzled.

These verses at the top of this chapter **tells you about a victory** that can be yours and mine. **It lets us know** that **victories** are not just something that happened to people who lived long ago and are long dead. **In fact,** this verse **teaches us that victory** can be a present tense experience. **Victory** comes through the Lord Jesus!

"**Victory**" is from the same **Greek root** as the word **translated "overcomes"** so many times in Revelation 2 and 3. **Overcoming is being victorious (to conquer)** over the pull of human nature against God in the self. This word 'overcomes' in the original language conveys the idea that the **believer in Christ has continual victory** over the world. **The Apostle Paul** has taken this entire chapter **to tell us** that Jesus has **given those who believe** in Him **absolute victory over death! Understand that** by entering death and rising again, **Jesus forever took away** the power of death. Because of a believer's union with Christ, they too partake of His victory. (Romans 8:37; II Corinthians 2:14).

You may be thinking, "Brother Glen, **how can we be thinking** of **winning** and **victory** with all the negatives in this world." **We live in a world** that is filled with doubt. **Very few people** seem to have any real certainty about anything. These **doubts arise concerning the economy.**

How high will **gas prices and milk prices** go? These doubts arise concerning the **war on terror.** How long will it last? **How large** will it grow? **How many lives** will be lost in pursuit of a victory? These **doubts arise** concerning the **future. What kind of life** will I have in the **future?** How long will I love? Will I get some **dread disease?** These doubts arise in just about every area of our lives. Negative, negative, negative ... **how can I be positive?** How can I be **assured of victory** in this world full of trouble?

When Paul mentions the 'world,' he is speaking of Satan's worldwide system of deception and wickedness. Satan and this world **try to keep us** from having that victory and entering God's Kingdom. The believer is victorious over the invisible system of demonic and human evil that Satan operates to capture mankind for hell.

The importance of this subject is this: that if we **wish to get to heaven** we must make sure that we **get out of Adam** and get into Christ. And that's what the **salvation of the gospel** tells us we must do. **There are these two Adams,** the **first** and the **last—Adam and Christ. We are born in Adam;** we must get out of Adam. **We are not born in Christ;** we must be born again to get into Christ. **Nobody is in both Adam and Christ,** that's the wrong way of thinking. **Those in Adam** are an **'old man';** those **in Christ** are a **'new man'.** When **we are "in Christ" we are a new man. A Christian is a new man** with indwelling sin. **The apostle Paul** then brings us this subject **when he says:** "As in Adam all die, even so in Christ shall all be made alive." **The new birth or being born again gives us victory!**

What the head of the family does affects the entire family. And that's what's meant by the fact that these are public persons. Now what was the framework within which these public persons acted? **The way the Bible puts this** to us is, **they were heads of two covenants.** Now **what's a covenant?** A covenant is an **arrangement made by God** upon which he will have friendly relations with us—that's what a covenant is. **It is a relationship ordained by God** on the basis of which **He will be our friend or our enemy. If we,** within a covenant, **act in a way which pleases God,** then He will have us as His people. He will be to us a God. And if we don't, He will not be our God!

We all have our family name, don't we? **Whether it's a Scotch name** or an **English** name or a **Welsh** name or a **Chinese** name, **we all love our family name.** But **the one family** which is **all important** to belong to is this one, **Christ's family.** The **Covenant of Grace,** is the **covenant** which

God has made with sinners **"in Christ"** by which, when we come to be in Him, we are **no longer regarded as in Adam.** In Adam we are guilty and liable to death and hell, **but "in Christ,"** and on our way to heaven and to glory. **Adam and Christ;** they are the **only two responsible persons** in the history of mankind who **will affect the human race** by their actions in that public way.

Why are we guilty in Adam? Why does **God categorize us as 'sinners'?** The answer lies in the way God constituted the human race at the beginning. God was in an **utterly unique relationship with Adam.** He was **made in the image** and **likeness of God.** More than that, with Adam there was a **special relationship;** this man and his Creator were **in a covenant union.** They are **not two individuals** any longer; the two have **become one flesh.** Their life and plans are in tandem. So God and Adam were in covenant; they were one and **they walked together** and planned their days with one another in mind. The blessings enjoyed in those first days and weeks should have been enjoyed for ever. The two were one in moral and covenantal unity. But that unity was put under a test during this period.

Adam failed the test. That is **the fall** or jumping into the forbidden pit. **Adam defied his God.** He was persuaded that if he disobeyed God and did it his own way he'd have more than what God was offering him, **and there are many today like that today.** They think, "If we give up on God we'll be much better off. We won't have **all the restrictions** a life with God brings. **We will be happier;** we will have more freedom." **The devil encouraged** them forcefully; "You won't die as the Lord says. **That is a myth.** Take the **forbidden fruit** from the tree. Nothing will happen **except new knowledge** and **self-confidence** that you are able to take on God and be wiser as a result." **So Adam jumped,** and he lost everything. **He lost all he had** with no possibility under heaven of getting it back. He was **driven out of the Garden** never to return. **He began to die** and there was no way he could prevent that happening.

When Adam was doing all that, you and I were in him. Adam was not acting on his own; **he was a public person;** he was the **representative of the human** race. The principal of representation runs right through the Bible. You can call it the principle of covenant headship; it is just the same relationship. **You may protest,** "But I didn't appoint him. **I didn't ask him** to be my head." **No, God did.** God appointed Adam, the wise and loving God made this choice, and so it was a **perfect choice,** the very best choice. **You could not have chosen** anyone more suitable. Your choice would have done been than Adam. The best man let us all down.

We are under the condemnation of God because we are sinners. In other words, we have the status of fallen, rebellious sons of Adam and we have the corresponding nature that goes with it. It is not that we are good men who have been given a bad name. **We are bad men** with a bad name. **Our nature** is alienated from God. **Our nature** is more than indifference to God; **we are at enmity with God.** (Ephesians 2:15, 16; James 4:4). We will not have the Lord rule over us. Our natures is at odds with God. **The apostle puts it like this,** "We are by nature the children of wrath." (Ephesians 2:3).

Listen: You do not become the children of wrath because you sin. **You sin** because you are a child of wrath. When a man lies or is unfaithful to his wife that is **only a symptom of the depraved nature** within him. **Paul describes that nature** and concludes **that we are dead in trespasses and sins.** (Ephesians 2:1). There is a coffin in your heart and your dead spirit lies within it. **Your physical ears** can hear what I am saying (writing), **and your brain** can follow my logic, **but your spirit does not respond** at all **because it is as lifeless as a stone.**

Let me explain with some simple thoughts. Why does a child have measles? Is it because he has **measles spots? No.** He has spots because he has the illness. The spots are the **symptoms** of measles. **We sin because we are sinners.** When we notice a **high temperature** we know the child is **not well.** We know that the **child isn't ill** because of a **temperature** over 100 degrees. **The high temperature** is the **symptom not** the cause. **When you take your child to the doctor** you want the **illness** to be dealt with. You **do not want a tube of make-up** to be given to you to **cover the measles spots.** You expect the virus, the bacteria, the infection that is causing the temperature to be dealt with. That's what God must do in us!

Let me end these thoughts by saying, I never had to sit any of **my children (all 4 of them),** down and say, "**Today we are going to have a lesson** in complaining, and answering back, and whining, and stamping your feet, and saying 'Me! Me! Me!, Stop It, Don't do that, He hit me,' Children, today I am going to teach you** how to be selfish and demand your own way, or how to be mean to your sister and brothers." **I never had to teach them those things,** any more **than I myself** had to have lessons in them. **We all do that** in an expert way. **We don't need** to be taught **how to sin. Sinning comes naturally** to us. It comes from **our nature.** We are the family followers of Adam, and we follow in his sinful path. "For as by one man (Adam), sin entered into the world, and death by sin, so death spread to all men, for all have sinned." (Romans 5:12).

Resistance to God's wise and good ways is second nature to us. Rather **we need to be taught to say,** "Please ... thank you ... no, you go first." **We need to be taught** self-control and to appreciate the achievements of others without envy. **Every child needs** this in every civilization in every culture in the world since the beginning.... because "there are none righteous, no not one," and, "all have sinned, and fallen short of the glory of God." (Romans 310, 23).

Because Jesus died and rose from the dead ... **He is a Victor!** He defeated Satan, our adversary. **Jesus is the victor** and the devil is the loser. **Jesus defeated sin and death.** Because Christ is already a victor, **we who are "in Christ"** are also **victors in Him.**

The late great Presbyterian pastor, Dr. D. James Kennedy wrote, "Some people have made transformational changes in one department of human learning or in one aspect of human life and their names are forever enshrined in the annals of human history. But the past shows that Jesus Christ, the greatest man Who ever lived, has changed virtually every aspect of human life."

I came across a cartoon of two Roman soldiers standing by the **empty tomb.** The stone was rolled away and **one soldier** was **looking very worried** because he knew they **had failed** in their responsibility. The **other one shrugged** and said, **"Don't worry about it.** A hundred years from now, no one will remember." **Well, he was dead wrong wasn't he! All mankind remembers** this historical fact. The impact of the **resurrection of Jesus** has been felt for over 2000 years now. **Because He is alive ... He can and does give life!**

Christ brings life to all those who believe in him. Look at my text, verse 22: "As in Adam all die, even so in Christ shall all be made alive." (I Corinthians 15:22) **Now the 'all'** in Adam means the **entire human race** who live and die in Adam. In the **second part** of the verse, **'all' "in Christ"**, means all those who come to **believe in Christ** in the course of their lifetime, all those **who are saved** by Christ, all **those who trust in Christ, all those who die** believing **in Christ** and in the Covenant of Grace.

Death is one of the greatest fears known to men. **We don't talk much about it,** but the thought of the eternal blink fills many hearts with fear! But, it shouldn't! **If you know Jesus Christ** as your personal Savior, friend, **He has forever pulled** the **stinger** out of death for you and me. **1 Corinthians 15:55-56 states,** "O death, where is your **sting?** O Hades, where is your victory? The **sting** of death is sin, and the strength of sin is the law."

Years ago, in the 1960's, while I was hiking in the mountains of California with my two youngest boys, **a bee stung Mark, the elder, on his forehead. He quickly brushed it away** and threw himself in the grass, kicking and screaming. **No sooner** had the bee **been brushed away** when it **went straight for the youngest son Joel,** and began **buzzing** around his head. **He ran and tried to hide** in the brush and began screaming for help. **I picked him up** and told him **not to worry,** the **bee** had **lost its stinger.**

This particular bee can sting only once. It had left its stinger in my oldest and had become harmless. So **I took my younger** son over to **his older brother** and **showed** him the **little black stinger** in his brother's **forehead,** as I pulled it out. I told him, "The **bee can still buzz and scare** you, but it is **powerless to hurt you.** Your brother took the sting away."

In 1 Corinthians 15:56, the apostle **Paul wrote** that "the **sting of death is sin."** But **Jesus took the sting for us** by dying in our place on the cross. **Death is now powerless** to hurt us because Jesus took its sting. **Death may "buzz around"** and **scare** us, but it **cannot hurt us** anymore. We need not fear God's judgment. **All death can do now** is open the door to Glory.

Psychologists tell us that of all the **obsessions and fears** named these days, one almost never hears of **the fear of death.** Yet it is **this fear** which **makes** virtual **slaves of all men.** The writer to the **Hebrews tells us** that the devil has a grip on men through their fear of death. **Death is the destiny of all men.** The **Son of God** took on humanity, flesh and blood at His incarnation, and then **by His death** and **resurrection** rendered death and the devil **powerless.** Those who have trusted in Christ need no longer live in fear of death. **Death and the fear of death** have been swallowed **up** by the **triumph of our Lord** over them.

In 1846, former President John Quincy Adams suffered a stroke. Although he returned to Congress the following year, **his health was clearly failing.** Webster described his **last meeting with Adams like this:** Someone, a friend of his, came in and made particular **inquiry of his health. Adams answered,** "I inhabit a weak, frail, decayed tenement; battered by the winds and broken in upon by the storms, and from all I can learn, **the landlord does not intend to repair." Why is it** that the landlord **did not intend** to **repair Adams' body?** "Flesh and blood cannot inherit the kingdom of God," he stated. **Victory over death is assured,**

but it has not yet fully come. However, as **Paul makes clear** throughout this text, **that victory is coming** for all those **who are "In Christ."**

How will this change take place? This change **will take place** "in a moment, in the twinkling of an eye." (I Corinthians 15:52). The change **victory over death** will bring will be **instantaneous.** There will not be enough time to make things right before God, as many plan on doing. The Return of Christ will overtake so many who are not ready. **"The day** of the Lord will **come like a thief,** and then the heavens will pass away with a roar, and the heavenly bodies will be burned up and dissolved, and the earth and the works that are done on it will be exposed" (2 Peter 3:10). We have no idea when a **thief is coming** and might break into our home, so we must always take **precautions to be ready. Likewise, we do not know** when the **Lord** is coming, so we must take precautions! Those **"in Christ"** will not be overcome by the Second Coming of Jesus!

Death is the last enemy but here is the comfort we have: **in the end when our Lord returns He will deal** with every enemy and the very last enemy is death. **Death itself shall cease to exist** and the people of God will enter in to the heavenly kingdom **where there is no dying.** We shall never know sickness, pain, temptation, or problems of any kind for there the people of God shall be with the Lord Himself. **He will feed them** and He will **lead them** to everlasting fountains of water.

Christopher Buckley considered himself to be an **agnostic,** but was caught off guard by his **five-year-old daughter, Caitlin,** who started **asking big questions** at a young age. That is what children do, isn't it? One day, **out of the blue, Caitlin asked,** "Dad, does everyone die?" Buckley, surprised, **tried to change the subject.** "Say, how about a Flintstones pop-up ice cream bar?" The **little girl asked,** "But Dad, am I going to die?" **Dad said,** "Well, uh, I guess everyone dies. I mean, it's part of . . . and he paused. **Caitlin persisted,** "But what happens after you die?" **Buckley, torn between** his **agnosticism** and his little girl's **question,** answered, "You go straight to heaven." What happens when we die? That is the big question, isn't it! How would you answer that question?

Friend, Jesus is preparing all of these things right now. In John 14:2b-3, Jesus said, "I go to prepare a place for you, and if I go to prepare a place for you, I will come again a receive you unto Myself, that where I am, there you may be also." **Let us therefore live** for His glory so that **when He comes again** He may find us busy doing the work of the Lord. **He will reward all** of us with the glories of heaven and the glories of God which His Word speaks about so abundantly.

Let's be real. The Word of God states, "It is appointed unto man once to die, and after death, the judgment." (Hebrews 9:27). **Death is coming for everyone of us,** but it does not need to be feared! **If you are saved,** death is merely your doorway **into the eternal presence of God,** (II Corinthians 5:1-8; II Timothy 4:6). **If, you are lost** and do not know Jesus Christ, then friend, **you have good reason to fear** death! For death is not your doorway into life, but it is your doorway into eternal damnation in the fires of Hell! **All those who have placed their faith** in Jesus need not fear death. **Christ** has **conquered death** for us. **He has pulled its stinger!** He has **given His children victory over death!** Thank God for His victory!

No one wants to die, but all of us eventually will. "It is appointed unto men, once to die . . ." (Hebrews 9:27). We all die! **It is God and God alone** who gives us the victory over death. We could never have gained the victory ourselves. No matter how hard we worked; no matter how hard we tried, we cannot have victory over death. **Ponce de Leon came to Florida** looking for the Fountain of Youth. **The legend** was that if you drank from the Fountain of Youth, you would have your youth restored. **Ponce de Leon was looking for a way** to overcome death, to undo the ravages time brings to bodies. **Ponce de Leon never found** that fountain, nor a way to outsmart death. He couldn't. Only God can have victory over death, & God has brought victory over death. **God brought victory** over death through our Lord Jesus Christ.

The day of Christ's return in power and great glory will be a great Day, **a day of rejoicing** for all who are trusting in Jesus Christ for the forgiveness of all their sins. For **those who have refused Jesus** Christ and His offer of salvation, **there will be judgment.** In the Bible's final chapter, we read of **the blessedness of those whose sins** have been washed away by the precious blood of Christ (Revelation 22:14). we also read of **those who do not enter the Heavenly City,** those who, because of their continuing in sin, are excluded from the glories of Heaven (Revelation 22:15).

We "rejoice in glorious hope," **but we must never forget** that, for some, **Jesus will come as "the Judge."** The Gospel comes to all men and women as a message of love, a gracious invitation. **All are invited to come** to the Savior, and **receive full salvation** through faith in Him. We dare not, however, forget that the Gospel also contains a warning to those who persist in their sin, **those who say "No"** to the offer of God's salvation

The History Channel carried a **special** about the **lost city of Cleopatra.** The **entire island** where she **built her palace** is **now**

underwater. **Divers** had discovered it. **One of the things I learned** from watching was that Cleopatra **adorned herself** like the **Egyptian goddess Isis** in human form. And then **believing she was a deity** she took on the persona of someone who was eternal. **But in the end,** as it happens to everyone, **Cleopatra** discovered that **she was no different** than anyone else. **She couldn't escape the call of death.**

Augustine wrote, "The end of life puts the longest life on a par with the shortest.... **Death becomes evil only** by the retribution which follows it. They, then, who are destined to die need not inquire about what death they are to die, but into what place death will usher them." **For those who trust Jesus Christ, death is not a sheriff** dragging us off to court, **but a servant ushering** us into the presence of a loving Lord. **The apostle Paul understood this.** He looked at life and death from Christ's perspective. **Since he knew where death** would take him, he could boldly declare, "**Death is swallowed up in victory**" (1 Corinthians 15:54). Every Christian can have that same courage. **Because of Christ's death and resurrection, we** who **place our faith in Him** can look at death not as a period but a comma that precedes a glorious eternity with our Lord. **The country preacher/evangelist Vance Havner once said, "If the Resurrection** of Jesus **is a myth,** then **I am MYTHtaken, MYTHstified, and MYTHerable." Well,** Havner was right.

As Paul says in our text, **without the resurrection,** the very **structure of our Christian faith falls** apart and the **gospel we proclaim** becomes null and void. **If Easter Sunday** had never dawned, I would be **wasting my life** as a minister. Remember Paul's words in 1st Corinthians 17:14 and 17? "If Christ has not been raised, our preaching is useless and so is your faith. And if Christ has not been raised, your faith is futile; you are still in your sins." Because of the resurrection of Jesus from the grave, we now understand the fact of life after death.

When I was growing up in South Texas, **I didn't understand death** at all. **A girl,** about my age, who lived down the road **died.** I wasn't allowed to go to the funeral. I didn't even know what a funeral was. I had so many questions. **I even tried to deny the reality of death.** It happened again later at **my papa's funeral.** Seeing his lifeless body in the casket, I recall thinking, "If that ever happens to me, I'm just gonna get up and walk away."

I am now in my late 70's, and I look at death differently. **I have officiated** at **many funerals.** I've said **farewell to both of my parents, my brother and sister,** almost all of my aunts and uncles, and many friends. In fact, almost all my school mates are no longer here. **I no longer deny** the harsh reality of death. **Death rips** apart life's closest bonds, **leaves hearts** broken, ushers in loneliness, and **opens floodgates** of tears. **Just using pleasant-sounding** words and calling funeral services **"celebrations"** does not change that.

There is a greater reality, though, that can **give us the will to go on living** with hope. **Jesus Christ broke** the power of death. He did "get up and walk away" from the grave. "But now is Christ risen from the dead, and has become the first fruits of those who have fallen asleep" (died) (I Corinthians 15:20). **And one day 'death,' the "last enemy,"** as Paul called it, **will be destroyed forever.** (15:26). **He said it like this:** "'Death is swallowed up in victory.' 'O Death, where is your sting? O Hades, where is your victory?' The sting of death is sin, and the strength of sin is the law. But thanks be to God, who gives us the victory through our Lord Jesus Christ" (vv.54-57). Praise God from Whom all Blessings Flow! **The death of death is sure! Hallelujah!**

Dr. Harry Rimmer was lecturing in a certain place and during the question and answer period, a **young Jewish man** stood up and asked Dr Rimmer, **"What did Jesus Christ do that no one else ever did?"** Dr Rimmer answered him this way, **"Sir, you are a Jew.** Would you agree with me that the **Romans crucified** nearly **30,000** young Jewish men?" The questioner answered, "yes." **Dr. Rimmer continued by asking,** "Alright, I will name one of those who were crucified and you name another. **I name Jesus Christ."** The **student said, "I can't name another." Do you know why** this young man could not name another Jew out of those 30,000? Because **time is the great leveler** of names and events.

Only one crucified Jew is known to men. His name is **Jesus! He is remembered** because He lives! **Listen:** Nobody hates a dead man! **When people die, hate is forgotten!** Yet, Satan hates Jesus, the world hates Jesus, the demons hate Jesus. Why attack a dead man? **If Jesus is dead,** than we are all crazy and ought to be locked up! **However, Jesus is alive and well . . . in His resurrection power!**

Burton Coffman, before his death, aptly **wrote on this text:** "Nearly two thousand years have passed since this apostolic lightning split the midnight darkness surrounding the tomb; and **even yet there is never a day passes** in any city anywhere which fails to shout this message over the dead. Here in Houston, where these lines are being written, it is certain that a hundred times **this very week these words** have echoed in the **chapels and cemeteries** where people gather to bury the dead; and so it is all over the world when Christ is known. **Victory in the presence** of death! If people wonder why the holy faith in Jesus Christ continues from age to age, let them find at least a part of the answer in these immortal words before us."

    Those in the Lord, "in Christ," shall be made alive (verse 22). We have **this sure hope,** a hope that is not in vain. Our labor, our work for the Lord and in the Lord is not in vain—**just as our faith in Christ** is not in vain (verse 14). **Our faith is not empty, because Jesus is alive.** Our work is therefore also not empty or useless, but productive, and fruitful, as we spread the good news of Jesus, the **triumph of victory** over sin and death. **Someone once wrote:** "Only one life, twill soon be past, only what's done for Christ will last."

    Paul also exhorts us to be "always abounding in the work of the Lord." (First Corinthians 15:58). His work is creating. **Scripture refers to God** several times as the **Potter,** and **we are the clay** that He is shaping. The difference between us and earthy clay is that **the clay God is working is alive**, having a mind and will of its own, it can choose to resist or yield.

    What is your greatest victory? If you're **"in Christ,"** then those business achievements, social achievements and sporting achievements or arguments, **pale into insignificance,** and **our greatest victory** is just around the corner—just a heartbeat away, **when we meet the Lord in death, or when the Lord returns,** and we **share in His victory** over death. How will you respond now?

    John Stott wrote . . . "Jesus is the resurrection of believers who die **and the life** of believers who live. He promises not that you will just survive, but that you will be resurrected. **When he says,** "you will never die," **it doesn't mean** that you will escape death, but that death will prove to be a trivial episode, **a transition** to the fullness of life.

    It is time for Christians to realize that **we are in a battle!** Although Satan is defeated, he still "walks about like a roaring lion, seeking whom he may devour." (I Peter 5:8).

    Although Satan is roaming, and tempting, and putting us through trials, **remember, he is on a short leash,** and one day soon he will be reeled in and cast away. Victory!

    Ever since the beginning of humankind, the devil has been deceiving mankind and is in a battle for mans soul. **Folks, we are in a battle! God's Word states,** "the weapons of our warfare are not carnal but mighty in God for pulling down strongholds, casting down arguments and every high thing that exalts itself against the knowledge of God, bringing every thought into captivity to the obedience of Christ."

"**Thanks be to God, who** gives us the **victory** through our Lord Jesus Christ." (verse 57). We have come to that time of the year where people pause to give "thanks." In a few weeks, we'll gather with family and friends to overeat, tell stories, and watch football. However, **there is no greater blessing** for which we can give thanks than the victory Jesus has brought over death! **It is God who gives us the victory.** We could never have gained the victory ourselves. No matter how hard we worked; no matter how hard we tried, **we cannot have victory over death.**

As a boy I studied about Ponce de Leon who came to Florida looking for the **Fountain of Youth.** The **legend was** that **if you drank** from the Fountain of Youth, you would have **your youth restored.** Ponce de Leon was looking for a way to **overcome death,** to **undo the ravages** time brings to bodies. Ponce de Leon **never found that fountain,** nor a way to **outsmart** death. **He couldn't. Only God can have victory over death,** and God has brought victory over death.

Right now, even as you read this, we are in a battle for our souls! **We must be prepared!** This is done by "putting on the whole armor of God," so that we can stand against the wiles (schemes) of the devil. **Listen carefully:** In our fight against Satan every day, we are already winners of that battle . . . because Christ has won, thus we have won. **The victor** has already been decided. **The end result has already been determined.** Although **we know the final outcome of this battle,** that does not mean there will no casualties. **This is victory!**

This battle is not like any other battle of this world. We don't know the outcome of a basketball or football game. The outcome is not predetermined for these or other games, **but for the Christian, who is "in Christ,"** the outcome is already determined. **Paul tells us that** Christians have already won that victory. **He wrote,** "I have fought a good fight, I have finished the race, I have kept the faith. Finally, there is laid up for me the crown of righteousness, which the Lord, the righteous Judge, will give to me on that Day, and not to me only, but also to all who have loved His appearing." (II Timothy 4:7-8).

All Christians must remember that salvation is a **sovereign work** of God. As already stated, 'works' are **not** necessary to earn salvation. However, the true salvation wrought by God will produce good works (that are its fruit). **As Jesus taught in Matthew 7:17,** "Even so, every good tree bears good fruit, but a bad tree bears bad fruit." Far **to many people**

believe their religion of "good works" is all they need to be a Christian. **Not true!** Paul wrote, "We are His workmanship, created in Christ Jesus for good works, which God prepared beforehand, that we should walk in them." (Ephesians 2:10).

As if he hasn't challenged us enough, Paul reiterates, "But thanks be to God, Who always leads us in His triumph in Christ, and manifests through us the sweet aroma of the knowledge of Him in every place." (II Corinthians 2:14) **And, those 'in Christ' have real estate in Heaven!** "Knowing in yourselves that ye have in Heaven a better and an enduring substance" (Hebrews 10:34).

God has given us a promise of **real estate** in **glory,** and that promise comes to our hearts with **such full assurance** of its certainty that we know in ourselves that we have an enduring substance there. **Yes, "we have" it even now.** Some say, "A bird in the hand is worth two in the bush," **but we have** our bird in the bush and in the hand, too. Heaven is even now our own. **We have the title deed** of it, we have the **earnest** (guarantee) of it, we have the **firstfruits** of it. We have heaven **in price,** in **promise,** and in **principle;** this **we know** not only by the hearing of the ear but "in ourselves," because of Christ Who lives in us.

Sir Winston Churchill arranged his own funeral. There were **stately hymns** in St. Paul's Cathedral and an **impressive liturgy.** But **at the end** of the service, Churchill had an **unusual event** planned. When they said the benediction, **a bugler** high **in the dome** of St. Paul's Cathedral on one side **played Taps,** the universal signal that the **day is over.** There was a long pause. **Then a bugler** on the other side **played Reveille,** the military **wake-up call.** And, that's the way it is with those of us who are **"In Christ."** Yes, **one day** this **old body** will fade and fall, but one day **the new body** will be raised up in resurrection power. **Hallelujah!**

The thought of the better substance on the other side of Jordan reconciles us to present losses in this world? Our spending money we may lose, but **our treasure is safe.** We have lost the shadows, but the **substance remains,** for our Savior lives, and **the place** which He has prepared for us abides. There is a better land, a better substance, a better promise; and all this comes to us by a better covenant; therefore, let us be in better spirits, **and say unto the LORD,** "Every day will I bless thee; and praise thy name forever and ever."

Faithful followers of Christ are on the right track. **There will be difficulties, heartbreaks, and trials** along the way, **but 'victory' is certain "in Christ."** (Romans 8:35-39). **"In Christ,"** we are partakers of the promise of God. (Ephesians 3:6). **And, even death is defeated** to the Christian who is "asleep in Jesus" because we await the resurrection. (I Thessalonians 4:13,14). **What a victory!**

Our spiritual bodies in eternity will be perfect. **Our spiritual bodies** will be more than we can understand as long as we are living on this earth. No longer will I be farsighted and almost colorblind. This 76 year old body will be able to do things I only dreamed of as a boy. **I won't have any more scars** from a broken nose, broken ankle, or shoulder surgery, or open heart quadruple by-pass surgery.

Helen Keller, the blind and deaf woman who lived such an inspiring life, put it this way. **She wrote:**

> There's so much I'd like to see, so much to learn.
> And death is just around the corner.
> Not that that worries me. On the contrary,
> it is no more than passing from one room into another.
> But there's a difference for me, you know.
> Because in that other room I shall be able to see.

"I shall be able to see." Can you imagine what that meant to a woman who had lived her entire life in darkness and silence! "I will be able to see." **Hallelujah!**

Our victory is complete, and forever! No replays, no rematches, no arguments, no appeals, because **Jesus has won** and **we share in his victory.** The result is sure, and we can celebrate now, as we stand firm in the truth of the resurrection, and spread the good news to others—**Thanks be to God, Who gives us the victory** through our Lord Jesus Christ.

This passage, and the others we have studied, is teaching that God has declared us to be **"in Christ,"** which, among other things, means we have died to what we were "in Adam." **What does this saying, "in Christ," mean?** It is easy to understand a similar statement; "Christ in me." I open my heart, and Christ enters as promised in Revelation 3:20 and elsewhere. But here **we are hearing** something completely different: **not Christ in me, but me in Christ!**

This is what theologians call "identification with Christ." It means God has acted in such a way that **we have become identified with Christ.** Therefore, as far as God is concerned, what is true of Christ's standing has become true of us. **Did Jesus die?** Then so did I. **Did Jesus rise** from the dead? Then I, too, rose from the dead. The comparisons can be pressed even further. **Did Jesus ascend** to the Father in heaven? Then according to my identification with Christ, I too ascended to heaven and took my seat at the right hand of the Father!

Michelangelo also had the **right perspective on death.** A friend commented on the **wonderful life** that Michelangelo had lived and said, "After such a good life it's hard to look death in the eye." **Michelangelo responded:** "Not at all. Since life was such a pleasure, **death, coming from the same great Source,** cannot displease us."

Paul didn't write First Corinthians 15 as **a scientific textbook.** Instead, **God** simply **gives us a glimpse into eternity,** and provides the promise that it will be wonderful. **Paul concludes:** "Thanks be to **God, who gives us the victory** through our Lord Jesus Christ." (v. 57). **This is expressly stated in Ephesians 2:5, 6:** "Even when we were dead in our sin and transgression [God] made us alive together with Christ, and raised us up with him, and seated us with him in the heavenly places in Christ." **Of course we have not** become the creators of the world, **nor** have we become deity, but the areas where we are identified with Christ go much further than many of us would think.

In I Corinthians 15:45 it says, "The first Adam became a living soul, the last Adam became a life giving spirit." **Jesus is the last Adam.** He is a second federal head. He is called the last Adam. Just as Adam gave rise to a fallen humanity, **Christ has become the source of a new,** righteous humanity. One humanity is doomed to die; the other humanity has already died. **One humanity lives** in alienation from God; **the other,** those '**in Christ," are alive to God, forever!**

Dr. David Seamands tells of a Muslim who became a Christian in Africa. Some of his **friends asked him,** "Why did you become a Christian?" **He answered,** "Well, it's like this. Suppose you were **going down the road** and suddenly the road **forked** in two directions and you didn't know which way to go, and there **at the fork** of the road were two men: one **dead** and one **alive. Which one would you ask for directions?"**

My friend, you are **not reading this by accident.** God has brought you to this book so that you could read **about the victory** that can only be found in the Lord Jesus Christ. **Have you trusted Him by faith?** Are you **walking in His victory** today? **Are you** saved, sealed and sure for Heaven? **If you died right now,** are you sure you would miss Hell and go to Heaven? Friend, you need to be sure!

God brought victory over death through our Lord Jesus Christ. When Jesus Christ came from the tomb, the shackles of death were broken once and for all! While death still hurts us, **we look beyond the tomb** in hope, knowing that our Victory is Christ! It is **reported that Martin Luther's final words** were these: "Our God is the God from whom cometh salvation: **God is the Lord** by whom we escape death." How glorious it is to know that our God is the God by whom we escape death! There is a **strong implication** here that **unless Jesus is our Lord,** we shall **not** have victory over death.

Maybe your life is a mess today. You know you are not right with God. You know that if you died, you would go to Hell forever. Friend, **it doesn't have to be that** way! **If you will come to Jesus** by faith, repent of your sins, and accept His death and resurrection as the payment for your sins, you will be saved. **Victory** can be yours today, if you will say yes to Him. Will you do it?

That strange and exciting passion within you now, is the **Spirit of God** leading you to the truth in Jesus. **He is calling you** to come to Him, and **I challenge you** and encourage you to **obey His voice.** Just do what He is calling you to do, and He will honor your response of faith, and, you will never be the same!

We have that promise of victory! Those of us **who have been redeemed,** by the precious blood of Jesus, have the "victory through our Lord Jesus Christ." **The apostle John wrote,** "For whatsoever is born of God overcomes the world. And this is the **victory** that has overcome the world—our faith." (I John 5:4).

I once heard of a captain of a ship who was describing **what it was like to go through a storm.** He described the ship **in the midst of mountainous seas,** the waves mounting on every side, and the wind blowing hard with the pitiless rain coming down. **The ship seems a helpless victim** of the storm, **caught up** in the power of these mighty elements that are raging on every side. **Its doom seems sure. But he said,** "I stand there on the bridge of the ship and I grasp the railing. I can feel the throb, throbbing of **the engines deep down inside** the hull. The storm, the wind, and the waves seem to be saying to the ship, 'You cannot come, you cannot come.' **But I hear the answering throb** of the engines saying, 'Yes, we shall, yes, we shall, yes, we shall.' **And so we do." That is the way the battle is won.** That is the **way we overcome the world.** That is why **we have total victory in Jesus.**

What is this victory I keep referring to? We are actually able **to take immortality onto our mortal flesh.** Do you know **what passage of God's Word** this combined teaching resembles? Romans 8:11 states, "For if the

Spirit of Him who raised Jesus from the dead dwells in you, He who raised Christ from the dead will also give life to your mortal bodies through His Spirit who dwells in you."

"Who is he that overcomes the world, but he that believes that Jesus is the Son of God?" (I John 5:5). That is, **that trusts in faith to Him,** Such **unfaltering reliance** on Him will lead to a wonderful experience in your life as a Christian, **victory** over sinful habits, **victory** over all temptations, **victory** over trying circumstances, **victory** over depressing feelings, **victory** over personal insufficiencies, **victory** over dominant self. **Victory all along the line,** by fighting for it? **No! "even our faith."** Truly, **"if ye have faith ... nothing shall be impossible unto you."** (Matthew 17:20).

What a powerful teaching. However, with that promise, there is responsibility. **Do we live in the resurrection power** that is available to us? **Pray** that God will **fill you up to overflowing** with the Holy Spirit and do so every day. We **can have real victory** over **real Sin, really. Listen to the authoritative Word of God:** "If the Spirit of Him Who raised Jesus from the dead dwells (lives) in you, He Who raised Christ Jesus from the dead will also give life to your mortal bodies through His Spirit who dwells in you." (Romans 8:11).

This week I read a little story about a **famous painting** that once hung in an art **gallery in Europe.** It's a depiction of **Faust playing chess with the devil.** And in the painting, **the devil has Faust checkmated** and is **claiming his soul** in victory. **Over the years people looked** at this painting and felt a certain identification with it. **They would go away** and feel like the artist had **captured their own hopeless** situation when it comes to death. **One day a great chess master came.** He stood there **looking at the painting studying** the game board for a long time. **Finally he disturbed everyone** in the gallery by stepping back and **shouting at the top** of his voice, **"It's a lie!** The **painting is wrong!** The **knight and the king** have another move!"

I'm not much of a chess player anymore, but **I understand** what it means to be **checkmated.** And many of us feel this way about death. **We feel that death** is the **last move** and **we can't win.** But the empty tomb of **our Lord says, "That's a lie! You do have another move!"** And if we take that move, **if we take the step of faith** and **put our faith in Jesus,** the **only One** Who conquered death for us, then we **can proclaim with the Apostle Paul,** "... Death is swallowed up in Victory. Where oh death, is your victory? Where oh grave, is your sting?" (I Corinthians 15:54b-55). Are you in the family of faith?

I asked you at the start of this chapter, **how many families are there?** Answer: two. **And my last question:** which family are you in? **Make sure it is Christ!**

Death is swallowed up in victory. The grave is defeated. Thanks be to God, **Who has done all this for each of us** who have allowed Jesus to become the Lord and Savior. **Yes, we have obtained eternal victory** through Jesus Christ our Lord.

The question now is, **Are you still in Adam or are you in Christ?** You must be in the one or the other, and **I am saying** that you **must ask God for life,** that he may take you out of Adam **and put you "in Christ."** You must **ask Him to deliver** you from the wrath of God, repent of your sins, and give your life to the Lord Jesus Christ. **What status are you in today?** I am **not asking you** to make a list of all your good points, or have you **covered over** and hidden every measles' spot of sin? **There is no help** at all in **cosmetic change. I'm asking you to come to Jesus!** Friend, can you say, "On Christ the solid rock I stand, all other ground is sinking sand?" That is the beginning of grace. That is salvation. **This is VICTORY!**

You hear a lot about victorious Christian living today, but you **see very little** of it. **Many Christians,** if they were honest, are **living defeated lives.** They're **asking the question:** "Is it possible to overcome the world?" This phrase "overcomes the **world,**" **"overcomes" in the original says, "has overcome," literally. It indicates a victory** which has **been achieved,** in the past, **once for all,** the effects of which we are still living with today. What it is **talking about is Calvary!** Is it possible to overcome the world? **Yes! It has been** overcome! **He has nailed it to His cross,** and your flesh, and the devil!

You may feel that you are not living in the victory of it, **but your faith,** the true effectual faith of God, rests squarely on the **fact that Jesus has defeated death,** and anybody who can defeat death can defeat anything! **You can't fight the world** and overcome it, **it doesn't come** through organizations and denominations, **it doesn't come** through government, **it doesn't come** through politics, **it doesn't come** even through reformation. **He that overcomes** the world must overcome it by faith. **Faith gives the victory, why?** Because **it joins us to Christ,** who **has won** the victory of the cross over the world, the flesh, and the devil. **We become united with Him by faith,** and therein overcome the world.

The Apostle John wrote, "Whoever is born of God overcomes the world; and this is the victory that has overcome the world—our faith."

(I John 5:4). **Just our faith. Not** great intellectual prowess, **not** degrees in theology, **not** membership of the deaconate or of the eldership—**but simply faith,** empty **hands** stretched out **embracing Jesus** as Lord and Savior. **That's the victory** that **overcomes** the **world,** that overcomes **sin,** that overcomes **temptation,** that overcomes **our failures,** that overcomes the **hostility** of Satan. **It's our faith** in Jesus Christ. **Faith** makes us **winners! Faith is the victory!**

Do you understand what John is saying? Do you want victory? **Don't look to yourself.** No, don't look to **yourself.** Don't look to your **attainments.** Don't look to your **past records.** Don't look to your **membership** of the First Presbyterian Church, or Baptist, or Catholic or Methodist Church. Don't look to the **place that you live** in this city. Look to Jesus! **Look to Jesus!**

The saints are reminded that **because Jesus lives,** they shall live also. They are reminded that **even if death** were to take these mortal bodies; we will live on in a new body in a new place called Heaven. What a truth! Years ago, **Bill Gaither penned the refrain to the song**

> "Because He Lives." That refrain goes like this:
> Because He lives I can face tomorrow.
> Because He lives all fear is gone.
> Because I know He holds the future
> and life is worth the living just because He lives.
>
> Gloria and William Gaither

That is what Paul is saying in these verses! **Because Jesus lives,** we can have a better life now. **Because Jesus lives,** we can everlasting life someday. **Because Jesus lives,** we have the hope of seeing our departed loved one again. **Because Jesus lives,** we hope in the hour of our death. **Because Jesus lives,** we will enjoy victory on our death beds and glory over the cemetery!

If you take your eyes off Jesus, you will always **fail. victory comes** in overcoming the world in its hostility towards us. **Victory comes,** friend, by looking to Jesus, **just as the old gospel song** by Helen Lemmel **says,** "Turn your eyes upon Jesus. Look full in His wonderful face, and the things of earth will grow strangely dim in the light of His glory and grace." May God challenge and bless His Word to us.

We've covered allot in this book, and you are almost through reading. Do you still need more motivation to "step it up?" Well if you do, **Paul leaves us** with a final encouragement. "(Know) that your toil is not in vain in the Lord." (First Corinthians 15:58). **Your service in the Lord** will never be a waste. You will be rewarded exponentially both in this life and in the life to come. The **great American missionary, Jim Elliot said,** "He is no fool who gives what he cannot keep, to gain what he cannot lose." **Is that your heart?**

I ask you when we began this chapter, **"What is your greatest victory?"** If you're in Christ, then those sporting, or family, or business achievements, or arguments pale into insignificance, **and our greatest victory** is just around the corner, just a heartbeat away, **when the Lord returns** and we share in His victory over death.

It is not at all unusual for victors in a sporting event to **have a drink in victory. After winning** the **1936 Indianapolis 500, Louis Meyer** asked for a **glass of buttermilk,** which his **mother urged** him to drink on hot days. It soon **became a tradition** for the **winner** to chug a bottle of **milk** after the Indy 500. In fact, the **American Dairy Association** now **pays $10,000** to have the winner **drink milk in victory** lane.

In this passage, **Paul declares** that **death** is going to be **chugged,** swallowed up in victory. **Death will be swallowed up in victory** when the mortal is no more. At that point, we will **no longer have** these bodies of flesh & blood, sickness & death, & morality & perishability. "Death is swallowed up in victory."

Whether it be in death or His return to earth, this world, as we now know it, is racing to the end of time. There will be **no forewarning.** There will be **no announcements** on TV, on radio, or in the papers. There will be **no proclamations** from the pulpits. **God will not proclaim** in a booming, **Charlton Heston voice** that the end is nearing. It will just happen! My friend, if you have ever listened to anything in your life, then **listen to this.** You **need to be ready! Jesus Himself said,** "Therefore be ye also ready: for in such an hour as ye think not the Son of man cometh." (Matthew 24:44).

My friend, you did not read this book by accident. God has brought you here so that **you could hear about the victory** that can only be found in the Lord Jesus Christ. Have you trusted Him by faith? **Are you walking in His victory?** Are you saved, sealed and sure for Heaven? If you died right now, are you sure you would miss Hell and go to Heaven?

Maybe your life is a mess today. You know you are **not right with God.** You know that if you died, you would go to Hell forever. Friend, it doesn't have to be that way! **If you will come to Jesus** by faith and accept His death and resurrection as the payment for your sins, **you will be saved.** Jesus will come into your heart and life, **He will change your life** and you will have a home in Heaven when you leave this world. Isn't that what you want? The peace of salvation can be yours! **Victory** can be yours today, if you will respond to Him. Will you do it now?

"In Christ," our victory is complete, and forever! No replays, no rematches, no appeals, **Jesus has won** and **we share in his victory.** The result is sure, and we can celebrate now, **as we stand firm** in the truth of the resurrection, and spread the good news to others. "Thanks be to God, **who gives us the victory** through our Lord Jesus Christ." (verse 57).

I've read the back of **the Book . . . the Bible, and WE WIN! Victory** is assured. If you keep looking to yourself, you won't know the score, **but when you look to Jesus,** you know: **"That the victory is already won." Our Lord Jesus Christ invites you** to **participate** in that **victory. He invites you** to come and to become a part of Him. **Receive him** as your Savior and Lord. **Let him give you the victory** over all things—in life or in death.

> "I heard an old, old story, how a Savior came from glory,
> How He gave His life on Calvary to save a wretch like me.
> I heard about His groaning, of His precious blood atoning,
> Then I repented of my sins and won the victory."
> "O victory in Jesus, my Savior forever!
> He sought me and bought me with His redeeming blood.
> He loved me ere I knew Him, and all my love is due Him.
> He plunged me to victory beneath the cleansing flood."
>
> Eugene Bartlett

IN CONCLUSION
My Main Question Now Is: "Are You "In Christ"?

We must never forget, it is **God's sovereign work**: "From God you are 'in Christ Jesus'" (1 Corinthians 1:30). Knowing this, we must also know that **it is through faith.** Christ dwells in our hearts **"through faith,"** (Ephesians 3:17). The life we live in union with his death and life "we live by faith in the Son of God" (Galatians 2:20). **We are united** in his **death** and **resurrection** "through faith" (Col. 2:12).

The Bible teaches that **justification by faith** is the **foundational truth** in Christianity. "For by grace you have been saved through faith, and that not of yourselves; it is the gift of God, not of works, lest anyone should boast." (Ephesians 2:8). **You cannot know** true rest and peace until you are convinced you can never be made right in God's eyes **by your own works** of righteousness.

Your own charity, morality, works and goodness are useless in receiving salvation from God. **The prophet Isaiah stated,** "all our righteousness is as filthy rags in God's sight. (Isaiah 64:6).

"For you are all one **in Christ Jesus,**" (Galatians 3:28). **When we turn to Jesus** with saving, self-emptying faith, we become one **"in Christ."** Being **"in Christ"** means God credits (imputes) Jesus' righteousness to us. All our sins are washed away because of His work, not ours! **Friend, no righteousness** of the flesh will ever stand before God. **Even the best people** among us, the most moral saints, have fallen short of God's glory. None of us will ever be accepted in the Father's eyes by our good works. **We are accepted** by Him **only** as we are **"in Christ."**

If grace is **"in Christ,"** and salvation is **"in Christ,"** (II Timothy 2:10), then **we need to understand** what the Bible teaches about **getting "into Christ."** "What must we do to become a child of God." **This is what Nicodemus,** the super-religious man who came to Jesus by night asked. **Jesus told him that** "he must be born again." (John 3:3-7). **In Acts 16:30-31** we also find the **searching question** from a prison cell, "Sirs, what must I do to be saved?" and they said, "Believe on the Lord Jesus Christ, and you will be saved..." **In John 8:24 Jesus said,** "If you do not believe that I am

He, you will die in your sins." **Jesus said,** "I am the way, the truth and the life, and no one comes to the Father, except by me." (John 14:6).

Friend, do you need Jesus as your Lord and Savior? In Acts 8 we see Phillip and the Ethiopian nobleman traveling down the road. Phillip had been teaching him about Jesus, salvation and baptism. **In that desert** they came to an **oasis** and the man said, "Here is water; what hinders me from being baptized?" **Phillip then said,** "If you believe with all your heart, you may." **The Ethiopian then made the good confession:** "I believe that Jesus is the Christ, the Son of God." **Romans 10:10 teaches:** that "with the heart one believes unto righteousness, and with the mouth confession is made unto salvation." **And, verse 13 says,** "For whoever calls on the name of the Lord shall be saved." **If you haven't done that, I pray you will, now!**

Victory, from the Greek word "**nikos,**" a word **borrowed** by the **athletic outfit "Nike."** A word used in the **language of the day** to denote a **military or legal victory.** Here, **a spiritual victory achieved by our Savior** and graciously shared with those who love Him.

The Apostle John records our glorious victory thanks to the work of Christ in Revelation 21. "And He will wipe away every tear from their eyes; and there will no longer be any death; there will no longer be any mourning, or crying, or pain; the first things have passed away" (Revelation 21:4).

No wonder Paul could say after this lengthy discourse in chapter 15 considering our grand redemption, "Thanks be to God, who gives us the **victory** through our Lord Jesus Christ" (1 Corinthians 15:57).

It is a wonderful truth, that you can have victory "In Christ." Hallelujah!

BRIEF BIOGRAPHY OF AUTHOR

Dr. Glen Clifton, became pastor of his first church at age 19 while attending Baylor University. He and his wife Dee have had four children. He has been pastor of Southern Baptist Churches in Texas (twice), Mississippi, and California (twice), with three Interim pastorates in Florida. He retired to the Treasure Coast of Florida, where he has been serving churches for the past 11 years.

A native Texan, Clifton is a graduate of Baylor University (B.A.), New Orleans Baptist Theological Seminary (MRE), and Louisiana Baptist University (DMin). He has also taught in public schools in 4 states, as well as Seminary Extension of N.O.B.T.S. He has had the privilege of speaking and preaching Revivals in almost 20 states.

Clifton has served as a Church Planter in areas with no church. Some of the churches have led their Association in baptisms, church growth and mission giving in California, Mississippi and Texas.

This is Clifton's second book. His first, "What All New Christians Should Know," is a quick-start book for new Christians. It is in its fourth printing.

Although retired, Clifton fills the pulpit almost every Sunday somewhere on the Southeast Coast of Florida. He may be contacted for speaking engagements at Glendeeclif@hotmail.com or (772) 336-3992.